MACHINE LEARNING FOR ALGORITHMIC TRADING

4 BOOKS IN 1

Learn the art of Programming with a complete crash course for beginners. Strategies to Master Data Science, Numpy, Keras, Pandas and Arduino like a Pro in 7 days

JASON TEST AND MARK BROKER

© **Copyright 2020 - All rights reserved.**

The content contained within this book may not be reproduced, duplicated or transmitted without direct written permission from the author or the publisher.

Under no circumstances will any blame or legal responsibility be held against the publisher, or author, for any damages, reparation, or monetary loss due to the information contained within this book. Either directly or indirectly.

Legal Notice:

This book is copyright protected. This book is only for personal use. You cannot amend, distribute, sell, use, quote or paraphrase any part, or the content within this book, without the consent of the author or publisher.

Disclaimer Notice:

Please note the information contained within this document is for educational and entertainment purposes only. All effort has been executed to present accurate, up to date, and reliable, complete information. No warranties of any kind are declared or implied. Readers acknowledge that the author is not engaging in the rendering of legal, financial, medical or professional advice. The content within this book has been derived from various sources. Please consult a licensed professional before attempting any techniques outlined in this book.

By reading this document, the reader agrees that under no circumstances is the author responsible for any losses, direct or indirect, which are incurred as a result of the use of information contained within this document, including, but not limited to, — errors, omissions, or inaccuracies.

TABLE OF CONTENTS

MACHINE LEARNING WITH ALGORITHM TRADING 1
PYTHON FOR BEGINNERS 1
Introduction 3
1. Python code optimization with ctypes 18
2. Finding the Perfect Toolkit: Analyzing Popular Python Project Templates 25
3. How are broad integer types implemented in Python? 34
4. Create a bot in Python to learn English 42
5. The thermal imager on the Raspberry PI 58
6. Finding a Free Parking Space with Python 67
7. Creating games on the Pygame framework | Part 1 84
Creating games on the Pygame framework | Part 2 90
Creating games on the Pygame framework| Part 3 97
8. Object-Oriented Programming (OOP) in Python 3 108
Conclusion 132
PYTHON FOR DATA SCIENCE 134
Introduction 136
Data Science and Its Significance 138
Python Basics 144
Functions 166
Lists and Loops 181
Adding multiple valued data in python 210
Adding string data in Python 218
Module Data 233
Conclusion 248
OPTIONS TRADING FOR BEGINNERS 250
Introduction 252
1. Options Trading Basics 254
2. Why Trade with Options 261
3. Major Option Trading Concepts 271
4. Options Trading Myths and Misconceptions 284
5. Top Options Trading Strategies 289
6. Top Qualities of a Successful Options Trader 301
7. How to Select the Right Option for a Major Gain 308
8. Important Tips & Tricks about Options Trading 319
9. Important FAQs of Options Trading 324
Conclusion 330
DAY AND SWING TRADING 331
INTRODUCTION 332
1. Difference between swing trading and day trading 336

2.How does it work?.. 345
3.Swing trading and day trading: tactics and strategies 358
4.Swing and day trading indicators.. 390
5.Pros and cons of swing and day trading 405
conclusion 413

PYTHON
FOR BEGINNERS

A crash course guide for machine learning and web programming. Learn a computer language in easy steps with coding exercises.

JASON TEST

INTRODUCTION

Design patterns are reusable model for solving known and common problems in software architecture.

They are best described as templates for working with a specific normal situation. An architect can have a template for designing certain types of door frames, which he fit into many of his project, and a software engineer or software architect must know the templates for solving common programming tasks.

An excellent presentation of the design pattern should include:

- Name
- Motivating problem
- Decision
- Effects

Equivalent Problems

If you thought it was a rather vague concept, you would be right. For example, we could say that the following "pattern" solves all your problems:

- Gather and prepare the necessary data and other resources

- Make the necessary calculations and do the necessary work
- Make logs of what you do
- Free all resources
- ???
- Profit

This is an example of too abstract thinking. You cannot call it a template because it is not an excellent model to solve any problem, even though it is technically applicable to any of them (including cooking dinner).

On the other hand, you may have solutions that are too specific to be called a template. For example, you may wonder if QuickSort is a template to solve the sorting problem.

This is, of course, a common program problems, and QuickSort is a good solutions for it. However, it can be applieds to any sorting problem with virtually no change.

Once you have this in the library and you can call it, your only real job is to make somehow your object comparable, and you don't have to deal with its entity yourself to change it to fit your specific problem.

Equivalent problems lie somewhere between these concepts. These are different problems that are similar enough that you can apply the same model to them, but are different enough that this model is significantly customized to be applicable in each case.

Patterns that can be applied to these kinds of problems are what we can meaningfully call design patterns.

Why use design patterns?

You are probably familiar with some design patterns through code writing practice. Many good programmers end up gravitating towards them, not even being explicitly trained, or they simply take them from their seniors along the way.

The motivation to create, learn, and use design patterns has many meanings. This is a way to name complex abstract concepts to provide discussion and learning.

They make communication within the team faster because someone can simply use the template name instead of calling the board. They allow you to learn from the experiences of people who were before you, and not to reinvent the wheel, going through the whole crucible of gradually improving practices on your own (and constantly cringing from your old code).

Bad decisions that are usually made up because they seem logical at first glance are often called anti-patterns. For something to be rightly called an anti-pattern, it must be reinvented, and for the same problem, there must be a pattern that solves it better.

Despite the apparent usefulness in this practice, designing patterns are also use ful for learning. They introduce you to many problems that you may not have considered and allow you to think about scenarios with which you may not have had hands-on experience.

They are mandatory for training for all, and they are an excellent learning resources for all aspiring architect and developing who may be at the beginning of their careers and who have no direct experience in dealing with the various problems that the industry provides.

Python Design Patterns

Traditionally, design models have been divided into three main categories: **creative, structural,** and **behavioral**. There are other categories, such as architectural patterns or concurrency patterns, but they are beyond the scope of this article.

There are also Python-specific design patterns that are created specifically around problems that the language structure itself provides, or that solve problems in unique ways that are only resolved due to the language structure.

Generating Patterns deal with creating classes or objects. They serve to abstract the specifics of classes, so that we are less dependent on their exact implementation, or that we do not have to deal with complex constructions whenever we need them, or that we provide some special properties of the instantiation. They are very useful for reducing dependency and controlling how the user interacts with our classes.

Structural patterns deal with assembling objects and classes into larger structures while keeping these structures flexible and efficient. They, as a rule, are really useful for improving the readability and maintainability of the code, ensuring the correct separation of functionality, encapsulation, and the presence of effective minimal interfaces between interdependent things.

Behavioral patterns deal with algorithms in general and the distribution of responsibility between interacting objects. For example, they are good practice when you may be tempted to implement a naive solution, such as busy waiting, or load your classes with unnecessary code for one specific purpose, which is not the core of their functionality.

Generative Patterns

- Factory
- Abstract factory
- Builder
- Prototype
- Singleton
- Object pool

Structural Patterns

- Adapter
- Bridge
- Composite
- Decorator
- Facade

- Flyweight
- Proxy

Behavioral patterns

- Chain of responsibility
- Command
- Iterator
- Mediator
- Memento
- Observer
- State
- Strategy
- Visitor

Python Specific Design Patterns

- Global object pattern
- Prebound method pattern
- Sentinel object pattern

Type Annotation in Python

First, let's answer the question: why do we need annotations in Python? In short, the answer will be this: to increase the information content of the source code and to be able to analyze it using specialized tools. One of the most popular, in this sense, is the control of variable types. Even though Python is a language with dynamic typing, sometimes there is a need for type control.

According to PEP 3107, there may be the following annotation use cases:

- type checking:
- expansion of the IDE functionality in terms of providing information about the expected types of arguments and the type of return value for functions:
- overload of functions and work with generics:
- interaction with other languages:
- use in predicate logical functions:
- mapping of requests in databases:
- marshaling parameters in RPC (remote procedure call)

Using annotations in functions

In functions, we can annotate arguments and the return value.

It may look like this:

def repeater (s: str, n: int) -> str:

*return s * n*

An annotation for an argument is defined after the colon after its name:

argument_name: annotation

An annotation that determines the type of the value returned by the function is indicated after its name using the characters ->

def function_name () -> type

Annotations are not supported for lambda functions

Access to function annotations Access to the annotations

Used in the function can be obtained through the __annotations attribute, in which annotations are presented in the form of a dictionary, where the keys are attributes, and the values are annotations. The main value to returned by the function is stored in the record with the return key.

Contents of repeater . annotations :

{'n': int, 'return': str, 's': str}

4 programming languages to learn, even if you are a humanist

The digital age dictates its own rules. Now, knowledge of programming languages is moving from the category of "too highly specialized skill" to must have for a successful career. We have compiled for you the four most useful programming languages that will help you become a truly effective specialist.

1. Vba

If you constantly work in Excel and spend time on the same routine operations every day, you should consider automating them. Macros - queries in the VBA language built into Excel will help you with this. Having mastered macros, you can not only save time, but also free up time for more interesting tasks (for example, to write new macros). By the way, to automate some operations, learning VBA is not necessary - just record a few actions using the macro recorder , and you can repeat them from time to time. But it's better to learn this language: macro recordings will give you only limited functionality.

Despite its attractiveness, macros have two drawbacks. Firstly, since a macro automatically does all the actions that you would do with your hands, it seriously loads RAM (for example, if you have 50,000 lines in a document, your poor computer may not withstand macro attacks). The second - VBA as a programming language is not very intuitive, and it can be difficult for a beginner to learn it from scratch.

2. SQL

In order to combine data from different databases, you can use the formulas VPR and INDEX (SEARCH). But what if you have ten different databases with 50 columns of 10,000 rows each? Chances are good to make a mistake and spend too much time.

Therefore, it is better to use the Access program. Like VPR, it is designed to combine data from various databases, but it does it much faster. Access automates this function, as well as quickly filters information and allows you to work in a team. In addition to Access, there are other programs for working with databases (DBMS), in most of which you can work using a simple programming language - SQL (Structured Query Language). Knowledge of SQL is one of the basic requirements for business analysts along with knowledge of Excel, so we advise you to take a closer look if you want to work in this area.

3. R

R is a good alternative to VBA if you want to make data processing easier. How is he good? Firstly, unlike a fellow, it is really simple and understandable even for those who have never had anything to do with programming in their life. Secondly, R is designed to work with databases and has wide functionality: it can change the structure of a document, collect data from the Internet, process statistically different types of information, build graphs, create tag clouds, etc. To work with Excel files, you will have to download special libraries, but it is most convenient to save tables from Excel in csv format and work in them. By the way, it is R that the program was written with which we make TeamRoulette in our championships. Thanks to her, we manage to scatter people on teams in five minutes instead of two hours.

To learn how to work in R, first of all, download a visual and intuitive programming environment - RStudio .

4. Python

Python is an even more powerful and popular programming language (by the way, it really has nothing to do with python). Like R, Python has special libraries that work with Excel files, and it also knows how to collect information from the Internet (forget about manually driving data into tables!). You can write endlessly about Python, but if in a nutshell - it's a really convenient and quick tool that is worth mastering if you want to automate routine operations, develop your own algorithmic thinking and generally keep up with technical progress.

Unlike R, Python does not have one of the most convenient programming environments - here everyone is free to choose to taste. For example, we recommend IDLE, Jupyter Notebook, Spyder, for more advanced programmers - PyCharm.

You can learn how to program in Python and analyze data using it in our online course "Python. Data Analysis" . The consultants from Big4 and Big3 will tell you how to work with libraries, create programs and algorithms for processing information.

Well, as it were, let's go

Well, if you (You, He, She, It, They) are reading this means we are starting our first Python lesson. Hooray (...) Today you will learn how to code. And what's more, you'll learn how to code in Python.

But to start coding you need Python. Where to get it?

Where to get Python?

But you think that now you can just sit down and cod. Well actually yes. BUT usually real hackers and programmers code in code editors. For working with Python We (I) recommend using a Jupyter Notebook or JupyterLab or Visual Studio Code. We (I) Will code in Visual Studio Code, but the other editors are no different.

Well, it's CODING time.

I'm too old for that

Everyone always writes the first code that displays "Hello World". Well, are we some kind of gifted? No, and therefore we will begin with this. In Python, the print () function is used to output text. To output "Hello World" we need to write the following:

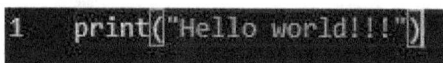

It's alife

Yes, you just wrote your first program. Now you are a programmer (NO).

Let's look at the structure of the print function. This function consists of the name - print, and the place where we throw what this function should output. If you want to display any text, you need to write it in quotation mark, either in single or double.

But now let's enter some text. For this, Python has an input function. To accept something, you need to write the following:

```
1    a=input()
2    print(a)
```

What does this program do for us? First we introduce some thing, at the moment we don't care what it is, text or numbers. After, our program displays what you wrote.

But how to make sure that we write the text before entering some thing? Really simple. There are two ways to do this.

```
1    print('             ')
2    a=input()
3    print(a)
```

How can, but not necessary

If you run the second program you will notice that you have to enter data in the same line in which the text is written.

```
1    a=input(            )
2    print(a)
```

How to do

But this is not aesthetically pleasing. We are here with you all the aesthetes. And so in order for you to enter values on a separate line, you can do the following:

Like cool, but why?

As we can see, \ n appeared at the end. This is a control character that indicates the passage to the next line. But it's too lazy for me to write it down every time, and therefore I prefer to type everything in the line where the text is written.

But where to apply it? Very simple, you can take math. There are some simple arithmetic operations in Python that I will tell you about now.

Python has the following arithmetic operations: addition, subtraction, multiplication, division, integer division, exponentiation, and the remainder of division. As everything is recorded, you can see below:

```
1   6+2
2   6-2
3   6*2
4   6/2
5   3//2
6   3**2
7   3%2
```

I will finally learn how to multiply

If you want to immediately print the result, then you just need to write an arithmetic operation in print:

```
1    print(6+2)
```

The result of this program will be 8

But how do we carry out operations with numbers that the user enters? We need to use input. But by default in Python, the values that input passes are a string. And most arithmetic operations cannot be performed on a line. In order for our program to work as we intended, we need to specify what type of value Python should use.

To do this, we use the int function:

```
1    a=int(input("      : "))
2    b=int(input("      : "))
3    print(a+b)
```

We add up the two numbers that the user enters. (Wow, I found out how much 2 + 2 will be)

1. PYTHON CODE OPTIMIZATION WITH CTYPES

Content:

1. Basic optimizations
2. Styles
3. Python compilation
4. Structures in Python
5. Call your code in C
6. Pypy

Basic optimizations

Before rewriting the Python source code in C, consider the basic optimization methods in Python.

Built-in Data Structures

Python's built-in data structures, such as set and dict, are written in C. They work much faster than your own data structures composed as Python classes. Other data structures besides the standard set, dict, list, and tuple are described in the collections module documentation.

List expressions

Instead of adding items to the list using the standard method, use list expressions.

```
#Slow
    mapped = []
    for value in originallist:
    mapped.append (myfunc (value))

# Faster
    mapped = [myfunc (value) in originallist]
```

ctypes

The ctypes module allows you to interact with C code from Python without using a module subprocessor another similar module to start other processes from the CLI.

There are only two parts: compiling C code to load in quality shared object and setting up data structures in Python code to map them to C types.

In this article, I will combine my Python code with LCS.c, which finds the longest subsequence in two-line lists. I want the following to work in Python:

```
list1 = ['My', 'name', 'is', 'Sam', 'Stevens', '!']
    list2 = ['My','name', 'is', 'Alex', 'Stevens', '.']

    common = lcs (list1, list2)

    print (common)
    # ['My', 'name', 'is', 'Stevens']
```

One problem is that this particular C function is the signature of a function that takes lists of strings as argument types and returns a type that does not have a fixed length. I solve this problem with a sequence structure containing pointers and lengths.

Compiling C code in Python

First, C source code (lcs.c) is compiled in lcs.so to load in Python.

```
gcc -c -Wall -Werror -fpic -O3 lcs.c -o lcs.o
    gcc -shared -o lcs.so lcs.o
```

- Wall will display all warnings:
- Werror will wrap all warnings in errors:
- fpic will generate position-independent instructions that you will need if you want to use this library in Python:
- O3 maximizes optimization:

And now we will begin to write Python code using the resulting shared object file .

Structures in Python

Below are two data structures that are used in my C code.

```
struct sequence
  {
    char ** items:
    int length:
  }:

  struct cell
  {
    int index:
    int length:
    struct Cell * prev:
  }:
```

And here is the translation of these structures into Python.

```
import ctypes
  class SEQUENCE (ctypes.Structure):
    _fields_ = [('items', ctypes.POINTER
(ctypes.c_char_p)),
            ('length', ctypes.c_int)]

  class CELL (ctypes.Structure):
    pass

  CELL._fields_ = [('index', ctypes.c_int), ('length',
ctypes.c_int),
            ('prev', ctypes.POINTER (CELL))]
```

A few notes:

- All structures are classes that inherit from ctypes.Structure.
- The only field _fields_ is a list of tuples. Each tuple is (<variable-name>, <ctypes.TYPE>).

- There ctypesare similar types in c_char (char) and c_char_p (* char).
- There is ctypesalso one POINTER()that creates a type pointer from each type passed to it.
- If you have a recursive definition like in CELL, you must pass the initial declaration, and then add the fields _fields_in order to get a link to yourself later.
- Since I did not use CELLPython in my code, I did not need to write this structure, but it has an interesting property in the recursive field.

Call your code in C

In addition, I needed some code to convert Python types to new structures in C. Now you can use your new C function to speed up Python code.

```python
def list_to_SEQUENCE (strlist: List [str]) -> SEQUENCE:
    bytelist = [bytes (s, 'utf-8') for s in strlist]
    arr = (ctypes.c_char_p * len (bytelist)) ()
    arr [:] = bytelist
    return SEQUENCE (arr, len (bytelist))


def lcs (s1: List [str], s2: List [str]) -> List [str]:
    seq1 = list_to_SEQUENCE (s1)
    seq2 = list_to_SEQUENCE (s2)

# struct Sequence * lcs (struct Sequence * s1, struct Sequence * s2)
common = lcsmodule.lcs (ctypes.byref (seq1), ctypes.byref (seq2)) [0]

    ret = []

    for i in range (common.length):
        ret.append (common.items [i] .decode ('utf-8'))
    lcsmodule.freeSequence (common)

    return ret

lcsmodule = ctypes.cdll.LoadLibrary ('lcsmodule / lcs.so')
lcsmodule.lcs.restype = ctypes.POINTER (SEQUENCE)

list1 = ['My', 'name', 'is', 'Sam', 'Stevens', '!']
list2 = ['My', 'name', 'is', 'Alex', 'Stevens', '.']

common = lcs (list1, list2)

print (common)

# ['My', 'name', 'is', 'Stevens']
```

ctypes.POINTER(SEQUENCE).

- To make a call with a reference to the Sequence structure, I use ctypes.byref()one that returns a "light pointer" to your object (faster than ctypes.POINTER()).
- common.items- this is a list of bytes, they can be decoded to get retin the form of a list str.
- lcsmodule.freeSequence (common) just frees the memory associated with common. This is important because the garbage collector (AFAIK) will not automatically collect it.

Optimized Python code is code that you wrote in C and wrapped in Python.

Something More: PyPy

Attention: I myself have never used PyPy.

One of the simplest optimizations is to run your programs in the PyPy runtime, which contains a JIT compiler (just- in-time) that speeds up the work of loops, compiling them into machine code for repeated execution.

2. FINDING THE PERFECT TOOLKIT: ANALYZING POPULAR PYTHON PROJECT TEMPLATES

The materials, the translation of which we publish today, is dedicated to the story about the tools used to create Python applications. It is designed for those programmers who have already left the category of beginners but have not yet reached the category of experienced Python developers.

For those who can't wait to start practice, the author suggests using Flake8, pytest , and Sphinx in existing Python projects. He also recommends a look at pre-commit, Black, and Pylint. Those who plan to start a new project, he advises paying attention to Poetry and Dependable.

Overview

It has alway been difficult for me to form an objective opinion about the "best practices" of Python development. In the world of technology, some popular trends are continually emerging, often not existing for long. This complicates the extraction of the "useful signal" from the information noise.

The freshest tools are often only good, so to speak, on paper. Can they help the practical programmer with something? Or their application only leads to the introduction of something new in the project, the performance of which must be maintained, which carries more difficulties than benefits?

I didn't have a clear understanding of what exactly I considered the "best practices" of development. I suppose I found something useful, based mainly on episodic evidence of "utility," and on the occasional mention of this in conversations. I decided to put things in order in this matter. To do this, I began to analyze all the templates of Python projects that I could find (we are talking about templates used by the cookiecutter command-line utility to create Python projects based on them).

It seemed to me that it was fascinating to learn about what auxiliary tools the template authors consider worthy of getting these tools into new Python projects created based on these templates.

I analyzed and compared the 18 most popular template projects (from 76 to 6300 stars on GitHub), paying particular attention to what kind of auxiliary tools they use. The results of this examination can be found in this table.

Below I want to share the main conclusions that I have made while analyzing popular templates.

De facto standards

The tools discussed in this section are included in more than half of the templates. This means that they are perceived as standard in a large number of real Python projects.

Flake8

I have been using Flake8 for quite some time, but I did not know about the dominant position in the field of linting that this tool occupies. I thought that it exists in a kind of competition, but the vast majority of project templates use it.

Yes, this is not surprising. It is difficult to oppose something to the convenience of linting the entire code base of the project in a matter of seconds. Those who want to use cutting-edge development can recommend a look at us make- python-styleguide . This is something like "Flake8 on steroids." This tool may well contribute to the transfer to the category of obsolete other similar tools (like Pylint).

Pytest and coverage.py

The vast majority of templates use pytest . This reduces the use of the standard unit test framework. Pytest looks even more attractive when combined with tox. That's precisely what was done in about half of the templates. Code coverage with tests is most often checked using coverage.py.

Sphinx

Most templates use Sphinx to generate documentation. To my surprise, MkDocs is rarely used for this purpose.

As a result, we can say that if you do not use Flake8, pytest, and Sphinx in your current project, then you should consider introducing them.

Promising tools

In this section, I collected those tools and techniques, the use of which in the templates suggested some trends. The point is that although all this does not appear in most project templates, it is found in many relatively recent templates. So - all this is worth paying attention to.

Pyproject.toml

File usage is pyproject.tomlsuggested in PEP 518. This is a modern mechanism for specifying project assembly requirements. It is used in most fairly young templates.

Poetry

Although the Python ecosystem isn't doing well in terms of an excellent tool for managing dependencies, I cautiously optimistic that Poetry could be the equivalent of npm from the JavaScript world in the Python world.

The youngest (but popular) project templates seem to agree with this idea of mine. Real, it is worth saying that if someone is working on some kind of library that he can plan to distribute through PyPI, then he will still have to use setup tools . (It should to be noted that after the publication of this material, I was informed that this is no longer a problem).

Also, be careful if your project (the same applies to dependencies) relies on Conda. In this case, Poetry will not suit you, since this tool, in its current form, binds the developer to pip and virtualenv.

Dependabot

Dependabot regularly checks project dependencies for obsolescence and tries to help the developer by automatically opening PR.

I have recently seen this tool more often than before. It seem like to me that it is an excellent tool: the addition of which to the project affects the project very positively. Dependabot helps reduce security risks by pushing developers to keep dependencies up to date.

As a result, I advised you not to lose sight of Poetry and Dependabot. Consider introducing these tools into your next project.

Personal recommendations

Analysis of project templates gave me a somewhat ambivalent perception of the tools that I will list in this section. In any case, I want to use this section to tell about them, based on my own experience. At one time, they were beneficial to me.

Pre-commit

Even if you are incredibly disciplined - do not waste your energy on performing simple routine actions such as additional code run through the linter before sending the code to the repository. Similar tasks can be passed to Pre- commit. And it's better to spend your energy on TDD and teamwork on code.

Pylint

Although Pylint is criticized for being slow, although this tool is criticized for the features of its settings, I can say that it allowed me to grow above myself in the field of programming.

He gives me specific instructions on those parts of the code that I can improve, tells me how to make the code better comply with the rules. For a free tool, this alone is already very much. Therefore, I am ready to put up with the inconvenience associated with Pylint.

Black

Black at the root of the debate over where to put spaces in the code. This protects our teams from an empty talk and meaningless differences in files caused by different editors' settings.

In my case, it brightens up what I don't like about Python (the need to use a lot of spaces). Moreover, it should be noted that the Black project in 2019 joined the Python Software Foundation, which indicates the seriousness and quality of this project.

As a result, I want to say that if you still do not use pre-commit, Black, and Pylint - think about whether these tools can benefit your team.

Subtotals

Twelve of the eighteen investigated templates were created using the cookiecutter framework. Some of those templates where this framework is not used have exciting qualities.

But given the fact that cookiecutter is the leading framework for creating project templates, those who decide to use a template that did not use a cookiecutter should have excellent reasons for this. Such a decision should be very well justified.

Those who are looking for a template for their project should choose a template that most closely matches his view of things. If you, when creating projects according to a precise template, continuously have to reconfigure them in the same way, think about how to fork such a template and refine it, inspired by examples of templates from my list.

And if you are attracted to adventure - create your template from scratch. Cookiecutter is an excellent feature of the Python ecosystem, and the simple process of creating Jinja templates allows you to quickly and easily do something your own.

Bonus: Template Recommendations

Django

Together with the most popular Django templates, consider using we make-django-template. It gives the impression of a deeply thought out product.

Data Processing and Analysis

In most projects aimed at processing and analyzing data, the Cookiecutter Data Science template is useful. However, data scientists should also look at Kedro.

This template extends Cookiecutter Data Science with a mechanism for creating standardized data processing pipelines. It supports loading and saving data and models. These features are very likely to be able to find a worthy application in your next project.

Here I would a also like to express my gratitude to the creators of the shablona template for preparing very high- quality documentation. It can be useful to you even if you end up choosing something else.

General Purpose Templates

Which general-purpose template to choose in some way depends on what exactly you are going to develop based on this template - a library or a regular application. But I, selecting a similar template, along with the most popular projects of this kind, would look very closely at Jace's Python Template.

This is not a well-known pattern, but I like the fact that it has Poetry, isort , Black, pylint, and mypy .

PyScaffold is one of the most popular non-cookiecutter based templates. It has many extensions (for example, for Django, and Data Science projects). It also downloads version numbers from

GitHub using setuptools-scm. Further, this is one of the few templates supporting Conda.

Here are a couple of templates that use GitHub Actions technology:

1. The <u>Python Best Practices Cookiecutter template</u>, which, I want to note, has most of my favorite tools.
2. The <u>Blueprint / Boilerplate For Python Projects</u> template, which I find pretty interesting, as the ability it gives them to find common security problems with Bandit, looks promising. Also, this template has a remarkable feature, which consists in the fact that the settings of all tools are collected in a single file setup.cfg.

And finally - I recommend taking a look at we make-python-package template. I think it's worth doing it anyway. In particular, if you like the Django template of the same developer, or if you are going to use the advanced, we make- python-styleguide instead of pure Flake8.

3. HOW ARE BROAD INTEGER TYPES IMPLEMENTED IN PYTHON?

When you write in a low-level language such as C, you are worried about choosing the right data type and qualifiers for your integers, at each step, you analyze whether it will be enough to use it simply in or whether you need to add long or even long double. However, when writing code in Python, you don't need to worry about these "minor" things, because Python can work with numbers of integer any size type.

In C, if you try to calculate 220,000 using the built-in function powl, you will get the output inf.

```
#include <stdio.h>
#include <math.h>

int main (void) {
  printf ("% Lf \ n", powl (2, 20000));
  return 0:
}

$ ./a.out
inf
```

But in Python, making this easier than ever is easy:

```
>>> 2 ** 20,000
39802768403379665923543072061912024537047727804924259387134 ...
... 6021 digits long ...
6309376
```

It must be under the hood that Python is doing something very beautiful, and today we will find out the exactly what it does to work with integers of arbitrary size!

Presentation and Definition

Integer in Python, this is a C structure defined as follows:

```
struct _longobject {
    PyObject_VAR_HEAD
    digit ob_digit [1];
};
PyObject_VAR_HEADIs a macro, it expands to PyVarObject, which has the following structure:
typedef struct {
    PyObject ob_base;
    Py_ssize_t ob_size; / * Number of items in variable part * /
} PyVarObject;
```

Other types that have PyObject_VAR_HEAD:

- PyBytesObject
- PyTupleObject
- PyListObject

This means that an integer, like a tuple or a list, has a variable length, and this is the first step to understanding how Python can support work with giant numbers. Once expanded, the macro _longobjectcan be considered as:

```
struct _longobject {
    PyObject ob_base;
    Py_ssize_t ob_size; / * Number of items in variable part * /
    digit ob_digit [1];
};
```

There PyObjectare some meta fields in the structure that are used for reference counting (garbage collection), but to talk about this, we need a separate article. The field on which we will focus this ob_digitand in a bit ob_size.

Decoding ob_digit

ob_digitIs a statically allocated array of unit length of type digit (typedef для uint32_t). Since this is an array, it ob_digitis a pointer primarily to a number, and therefore, if necessary, it can be increased using the malloc function to any length. This way, python can represent and process very large numbers.

Typically, in low-level languages such as C, the precision of integers is limited to 64 bits. However, Python supports integers of arbitrary precision. Starting with Python 3, all numbers are presented in the form bignum and are limited only by the available system memory.

Decoding ob_size

ob_sizestores the number of items in ob_digit. Python overrides and then uses the value ob_sizeto to determine the actual number of elements contained in the array to increase the efficiency of allocating memory to the array ob_digit.

Storage

The most naive way to store integer numbers is to store one decimal digit in one element of the array. Operation such as additional and subtractions can be performed according to the rules of mathematics from elementary school.

With this approach, the number 5238 will be saved like this:

This approach is inefficient because we will use up to 32-bit digits (uint32_t) for storing a decimal digit, which ranges from 0 to 9 and can be easily represented with only 4 bits. After all, when writing something as universal like python, the kernel developer needs to be even more inventive.

So, can we do better? Of course, otherwise, we would not have posted this article. Let's take a closer look at how Python stores an extra-long integer.

Python path

Instead of storing only one decimal digit in each element of the array ob_digit, Python converts the numbers from the number system with base 10 to the numbers in the system with base 230 and calls each element as a number whose value ranges from 0 to 230 - 1.

In the hexadecimal number system, the base 16 ~ 24 means that each "digit" of the hexadecimal number ranges from 0 to 15 in the decimal number system. In Python, it's similar to a "number" with a base of 230, which means that the number will range from 0 to 230 - 1 = 1073741823 in decimal.

In this way, Python effectively uses almost all of the allocated space of 32 bits per digit, saves resources, and still performs simple operations, such as adding and subtracting at the math level of elementary school.

Depending on the platform, Python uses either 32-bit unsigned integer arrays or 16-bit unsigned integer arrays with 15-bit digits. To perform the operations that will be discussed later, you need only a few bits.

Example: 1152921504606846976

As already mentioned, for Python, numbers are represented in a system with a base of 2^{30}, that is, if you convert 1152921504606846976 into a number system with a base of 2^{30}, you will get 100.

1152 9215 0460 6846 976 = 1 * ((2^{30}) 2 + 0) * ((2^{30}) 1 + 0) *((2^{30}) 0)

Since it is the ob_digitfirst to store the least significant digit, it is stored as 001 in three digits. The structure _longobjectfor this value will contain:

- ob_size like 3
- ob_digit like [0, 0, 1]

We created a demo REPL that will show how Python stores an integer inside itself, and also refers to structural members such as ob_size, ob_refcountetc.

Integer Long Operations

Now that we have a pure idea of how Python implements integers of arbitrary precision, it is time to understand how various mathematical operations are performed with them.

Addition

Integers are stored "in numbers," which means that addition is as simple as in elementary school, and the Python source code shows us that this is how addition is implemented. A function with a name x_addin a file longobject.cadds two numbers.

```
For (i = 0; i < size_b; ++i) {
    carry += a->ob_digit[i] + b->ob_digit[i];
    z->ob_digit[i] = carry & PyLong_MASK;
    carry >>= PyLong_SHIFT;
}
For ( ; i < size_a; ++i) {
    carry += a->ob_digit[i];
    z->ob_digit[i] = carry & PyLong_MASK;
    carry >>= PyLong_SHIFT;
}
z->ob_digit[i] = carry;
```

The code snippet above is taken from a function x_add. As you can see, it iterates over a number by numbers and performs the addition of numbers, calculates the result and adds hyphenation.

It becomes more interesting when the result of addition is a negative number. The sign ob_sizeis an integer sign, that is, if you have a negative number, then it ob_sizewill be a minus. The value ob_sizemodulo will determine the number of digits in ob_digit.

Subtraction

Just as addition takes place, subtraction also takes place. A function with a name x_subin the file longobject.csubtracts one number from another.

```
For (i = 0; i < size_b; ++i) {
  borrow = a->ob_digit[i] - b->ob_digit[i] - borrow;
  z->ob_digit[i] = borrow & PyLong_MASK;
  borrow >>= PyLong_SHIFT;
  borrow &= 1; /* Keep only one sign bit */
}
for (; i < size_z; ++i) {
  borrow = a->ob_digit[i] - borrow;
  z->ob_digit[i] = borrow & PyLong_MASK;
  borrow >>= PyLong_SHIFT;
  borrow &= 1; /* Keep only one sign bit */
}
```

The code snippet above is taken from a function x_sub. In it, you see how the enumeration of numbers occurs and subtraction is performed, the result is calculated and the transfer is distributed. Indeed, it is very similar to addition.

Multiplication

And again, the multiplication will be implemented in the same naive way that we learned from the lessons of mathematics in elementary school, but it is not very efficient. To maintain efficiency, Python implements the Karatsuba algorithm , which multiplies two n-digit numbers in O (nlog23) simple steps.

The algorithm is not simple and its implementation is beyond the scope of this article, but you can find its implementation in functions and in the file .k_mul k_lopsided_mullongobject.c

Division and other operations

All operations on integers are defined in the file longobject.c, they are very simple to find and trace the work of each.

Attention: A detailed understanding of the work of each of them will take time, so pre-stock up with popcorn.

Optimizing Frequently Used Integers

Python preallocates a small number of integers in memory ranging from -5 to 256. This allocation occurs during initialization, and since we cannot change integers (immutability), these pre-allocated numbers are singleton and are directly referenced instead of being allocated. This means that every time we use / create a small number, Python instead of reallocation simply returns a reference to the previously allocated number.

Such optimization can be traced in the macro IS_SMALL_INTand function get_small_intc longobject.c. So Python saves a lot of space and time in calculating commonly used integer numbers.

4. CREATE A BOT IN PYTHON TO LEARN ENGLISH

No, this is not one of the hundreds of articles on how to write your first Hello World bot in Python. Here you will not find detailed instructions on how to get an API token in BotFather or launch a bot in the cloud. In return, we will show you how to unleash the full power of Python to the maximum to achieve the most aesthetic and beautiful

code. We perform a song about the appeal of complex structures - we dance and dance. Under the cut asynchrony, its system of saves, a bunch of useful decorators, and a lot of beautiful code.

Disclaimer: People with brain OOP and adherents of the "right" patterns may ignore this article.

Idea

To understanding what it is like not to know English in modern society, imagine that you are an 18th-century nobleman who does not know French. Even if you are not very well versed in history, you can still imagine how hard it would be to live under such circumstances. In the modern world, English has become a necessity, not a privilege, especially if you are in the IT industry.

The project is based on the catechism of the future: the development of a neural network as a separate unit, and education, which is based on games and sports spirit. Isomorphic paradigms have been hanging in the air since ancient times, but it seems that over time, people began to forget that the most straightforward solutions are the most effective.

Here is a shortlist of the basic things I want to put together:

- Be able to work with three user dictionaries
- Ability to parse youtube video/text, and then add new words to the user's dictionary
- Two basic skills training modes
- Flexible customization: full control over user dictionaries and the environment in general
- Built-in admin panel

Naturally, everything should work quickly, with the ability to easily replenish existing functionality in the future. Putting it all together, I thought that the best embodiment of my idea into reality would be a Telegram bot. My tale is not about how to write handlers for the bot correctly - there are dozens of such articles, and this is simple mechanical work. I want the reader to learn to ignore the typical dogmas of programming. Use what is profitable and effective here and now.

"I learned to let out the cries of unbelievers past my ears because it was impossible to suppress them."

Base structure

The bot will be based on the python-telegram-bot (ptb) library. I use loguru as a logger, though there is one small snag here. The fact is that ptb by default uses a different logger (standard logging) and does not allow you to connect your own. Of course, it would be possible to intercept all journal messages globally and send them to our registrar, but we will do it a little easier:

```
from loguru import logger
import sys

# Configure dual-stream output to the console and to the file
config = {
    'handlers': [
        {'sink': sys.stdout, 'level': 'INFO'},
        {'sink': 'logs.log', 'serialize': False, 'level': 'DEBUG'},
    ]
}
logger.configure(**config)

# ...

updater = Updater('YOUR_TOKEN')
dp = updater.dispatcher

# Roughly fasten your logger. Cheap and cheerful
updater.logger = logger
dp.logger = logger
```

Unfortunately, I don't have the opportunity to deploy my bot on stable data centers, so data security is a priority. For these purposes, I implemented my system of saves. It provides flexible and convenient work with data - statistics collection, as an example of easy replenishment of functionality in the future.

```python
from __future__ import annotations # In the future, I will omit this import
from loguru import logger

import inspect
import functools
import os

def file_is_empty(path: str) -> bool:
    return os.stat(path).st_size == 0

def clear_file(path: str) -> None:
    with open(path, 'w'): pass

def cache_decorator(method):
    @functools.wraps(method)
    def wrapper(self, *args, **kwargs):
        res = method(self, *args, **kwargs)
        Cache.link.recess(self, {'method_name': method.__name__}) # (1)
        # During testing, multiple calls can slow down
        # program work; opt avoids this
        logger.opt(lazy=True).debug(f'Decorator for {method.__name__} was end ')
        return res
    return wrapper

class cache:
    """
```

+ cache_size - Std thfDtlgh 'hi ch dl data will be su'ed

+ cache_files - Dump file in w'hich all intermediate operations on data are stored

link = None

def init   (self. cache_size = 10):
= Save all screw'ed cl asses. Thi s all or's you t o fl exibl>' vork with data.
sel f. cl asses = []
=Files matching classes
sel f._cache_files = []
= (1). A sm dl hack that dl or's you to cd1 a specifi c instance thrDtlgh a common class
= Thi s w'wks because w'e oril \' have one instance Df the cl ass. 'hi ch
= implements d 1 the logic of 'orking with data. In additi on. it is convenient ari d all o 's
= st gum cantl>' expand the functl Dflallt>' in the future
sel f. cl ass .link = self

self._counter = 0

```
self.CACHE SIZE = cache st ze
def add (self, d s: class, file: str) -> NDne:

    All or's to fasten a class to a sa ver

    + cls - Inst an ce of the class
    + file - The fil e the instari ce is 'orking with

    self._cache_files.append (file)
    self._cl asses.append (cls)

    if file i s eotptl' (file): return hDne

    l ogger. opt d an.' = True) .debug (fT or {cl s . class
    names) file (file) is not empty' ')

    fa data in sells oad(file):
        is.save nDn Caclti ng (data)


    cl ear_file (file)
    sel f._counter = 0


def recess (self, cls: ct ass, data diet) —> Ncri e:

    The main method that performs the basi c l o c of saves


    if self. counter + 1/ = self.CACHE SIZE:
            self.save all 0
    el se:
            self._counter + = I
            fil ename = self._cache_files [self._classes.index
    (cls)]
            self.save (data. fil enam e = filename)


= For simplicit>', save_d1, save, load methods are omitted
```

Now we can create any methods that can modify data, without fear of losing important data:

```
@cache_decorator
def add_smth_important(* args, ** kwargs) -> Any:
    # ...
    # We make some important actions on the data ...
    # ...
```

Now that we have figured out the basic structure, the main question remains: how to put everything together. I implemented the main class - EnglishBot, which brings together the entire primary structure: PTB, work with the database, the save system, and which will manage the whole business logic of the bot. If the implementation of Telegram commands were simple, we could easily add them to the same class. But, unfortunately, their organization occupies most of the code of the entire application, so adding them to the same class would be crazy. I also did not want to create new classes/subclasses, because I suggest using a very simple structure:

```
# Import the main class
from modules import EnglishBot
# Import classes that implement Telegram commands
from modules.module import start
# ...

if __name__ == '__main__':
    # Initialize the bot
    tbot = EnglishBot (
        # ...
    )

    # Add handlers to the stack
    tbot.add_command_handler (start, 'start')
    # ...
```

How command modules get access to the main class, we will consider further.

All out of nothing

Ptb handlers have two arguments - update and context, which store all the necessary information stack. Context has a wonderful chat_data argument that can be used as a data storage dictionary for chat. But I do not want to constantly refer to it in a format context.chat_data['data']. I would like something light and beautiful, say context.data. However, this is not a problem.

```
from telegram.ext import CommandHandler

def a (self, key: str):
    # First, check if the class has the required value
    # If not, then try to return it from chat_data
    try:
        return object.__getattribute__(self, key)
    except:
        return self.chat_data [key]

def b (self, key: str, data = None, replace = True):
    #Small hack: if replace = False and data exists, then overwriting does not occur
    # In this case, if the data is not specified, then they are put in None
    if replace or not self.chat_data.get (key, None):
        self.chat_data [key] = data

# Bindim context to receive data in the format context.data
CallbackContext.__getattribute__ = a
# As well as a convenient setter for your needs
CallbackContext.set = b
```

We continue to simplify our lives. Now I want all the necessary information for a specific user to be in quick access context.

```
def bind_context (func):
    def wrapper (update, context):
        context._bot.bind_user_data (update, context) # (2)
        return func (update, context)
    return wrapper

class EnglishBot:
    # ...

    def bind_user_data (self, update, context) -> dict:
        context.set ('t_id', update.message.chat_id, replace = False)
        context.set ('t_ln', update.message.from_user.language_code, replace = False)
        #
        # Set all the necessary information that we want to have quick access from context
        # For example, something from the database
        #
```

Now we'll completely become impudent and fasten our bot instance to context:

```
class EnglishBot:
    # ...

    def __init__ (self, * args, ** kwargs):
        # ...
        # (2): Now we can access the instance in the format context._bot
        CallbackContext._bot = self
```

We put everything in place and get a citadel of comfort and convenience in just one call.

```
from EnglishBot import bind_context

@bind_context
def start (update, context):
    # Now we have access to everything from one place
    # For example, we can easily add a new user to the database
    # Check if the user is in our database
    if not context._bot.user_exist (context.t_id):
        # For example, add some important notifications
        context.set ('push_notification', True)
        # And then add the user to the database
        context._bot.new_user (context.t_id, context.t_ln)

    return update.message.reply_text ('Welcome')
# ...
```

Decorators are our everything

Most often, it turns out that the name of the function coincides with the name of the command to which we want to add a handler. Why not use this statistical feature for your selfish purposes.

```
class EnglishBot:
    # ...

    def add_command_handler (self, func: function, name = None) -> None:
        """
        Function that adds a command handler
        """
        name = name or func.__name__
        self.dp.add_handler (CommandHandler (name, func))
# ...

# In the main file:
tbot.add_command_handler (start) # Instead of tbot.add_command_handler (start, 'start')
```

It looks cool, but it doesn't work. It's all about the bind_context decorator, which will always return the name of the wrapper function. Correct this misunderstanding.

```
import functools

def bind_context (func):
    # functools.wraps from stdlib saves signatures since Python 3.4
    @functools.wraps (func)
    def wrapper (update, context):
        context._bot.bind_user_data (update, context)
        return func (update, context)
    return wrapper
```

There are many message handlers in the bot, which, by design, should cancel the command when entering zero. Also I need to discard all edited posts.

```
import functools

END = -1

def zero_exiter (func):
    @functools.wraps (func)
    def wrapper (update, context):
        if update.to_dict () ['message']. get ('text', None) == '0':
            update.message.reply_text ('Sending some message')
            return END

        return func (update, context)
    return wrapper

def skip_edited (func):
    @functools.wraps (func)
    def wrapper (update, context):
        # This works in all cases, because None returned
        # in the conversation_handler stack, leaves the function in its current state
        if not update.to_dict (). get ('edited_message', None):
            return func (update, context)
    return wrapper
```

We do not forget at the same time about the most important decorator - @run_asyncon which asynchrony is based. Now we collect the heavy function.

```
from telegram.ext.dispatcher import run_async
from EnglishBot import skip_edited

@run_async
@skip_edited
def heavy_function (update, context):
    # ...
    # A heavy computing function that needs asynchrony
    # Has post edit protection
    # ...
```

Remember that asynchrony is a Jedi sword, but with this sword, you can quickly kill yourself.

Sometimes programs freeze without sending anything to the log. @logger.catch, the last decorator on our list, ensures that any error is correctly reported to a logger.

```
from loguru import logger

@logger.catch
def heavy_function2 (update, context):
    # ...
    # Another heavy computing function on which a program may hang
    # ...
```

Admin panel

Let's implement an admin panel with the ability to receive/delete logs and send a message to all users.

```
from EnglishBot import bind_context
from Cache import file_is_empty
from telegram import ReplyKeyboardMarkup
from loguru import logger

LOG_FILE = 'logs.log'
SENDING, MAIN, END = range (1, -2, -1)

buttons = ReplyKeyboardMarkup (
    [('Get logs', 'logs'), ('Clear logs', 'clear')],
    [('Send message', 'send')],
    # [..],
)

@bind_context
def admin_panel (update, context):
    # Check user admin rights
    if not context._bot_acess_check (context.t_id):
        # A good security practice is to show the user that such a command does not exist
        return update.message.reply_text (f'Unknown command {update.message.text} ')

    update.message.reply_text ('Choose an option', reply_markup = buttons)

    return MAIN
```

log s methods

```
def get logs (update context).
    if file is empU.' (LOG FILE).
        update.cd1back quo.'.rep1)' text       are empU.") else.
      = Show' document loading
        context.bot.send chat acti (xi (chat id = context.t icL action = 'upload documcut')
        context.bot.sendDocument (chat i d = context.t icL docimi cut = open (L OG FILE
        'rb') name = L Ohr FILE
time(xit = 1000)
```

= Since we do not cl ose the admin panel you need to rem ove the dourload icon on the button update.cd1back quell'.answer (text = ")
= B asicd1\' thi s is urin ecessm.'. As I sai d earli er None does not change the positi on of the hand er
= But this was' the code locks much m(xe readabl e return ñIAIN

```
def logs d ear (update context).
    with open (LOG FILE 'u") as fi l e. update.cd1back quo.'.rep1)' text ('O ear ed)
        update.cd1back quo.'.answer (text = ")

        return ñIAIN
```

= Send methods

```
def take message (update context).
    update.cd1back quell'.rep1)' text ('Send m essag e) update.cd1back quell'.answer (text = ")

        return SENDING

!fi ero exiter
def send d1 (updast   context).
    count = 0
```

Get user identifi cfs from the database for id in li st (context. bot.get user ids Q).
  = It may' happen that some user has added a bet to the em ergenc\'
  = Then when to.'ing to send him a message an error u4l1 be caught to.'.
    = fi'e do not setid a message to oursel ves if i d   context.t icL continue
    = Be sure to use ñlarkdour to save message formatting
    context.bet.send message (context.t icL text = update.message.text markdour
    parse mode = ñlarkdour') count + = 1
  except. pass

update.cd1back quell'.repl>' text (£Sent to { count) pecpl e ') update.cd1back
quell'.answer (text = ")

```
# ...
# In the main file:
tbot add_conversation_handler (
    entry_points = [('admin', admin)],
    # The regularity for send_alk allows you to process any message that does not start with /
    states = [[(logs, " logs $'), (logs_clear, " clear $'), (send, " send $')], [(send_alk, '@ ^ ((?! .* (( ^ \ /) +$. *)( . +}$
    )]]
)
```

The add_conversation_handler function allows you to add a conversation handler in a minimalistic way:

```
class EnglishBot:
    # ...
    def add_conversation_handler (self, entry_points: list, states: list, fallbacks: list) -> None:
        fallbacks = [CommandHandler (name, func) for name, func in fallbacks]
        entry_points = [CommandHandler (name, func) for name, func in entry_points]
        r_states = {}

        for i in range (len (states)):
            r_states [i] = []

            # Each array describes functions of one state
            for func, pattern in states [i]:
                # If the regular starts with the @ symbol, then we add a message handler
                # Otherwise, a regular button handler
                if pattern [0] == '@':
                    r_states [i].append (MessageHandler (Filters.regex (pattern [1:]), func))
                else:
                    r_states [i].append (CallbackQueryHandler (func, pattern = pattern))

        conv_handler = ConversationHandler (entry_points = entry_points, states = r_states, fallbacks = fallbacks)
        dp.add_handler (conv_handler)
```

Main functionality

Let's teach our bot to add new words to user dictionaries.

```python
from EnglishBot import bind_context, skip_edited, zero_exiter
from youtube_transcript_api import YouTubeTranscriptApi
from telegram.ext.dispatcher import run_async

START_OVER, ADDING, END = range (1, -2, -1)

re_youtube = re.compile ('^ (http (s)?: \/\/)? ((w) {3}.)? youtu (be | .be)? (\. com)? \/.+')
re_text = re.compile ('^ [az] {3,20} $')

def is_youtube_link (link: str) -> bool:
    if re_youtube.match (link) is not None: return True

def clear_text (text: str) -> str:
    bad_symbols = '! @ #% $ ^ & * () _ + 1234567890 - = /| %?> <., ":' ~ [] {}'
```

for s in bad_symbols:

```
        text = text.replace (s, ")

    return text.stra     ()  IDS'& ()

!@skip_edited
:@bind_context
def add_w'ords (update, context),
    update.message.reply' text ('Enter text:')
    return ADDING

:H uri_asx'nc
:@skip_edit ed
:@zero_exiter
def parse_text (update, context):
    DDDM DZténg takes soote titzte, sD ñ'ou need tD T1ctT1' the user that e\' .'thing is fine
    message = update.message.repl>'_text('L oad rig ...')

    if is 'outube_link (update.message.text):
        = If the video is irivdid or there are no subtitles in it, then we will catch ari  error
        to.':
            transcript list = Y en TubeTranscriptApi list transcripts (get ski deD id (update.message.text))
            t = tr ariscript_listfnd_transcript (['en'])
            _tmt = clear_tmt ('.' .j » ([i [tmt'] fur i in tletJ 0])} split ()
        except:
            otessag z edtt text ('k\'âtid x'ideD. To.' again:')
            return ADD UG
    else:
        _text = clear_tnt (update.message.text) .split ()

    = ¥Ve get a link to the words the user alread>' has
        T'& ds.' CDotext. bDt.get ck ct 'ords (cDIttWt.t id)
        l 'ards tD be ad6ed
        good_w'ords = []
    = Discarded words
        bad_words = Q

    = First, w'e discard duplicates
    for word in set  text):
        = Then w'e check the correctness of the w'ord regular
        z = re_text.match (word)
        if z:
            = Add a vord onl>' if it is n ot already' in the user ñ ation m.'
            if z.group () net in _w'ords:
                good_wcrds.append (word)
            el se:
                bad_words.append ('ord)

    = The Dnl >' thi Hg left 1 S tD suggest the user tD Add ends
    = And then add them t o the di cti Dfl .'
```

```
.. In the main file:
    tbot.add_coriversation_handler(
        entry'   oints = [('add wcrds', add   'crds)],
states = {
    [(parse_text, '@ * ((?L * (( \ () +)). *)(. +) $)],
    # ...
    ])
```

We pack the bot

Before we pack our bot, add proxy support and change log levels from the console.

```
# In the main file:

import argparse

parser = argparse.ArgumentParser ()
parser.add_argument ('-l', '--level', default = 'INFO',
        choices = ['TRACE', 'DEBUG', 'INFO', 'SUCCESS', 'WARNING', 'ERROR', 'CRITICAL'],
        help = 'Allows you to enable the bot in a given mode')
parser.add_argument ('- p', '--proxy', help = 'Allows you to enable bot with proxy')
args = parser.parse_args ()

config = {
  'handlers': [
    {'sink': sys.stdout, 'level': args.level},
    # It's not a mistake. In the file I collect logs of level DEBUG and higher
    {'sink': logs.log', 'serialize': False, 'level': 'DEBUG'},
  ],
}
logger.configure (** config)

if args.proxy:
    t_proxy = {'proxy_url': args.proxy, 'read_timeout': 1000, 'connect_timeout': 1000}
    # ...
    # Proxies for other services
    # ...
else:
    t_proxy = None
```

Python 3.5+ supports the ability to pack a directory into a single executable file. Let's take this opportunity to be able to deploy your work environment on any VPS easily. First, get the dependency file. If you are using a virtual environment, it can be done with one command: pip freeze > requirements.txt. If the project does not have a virtual environment, then you will have to tinker a bit. You can try to use pip freeze and manually isolate all the necessary packages. Still, if too many packages are installed on the system, then this method will not work. The second option is to use ready-made solutions, for example, pipreqs.

Now that our dependency file is ready, we can pack our directory into a .pyzfile. To do this, enter the command py - m zipapp "ПУТЬ_К_КАТАЛОГУ" -m "ИМЯ_ГЛАВНОГО_ФАЙЛА:ГЛАВНАЯ_ФУНКЦИЯ" -o bot.pyz, it will create the bot.pyz file in the project folder. Please note that the code in init .py must be wrapped in some function, otherwise the executable file will be impossible to compile.

```
# Sample __init__.py file
# py -m zipapp "PATH_TO_CATALOG" -m "__init__.py:main" -o bot.pyz

def main():
    # ...

if __name__ == '__main__':
    main()
```

We wrap the files in the archive zip bot.zip requirements.txt bot.pyzand send it to our VPS.

5. THE THERMAL IMAGER ON THE RASPBERRY PI

Well-known thermal imaging modules appeared on the famous Chinese site. Is it possible to assemble an exotic and, possibly, even useful thing - a home-made thermal imager? Why not, like Raspberry was lying somewhere. What came of it – I will tell you under the cut.

MLX90640. What is it?

And this, in fact, is a thermal imaging matrix with a microcontroller on board. Production of the previously unknown company Melexis. The thermal imaging matrix has a dimension of 32 by 24 pixels. This is not much, but when interpolating the image, it seems to be enough to make out something, at least.

There are two type of sensor is available version, the cases of which differ in the viewing angle of the matrix. A more squat structure A overlooks the outside world at an angle of 110 (horizontal) at 75 (vertical) degrees. B - under 55 by 37.5 degrees, respectively. The device case has only four outputs - two for power, two for communicating with the control device via the I2C interface. Interested datasheets can be downloaded here.

And then what is the GY-MCU90640?

Chinese comrades put the MLX90640 on board with another microcontroller on board (STM32F103). Apparently, for easier matrix management. This whole farm is called GY-MCU90640. And it costs at the time of acquisition (end of December 2018) in the region of 5 thousands $. As follows:

As you see, there are two types of boards, with a narrow or wide-angle version of the sensor onboard.

Which version is best for you? A good question, unfortunately, I had it only after the modules was already ordered and received. For some reason, at this time of the orders, I did not pay attention to these nuances. But in vain.

A wider version will be useful on self-propelleds robots or in security system (the field of view will be larger). According to the datasheets, it also has less noise and higher measurement accuracy.

But for visualization tasks, I would more recommend a more "long-range" version of B. For one very significant reason. In the future, when shooting, it can be deployed (manually or on a platform with a drive) and take composite "photos," thereby increasing the more than a modest resolution of 32 by 24 pixels. Collects thermal images 64 by 96 pixels, for example. Well, all right, in the future, the photos will be from the wide-angle version A.

Connect to Raspberry PI

There are two ways to control the thermal imaging module:

1. Shorten the "SET" jumper on the board and use I2C to contact the internal microcontroller MLX90640 directly.
2. Leave the jumper alone and communicate with the module through a similar interface installed on the STM32F103 board via RS-232.

If you write in C ++, it will probably be more convenient to ignore the extra microcontroller, short-circuit the jumper and use the API from the manufacturer, which lies here.

Humble pythonists can also go the first way. It seems like that there are a couple of Python libraries (here and here). But unfortunately, not a single one worked for me.

Advanced pythonists can write a module control driver in Python. The procedure for obtaining a frame is described in detail in the datasheet. But then you will have to prescribe all the calibration procedures, which seems slightly burdensome. Therefore, I had to go the second way. It turned out to be moderately thorny, but quite passable.

Thanks to the insight of Chinese engineers or just a happy coincidence, the shawl turned out to have a perfect location of the conclusions:

It remains only to put the block and insert the scarf into the raspberry connector. A 5 to 3 Volt converter is installed on the board, so it seems that nothing threatens Raspberry's delicate Rx and Tx terminals.

It should be added that the connection according to the first option, is also possible, but requires more labor and solder skill. The board must be installed on the other side of the Raspberry connector (shown in the title photo of this post).

Soft

On a well-known Chinese site, such a miracle is offered to access the GY-MCU90640:

Most likely, there should be some description of the interaction protocol with the microcontroller installed on the board, according to which this software product works! After a brief conversation with the seller of scarves (respect to these respected gentlemen), such a protocol was sent to me. It appeared in pdf and pure Chinese.

Thanks to Google's translator and active copy-paste, after about an hour and a half, the protocol was decrypted, anyone can read it on Github. It turned out that the scarf understands six basic commands, among which there is a frame request on the COM port.

Each pixel of the matrix is, in fact, the temperature value of the object that this pixel is looking at. The temperature in degrees Celsius times 100 (double-byte number). There is even a special mode in which the scarf will send frames from the matrix to the Raspberry 4 times per second.

Copyright (c) 2019

Perinissicm is hereby **granted**, free **of** &arge, to any person obtaining **a cry** of this **sofiware and associaed** «kxtunentation files **(the "Software'),** to deal in the Software without restrictioxi, inclu£ng without limitation the rights to **vse, cry, zaodify,** tzsergc. pablisk.. @stribute.. **sablicease,** aad .* a sdl copies **oftbc** Software. azxJ to pmait soas to wtxxa tbc **Softwac** is fñmisked to do so, sabject to the followiag coaxJitioas:

The **above** copyright notice and this **permission notice** shall be induded in all **copies or** mbstaotial portions of the SoRware.

THE SOFTWARE IS PROVIDED 'AS IS', WITHOUT WARRANTY OF ANY KIND, EXPRESS OR IMPLIED. INCLUDING BUT NOT LIMITED TO THE WARRANTIES OF MERCHANTABILITY, FITNESS FOR A PARTICULAR PURPOSE AND NONINFRINGEMENT. IN NO EVENf SHALL THE AUTHORS OR COPYRIGHT HOLDERS BE LIABLE FOR ANY CLAIM, DAMAGES Ofi OTHER LIABILITY, WHETHER IN ANACTION OF CONTRACT, TORT OR OTHERWISE, ARISING FROM, OUT OF OR IN CONNECTION WITH THE SOFTWARE OR THE USE OR OTHER DEALINGS IN THE SOFTWARE. " "

```
import numpy as np
import cv2
```

d function to get Emissivity from MCU
```
def get_emissivity ():
    ser.write (semi d .to_bytes ([0xA5,Dx55 ,0xOl ,OxFB]))
```

read = ser.read (4) return read [2] / 100

d function to ga temperatures from MCU (Celsius degree x 100)
‹Ref ga_temp_oray (d):

# getting ambient tame
T_a = (iot (d[1540]) + int (d [1541]) • 256) / 100

# getting raw array of pixels temperie
raw_data = d [4: 1540]
T_array = npJrombtdfa (raw_   . ype = up.intl6)

rctura T_a, T_anay

fiioaion to convert temples to pixels oa image
def td_to_image (f).
norm = up.nint8 ((f. 100 - Twin) • 255, (Tmax-Tmin))
norm.shy = (24.32)

========================= Main cycle =========================
Color map range

JASON TEST

```
Tn   = 40
Tmin =20


 print ('Corifi guring Seri d port')
 ser = seri d .Seri d (' dev ." seri d 0')
 ser.baucYate = 115200

= set frequency' of module to 4 Hz
 ser.site (seri d.to baies ([0xA5 0x25 0x01 0xCB]))
 time.sleep (0.1)

= Starting automatic data colection
 ser.site (seri d.to baies ([0xA5 0x35 0x02 0xD/))
 t0 = time.time  Q


 while True.
= waiting for data frame
  data = ser.read (1544)


= The data is ready' l et's handle it!
  To tanp array' = get temp array' (data)
  ta img = td to image (temp array')

= Guage processing
  img = cv2.applvColorñIap (ta img cv2.COL ORñfAP JE T)
  img = cv2.rest ze (inn g (320 240) interpolati on = cv2.IhMR GB IC)
  img = cv2 Hi p (inn g l)
  text = Tmin = {. +. lf) Tmax = {. +. lf) FPS = {. .2f)'. format (temp
  array'.min ()." 100 temp array'.max Q ." 100
  1 ." (time .time Q - t0))
  cv2.putText (img text (5 15) cv2.FONT HERSHEY SET&LE X 0.45 (0
  0 0) 1)
  cv2.imshou' ('Output' img)


  * if 's' is pressed - savi ng of picture key' = cv2.waitKe\' (1) & 0xFF
  if key'    ord (" s").
   fname = 'pic ' + dt.datetime.now' Q. strfli me (". o Y-°. o m-°. » d °. » H-°. » ñI-
   °. » S) + '.jpg' cv2.imuñte (fnam e img)
   print ('Savi rig image' fnam e) t0 = time.time  Q

except KevboardInterrupt.
 * to terminate the cycle
 ser.site (seri d.to baies ([0xA5 0x35 0x01 0xDB])) ser.close  Q
 cv2.destrovAllfi'indows  Q print ('Stopped)

= just in case ser.close  Q
 cv2.destrovAllfi'indows  Q
```

Results

The script polls the thermal imaging matrix and outputs the frames to the monitor console on which the Raspberry PI is connected, four times per second. This is enough not to experience significant discomfort when shooting objects. To visualize the frame, the OpenCV package is used. When the "s" button is pressed, the thermal imaging "heat maps" in jpg format are saved in the folder with the script.

For more information, I deduced the minimum and maximum temperatures on the frame. That is, looking at the color, you can see what approximately the temperature of the most heated or chilled objects. The measurement error is approximately a degree with a larger side. The thermal range is set from 20 to 40 degrees. Exit the script by pressing Ctrl + C.

The script works approximately the same on both the Raspberry Pi Zero W and the Pi 3 B +. I installed the VNC server on the smartphone. Thus, picking up raspberries connected to a power bank and a smartphone with VNC running, you can get a portable thermal imager with the ability to save thermal images. Perhaps this is not entirely convenient, but quite functional.

After the first start, an incorrect measurement of the maximum temperature is possible. In this case, you need to exit the script and rerun it.

That is all for today. The experiment with a home-made thermal imager turned out to be successful. With the helping of this device, it is quite possible to conduct a thermal imaging inspection of the house on your own, for example.

Due to the lower temperature contrast than indoors, the pictures were not very informative. In the photo above, the whole house is on two sides. On the bottom - photos of different windows.

In the code, I changed only the temperature range. Instead of +20 ... + 40, I set -10 ... + 5.

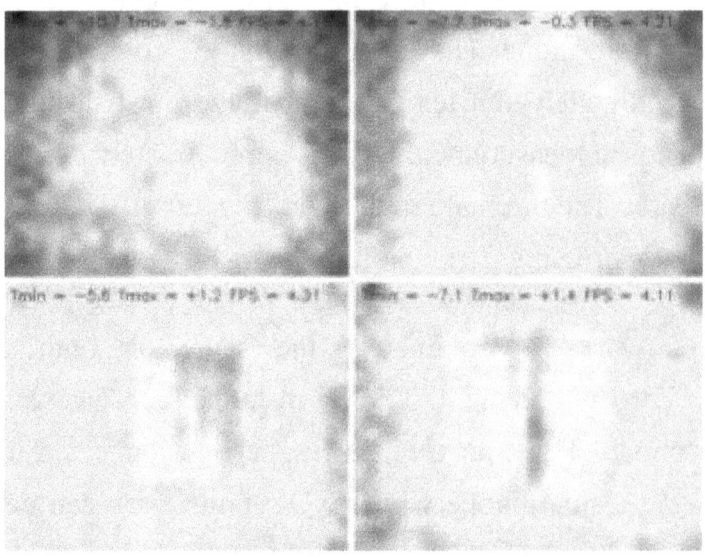

6. FINDING A FREE PARKING SPACE WITH PYTHON

I live in a proper city. But, like in many others, the search for a parking space always turns into a test. Free spaces quickly occupy, and even if you have your own, it will be difficult for friends to call you because they will have nowhere to park.

So I decided to point the camera out the window and use deep learning so that my computer tells me when the space is available:

It may sound complicated, but writing a working prototype with deep learning is quick and easy. All the necessary components are already there - you just need to know where to find them and how to put them together.

So let's have some fun and write an accurate free parking notification system using Python and deep learning

Decomposing the task

When we have a difficult task that we want to solve with the help of machine learning, the first step is to break it down into a sequence of simple tasks. Then we can use various tools to solve each of them. By combining several simple solutions, we get a system that is capable of something complex.

Here is how I broke my task:

The video stream from the webcam directed to the window enters the conveyor input: Through the pipeline, we will transmit each frame of the video, one at a time.

The first point is to recognize all the possible parking spaces in the frame. Before we can look for unoccupied places, we need to understand in which parts of the image there is parking.

Then on each frame you need to find all the cars. This will allow us to track the movement of each machine from frame to frame.

The third step is to determine which places are occupied by machines and which are not. To do this, combine the results of the first two steps.

Finally, the program should send an alert when the parking space becomes free. This will be determined by changes in the location of the machines between the frames of the video.

Each of the step can be completed in different ways using different technologies. There is no single right or wrong way to compose this conveyor: different approaches will have their advantages and disadvantages. Let's deal with each step in more detail.

We recognize parking spaces

Here is what our camera sees:

We need to scan this image somehow and get a list of places to park:

The solution "in the forehead" would be to simply hardcode the locations of all parking spaces manually instead of automatically recognizing them. But in this case, if we move the camera or want to look for parking spaces on another street, we will have to do the whole procedure again. It sounds so-so, so let's look for an automatic way to recognize parking spaces.

Alternatively, you can search for parking meters in the image and assume that there is a parking space next to each of them:

However, with this approach, not everything is so smooth. Firstly, not every parking space has a parking meter, and indeed, we are more interested in finding parking spaces for which you do not have to pay. Secondly, the location of the parking meter does not tell us anything about where the parking space is, but it only allows us to make an assumption.

Another idea is to create an object recognition model that looks for parking space marks drawn on the road:

But this approach is so-so. Firstly, in my city, all such trademarks are very small and difficult to see at a distance, so it will be difficult to detect them using a computer. Secondly, the street is full of all sorts of other lines and marks. It will be challenging to separate parking marks from lane dividers and pedestrian crossings.

When you encounter a problem that at first glance seems complicated, take a few minutes to find another approach to solving the problem, which will help to circumvent some technical issues. What is the parking space? This is just a place where a car is parked for a long time. Perhaps we do not need to recognize parking spaces at all. Why don't we acknowledge only cars that have stood still for a long time and not assume that they are standing in a parking space?

In other words, parking spaces are located where cars stand for a long time:

Thus, if we can recognize the cars and find out which of them do not move between frames, we can guess where the parking spaces are. Simple as that - let's move on to recognizing cars!

Recognize cars

Recognizing cars on a video frame is a classic object recognition task. There are many machine learning approaches that we could use for recognition. Here are some of them in order from the "old school" to the "new school":

- You can train the detector based on HOG (Histogram of Oriented Gradients, histograms of directional gradients) and walk it through the entire image to find all the cars. This old approach, which does not use deep learning, works relatively quickly but does not cope very well with machines located in different ways.

- You can train a CNN-based detector (Convolutional Neural Network, a convolutional neural network) and walk through the entire image until you find all the cars. This approach works precisely, but not as efficiently since we need to scan the image several times using CNN to find all the machines. And although we can find machines located in different ways, we need much more training data than for a HOG detector.

- You can use a new approach with deep learning like Mask R-CNN, Faster R-CNN, or YOLO, which combines the accuracy of CNN and a set of technical tricks that significantly increase the speed of recognition. Such models will work relatively quickly (on the GPU) if we have a lot of data for training the model.

In the general case, we need the simplest solution, which will work as it should and require the least amount of training data. This is not required to be the newest and fastest algorithm. However, specifically in our case, Mask R- CNN is a reasonable choice, even though it is unique and fast.

Mask R-C-N-N architecture is designed in such a way that it recognizes objects in the entire image, effectively spending resources, and does not use the sliding window approach. In other words, it works pretty fast. With a modern GPU, we can recognize objects in the video in high resolution at a speed of several frames per second. For our project, this should be enough.

Also, Mask R-CNN provides a lot of information about each recognized object. Most recognition algorithms return only a bounding box for each object. However, Mask R-CNN will not only give us the location of each object but also its outline (mask):

To train Mask R-CNN, we need a lot of images of the objects that we want to recognize. We could go outside, take pictures of cars, and mark them in photographs, which would require several days of work. Fortunately, cars are one of those objects that people often want to recognize, so several public datasets with images of cars already exist.

One of them is the popular SOCO dataset (short for Common Objects In Context), which has images annotated with object masks. This dataset contains over 12,000 images with already labeled machines. Here is an example image from the dataset:

Such data is excellent for training a model based on Mask R-CNN.

But hold the horses, there is news even better! We are not the first who wanted to train their model using the COCO dataset - many people had already done this before us and shared their results. Therefore, instead of training our model, we can take a ready-made one that can already recognize cars. For our project, we will use the open-source model from Matterport.

If we give the image from the camera to the input of this model, this is what we get already "out of the box":

The model recognized not only cars but also objects such as traffic lights and people. It's funny that she recognized the tree as a houseplant.

For each recognized object, the Mask R-CNN model returns four things:

- Type of object detected (integer). The pre-trained COCO model can recognize 80 different everyday objects like cars and trucks. A complete list is available here.

- The degree of confidence in the recognition results. The higher the number, the stronger the model is confident in the correct recognition of the object.

- Abounding box for an object in the form of XY-coordinates of pixels in the image.

- A "mask" that shows which pixels within the bounding box are part of the object. Using the mask data, you can find the outline of the object.

Below is the Python code for detecting the bounding box for machines using the pre-trained Mask R-CNN and OpenCV models:

```
import nump\' as up

import mrcnn config import mrcnn.utils
from mrcnn.model import ñlaskRCNN from pathli b import Path
```

= The corfi gur ati on that the flask-RCNN librm.' u4 1 1 use. class ñlaskRCNNCorfi g (mrcnn config Colt g.
   DUE = " coco retr ained model corifi g" EvfAGES PER GPL = 1
   GPL COLNT 1
   h I CLASSES = 1 + 80= in the COCO dataset there are 80 classes + 1 background class. DETECTION UHN CONFIDENCE = 0.6

= fi'e filter the list of r ecogniti on results so that on1\' cars remain. def get car boxes (boxes class i ds).
   car boxes = Q

   for i box in enumerate (boxes).
     = If the found obj eO is not a car them skip it. if class ids [i] in [3 8 6].
       car boxes. append (box) return up. array' (car boxes)

= The root direct‹x\' of the project. ROOT DIR = Path (".")

= Dir eO w.' for savi rig logs and trained model. ñIODEL DIR = ROOT DIR ." " logs"

* Locd path to the fi1e with trained weights.
COCO ñIODEL PATH = ROOT DIR ." " mask rem coco.h5"

= Dourload COCO dataset if necessary'. if not COCO ñIODEL PATH.exists Q.
   mrcnn.uti1s.dourload trained weights (COCO ñIODEL PATH)

= Dir eO w.' with images for processing. EvfAGE DIR = ROOT DIR ." "images"

= \'i deo fi1e or camera for processing - insert a vd ue of 0 if you want to use a cam era not a video file. VIDEO SOFF CE " test images ." parking.m@"

= Create a flask-RCNN model in output mode.
model = ñlaskR WU (mode = " inference" model dir = ñIODEL DIR corifi g = ñlaskR C UCorifi g Q)

= Dourload the pre-train ed model.
modd. load weights (COCO ñIODEL PATH b\' name = True)

* Locati ‹xi of parking spaces.
```
```
pznked cr boies=hone
```
```

```python
# Download the video file for which we want to run recognition.
video_capture = cv2.VideoCapture(VIDEO_SOURCE)

# We loop through each frame.
while video_capture.isOpened():
    success, frame = video_capture.read()
    if not success:
        break

    # Convert the image from the BGR color model (used by OpenCV) to RGB.
    rgb_image = frame[:, :, ::-1]

    # We supply the image of the Mask R-CNN model to get the result.
    results = model.detect([rgb_image], verbose=0)

    # Mask R-CNN assumes that we recognize objects in multiple images.
    # We transmitted only one image, so we extract only the first result.
    r = results[0]

    # The variable r now contains recognition results:
    # - r['rois'] - bounding box for each recognized object.
    # - r['class_ids'] - identifier (type) of the object.
    # - r['scores'] - degree of confidence.
    # - r['masks'] - masks of objects (which gives you their outline).

    # Filter the result to get the scope of the car.
    car_boxes = get_car_boxes(r['rois'], r['class_ids'])

    print("Cars found in frame of video:")

    # Display each frame on the frame.
    for box in car_boxes:
        print("Car:", box)

        y1, x1, y2, x2 = box

        # Draw a frame.
        cv2.rectangle(frame, (x1, y1), (x2, y2), (0, 255, 0), 1)

    # Show the frame on the screen.
    cv2.imshow('Video', frame)

    # Press 'q' to exit.
    if cv2.waitKey(1) & 0xFF == ord('q'):
        break

# We clear everything after completion.
video_capture.release()
cv2.destroyAllWindows()
```

After running this script, an image with a frame around each detected machine will appear on the screen: Also, the coordinates of each machine will be displayed in the console:

Cars found in frame of video:
Car: [492 871 551 961]
Car: [450 819 509 913]
Car: [411 774 470 856]

So we learned to recognize cars in the image.

We recognize empty parking spaces

We know the pixel coordinates of each machine. Looking through several consecutive frames, we can quickly determine which of the cars did not move and assume that there are parking spaces. But how to understand that the car left the parking lot?

The problem is that the frames of the machines partially overlap each other:

Therefore, if you imagine that each frame represents a parking space, it may turn out that it is partially occupied by the machine, when in fact it is empty. We need to find a way to measure the degree of intersection of two objects to search only for the "most empty" frames.

We will use a measure called Intersection Over Union (ratio of intersection area to total area) or IoU. IoU can be found by calculating the number of pixels where two objects intersect and divide by the number of pixels occupied by these objects:

So we can understand how the very bounding frame of the car intersects with the frame of the parking space. make it easy to determine if parking is free. If the IoU is low, like 0.15, then the car takes up a small part of the parking space. And if it is high, like 0.6, then this means that the car takes up most of the space and you can't park there.

Since IoU is used quite often in computer vision, it is very likely that the corresponding libraries implement this measure. In our library Mask R-CNN, it is implemented as a function mrcnn.utils.compute_overlaps ().

If we have a list of bounding boxes for parking spaces, you can add a check for the presence of cars in this framework by adding a whole line or two of code:

```
# Filter the result to get the scope of the car.
car_boxes = get_car_boxes (r ['rois'], r ['class_ids'])

# We look how much cars intersect with well-known parking spaces.
overlaps = mrcnn.utils.compute_overlaps (car_boxes, parking_areas)

print (overlaps)
```

The result should look something like this:

```
[
[1. 0.07040032 0. 0.]
[0.07040032 1. 0.07673165 0.]
[0. 0. 0.02332112 0.]
]
```

In this two-dimensional array, each row reflects one frame of the parking space. And each column indicates how strongly each of the places intersects with one of the detected machines. A result of 1.0 means that the entire space is entirely occupied by the car, and a low value like 0.02 indicates that the car has climbed into place a little, but you can still park on it.

To find unoccupied places, you just need to check each row in this array. If all numbers are close to zero, then most likely, the place is free!

However, keep in mind that object recognition does not always work correctly with real-time video. Although the model based on Mask R-CNN is wholly accurate, from time to time, it may miss a car or two in one frame of the video. Therefore, before asserting that the place is free, you need to make sure that it remains so for the next 5-10 next frames of video. This way, we can avoid situations when the system mistakenly marks a place empty due to a glitch in one frame of the video. As soon as we make sure that the place remains free for several frames, you can send a message!

Send SMS

The last part of our conveyor is sending SMS notifications when a free parking space appears.

Sending a message from Python is very easy if you use Twilio. Twilio is an accessible API that allows you to send SMS from almost any programming language with just a few lines of code. Of course, if you prefer a different service, you can use it. I have nothing to do with Twilio: it's just the first thing that come to brain .

To using Twilio, sign-up for a trial account, create a Twilio phone number, and get your account authentication information. Then install the client library:

```
$ pip3 install twilio
```

After that, use the following code to send the message:

```
from twilio.rest import Client

# Twilio account details.
twilio_account_sid = 'Your Twilio SID'
twilio_auth_token = 'Your Twilio Authentication Token'
twilio_source_phone_number = 'Your Twilio Phone Number'

# Create a Twilio client object.
client = Client(twilio_account_sid, twilio_auth_token)

# Send SMS.
message = client.messages.create(
    body = "Message body",
    from_ = twilio_source_phone_number,
    to = "Your number where the message will come"
)
```

To add the ability to send messages to our script, just copy this code there. However, you need make sure that the message is not sent on every frame, where you can see the free space. Therefore, we will have a flag that in the installed state will not allow sending messages for some time or until another place is vacated.

Putting it all together

```python
import numpy as np
import cv2
import mrcnn.config
import mrcnn.utils
from mrcnn.model import MaskRCNN
from pathlib import Path
from twilio.rest import Client

# The configuration that the Mask-RCNN library will use.
class MaskRCNNConfig(mrcnn.config.Config):
    NAME = "coco_pretrained_model_config"
    IMAGES_PER_GPU = 1
    GPU_COUNT = 1
    NUM_CLASSES = 1 + 80  # in the COCO dataset there are 80 classes + 1 background class.
    DETECTION_MIN_CONFIDENCE = 0.6

# We filter the list of recognition results so that only cars remain.
def get_car_boxes(boxes, class_ids):
    car_boxes = []

    for i, box in enumerate(boxes):
        # If the found object is not a car, then skip it.
        if class_ids[i] in [3, 8, 6]:
            car_boxes.append(box)

    return np.array(car_boxes)

# Twilio configuration.
twilio_account_sid = 'Your Twilio SID'
twilio_auth_token = 'Your Twilio Authentication Token'
twilio_phone_number = 'Your Twilio Phone Number'
destination_phone_number = 'Number where the message will come'
client = Client(twilio_account_sid, twilio_auth_token)

# The root directory of the project.
ROOT_DIR = Path(".")

# Directory for saving logs and trained model.
MODEL_DIR = ROOT_DIR / "logs"

# Local path to the file with trained weights.
COCO_MODEL_PATH = ROOT_DIR / "mask_rcnn_coco.h5"

# Download COCO dataset if necessary.
if not COCO_MODEL_PATH.exists():
    mrcnn.utils.download_trained_weights(COCO_MODEL_PATH)

# Directory with images for processing.
IMAGE_DIR = ROOT_DIR / "images"

# Video file or camera for processing - insert the value 0 if using a camera, not a video file.
VIDEO_SOURCE = "test_images / parking.mp4"

# Create a Mask-RCNN model in output mode.
model = MaskRCNN(mode="inference", model_dir=MODEL_DIR, config=MaskRCNNConfig())

# Download the pre-trained model.
model.load_weights(COCO_MODEL_PATH, by_name=True)
# Location of parking spaces.
```

```
parked_car_boxes= None
```

Doumload the stdeo file for vhlch ve vant tD run recDgMtior.
```
video_capture = eve.\'ideoCapture/fiDEO_SOURCE)
```

=. How' mans' frames in a row' math an mnpR.' place we have already' seen.
```
free space frames = 0
```

=. Have w'e d ready sent SMS?
```
sms sent = Fd se
```

"e l cop thfDugh each frame.
```
while s4 deD Capture.isOpened ()
    success, frame = video_capture.read ()
    if not success:
        break
```

Corivert the image from the BGR col or model to RGB.
```
rgb_mage = frame [.... .: – I]
```

fi'e supply' the image of the flask R—Ch model to get the result.
```
results = mDdel.detect ([rgb image], s erbDse = 0)
```

flask R-CA assumes that 'e recognize objects in multiple images.
= fi'e tr aris iitted onl>' one image, sD we extract Ofll\' the fir st result.
```
r = results [0]
```

= The variable r now' contains recogniti on results.
  = - r rois'] - bounding box for each recognized object:
    - r class ids'] - identifier (type) of the object:
    - r § scar est - degree Df cDn 1dence:
= - r masks   masks of objects ('hich gi yes von their outline).

```
if parked car boxes is None:
```
    = This is the first frame Df the videD - let's say' that all detected cars are in the parking lot.
    = Save the locad on of each car as a parking space and move on tD the next fratne.
```
    parked_car_boxes = get_car_boxes (•L•ois'], rcl ass_i ds'])
else:
```
    = XVe dread>' knor' where the places are. Check if there are an>'.

    = U'e ar e l DDki fly for KOf.S Dn the oirr aut frame.
```
    car_boxes = get_car_boxes (r ['r(x sd . L+        '])
```

        1'e lDok hDT' rauch these cars Intersect a'tth 'ell-knDTW parking
```
        DS'erlaps = rarcnn.utils.co tpute_a'erl aps {parked_car_bDxes, car_boxes)
```

    = XVe assume that there are no emph.' seats until 'e find at least one.
```
    free_space = Fal se
```

    = XVe go through the cycle for each well-known parking space.
```
    fa parking area. overlap areas in zip (parked car boxes. overl aps):
```

= fi'e are IDDkiflg for the maximum seal ue of the intersectiDH Flth an>' detected
Dn the frame b5' the machine (no matter w'hich).
max I oU overl ap = up.max (overlap areas)

```
# We get the upper left and lower right coordinates of the parking space.
    y1, x1, y2, x2 = parking_area

    # Check if space is free by checking the IoU value.
    if max_IoU_overlap < 0.15:
        # Place is free! Draw a green frame around it.
        cv2.rectangle (frame, (x1, y1), (x2, y2), (0, 255, 0), 3)
        # We note that we found at least it is free space.
        free_space = True
    else:
        # The place is still taken - we draw a red frame.
        cv2.rectangle (frame, (x1, y1), (x2, y2), (0, 0, 255), 1)

    # Write the IoU value inside the frame.
    font = cv2.FONT_HERSHEY_DUPLEX
    cv2.putText (frame, f"{max_IoU_overlap: 0.2}", (x1 + 6, y2 - 6), font, 0.3, (255, 255, 255))

# If at least one place was free, we begin to count frames.
# This is to make sure that the place is really free
# and do not send another notification.
if free_space:
    free_space_frames += 1
else:
    # If everything is busy, reset the counter.
    free_space_frames = 0

# If the place is free for several frames, we can say that it is free.
if free_space_frames > 10:
    # Display SPACE AVAILABLE !! at the top of the screen.
    font = cv2.FONT_HERSHEY_DUPLEX
    cv2.putText (frame, f"SPACE AVAILABLE!", (10, 150), font, 3.0, (0, 255, 0), 2, cv2.FILLED)

    # Send a message if you have not done so already.
    if not sms_sent:
        print ("SENDING SMS !!!")
        message = client.messages.create (
            body = "Parking space open - go go go!",
            from_ = twilio_phone_number,
            to = destination_phone_number
        )
        sms_sent = True

# Show the frame on the screen.
cv2.imshow ('Video', frame)

# Press 'q' to exit.
if cv2.waitKey (1) & 0xFF == ord ('q'):
    break

# Press 'q' to exit.
video_capture.release ()
cv2.destroyAllWindows ()
```

To run that code, you first need to install Python 3.6+, Matterport Mask R-CNN, and OpenCV.

I specifically wrote the code as simple as possible. For example, if he sees in the first frame of the car, he concludes that they are all parked. Try experiment with it and see if you can improve its reliability.

Just by changing the identifiers of the objects that the model is looking for, you can turn the code into something completely different. For example, imagine that you are working at a ski resort. After making a couple of changes, you can turn this script into a system that automatically recognizes snowboarders jumping from a ramp and records videos with cool jumps. Or, if you work in a nature reserve, you can create a system that counts zebras. You are limited only by your imagination.

7. CREATING GAMES ON THE PYGAME FRAMEWORK | PART 1

Hi, Python lover!

This is the first of a thired-part tutorial on creating games using Python 3 and Pygame. In the second part, we examined the class TextObjectused to render text to the screen is created to the main window, and learned how to draw objects: bricks, ball, and racket.

In this part, we will the dive deeper into the heart of Breakout, and learn how to handle events, get acquainted with the main Breakout class, and see how to move various objects in the game.

Event handling

Breakout has three types of events: keystroke events, mouse events, and timer events. The main loop in the Game class handles keystrokes and mouse events and passes them to subscribers (by calling a handler function).

Although the Game class is very general and does not have knowledge about Breakout implementation, the subscription and event handling methods are very specific.

Breakout class

The Breakout class implements most of the knowledge about how Breakout is controlled. In this tutorial series, we will meet the Breakout class several times. Here are the lines that various event handlers register.

It should be noted that all key events (for both the left and right "arrows") are transmitted to one racket handler method.

```
# Register the handle_mouse_event () method of the button object
self.mouse_handlers.append (b.handle_mouse_event)

# Register racket handle () method for handling key events
self.keydown_handlers [pygame.K_LEFT] .append (paddle.handle)
self.keydown_handlers [pygame.K_RIGHT] .append (paddle.handle)
self.keyup_handlers [pygame.K_LEFT] .append (paddle.handle)
self.keyup_handlers [pygame.K_RIGHT] .append (paddle.handle)
```

Keystroke handling

The Game class calls registered handlers for each key event and passes the key. Note that this is not a Paddle

class. Into Breakout, the only object that is interested in such events is a racket. When you press or release a key, its method is `handle()` called. The Paddle object does not need to know if this was a key press or release event, because it controls the current state using a pair of Boolean variables: `moving_left` and `moving_right`. If `moving_left` True, it means that the "left" key was pressed, and the next event will be the release of the key, which will reset the variable. The same applies to the right key. The logic is simple and consists of switching the state of these variables in response to any event.

```
def handle (self, key):
    if key == pygame.K_LEFT:
        self.moving_left = not self.moving_left
    else:
        self.moving_right = not self.moving_right
```

Mouse event handling

Breakout has a game menu that we will meet soon. The menu button controls various mouse events, such as movement and button presses (mouse down and mouse up events). In the response to these events, the button updates the internal state variable. Here is the mouse processing code:

```
def handle_mouse_event (self, type, pos):
    if type == pygame.MOUSEMOTION:
        self.handle_mouse_move (pos)
    elif type == pygame.MOUSEBUTTONDOWN:
        self.handle_mouse_down (pos)
    elif type == pygame.MOUSEBUTTONUP:
        self.handle_mouse_up (pos)

def handle_mouse_move (self, pos):
    if self.bounds.collidepoint (pos):
        if self.state! = 'pressed':
            self.state = 'hover'
    else:
        self.state = 'normal'

def handle_mouse_down (self, pos):
    if self.bounds.collidepoint (pos):
        self.state = 'pressed'

def handle_mouse_up (self, pos):
    if self.state == 'pressed':
        self.on_click (self)
        self.state = 'hover'
```

Notice that the method `handle_mouse_event()` registered to receive mouse events checks the type of event and redirects it to the appropriate method that processes this type of event.

Handling Timer Events

Timer events are not processed in the main loop. However, since the main loop is called in each frame, it is easy to check whether the time has come for a particular event. You will see this later when we discuss temporary special effects.

Another situation is the need to pause the game. For example, when displaying a message that the player must read and so that nothing distracts him. The show_message()Breakout class method takes this approach and to calls time.sleep(). Here is the relevant code:

```
import config as c

class Breakout (Game):
    def show_message (self,
                text,
                color = colors.WHITE,
                font_name = 'Arial',
                font_size = 20,
                centralized = False):
        message = TextObject (c.screen_width // 2,
                c.screen_height // 2,
                lambda: text, color,
                font_name, font_size)
        self.draw ()
        message.draw (self.surface, centralized)
        pygame.display.update ()
        time.sleep (c.message_duration)
```

Game process

Gameplay (gameplay) is where the Breakout rules come into play. The gameplay consists in moving various objects in response to events and in changing the state of the game based on their interactions.

Moving racket

You saw earlier that the Paddle class responds to arrow keys by updating its

fields `moving_left` and `moving_right`. The movement itself occurs in a method `update()`. Certain calculations are performed here if the racket is close to the left or right edge of the screen. We do not want the racket to go beyond the boundaries of the screen (taking into account a given offset).

Therefore, if the movement moves the object beyond the borders, then the code adjusts the movement so that it stops right at the border. Since the racket only moves horizontally to the vertical component of the movement is always zero.

```python
import pygame

import config as c
from game_object import GameObject

class Paddle(GameObject):
    def __init__(self, x, y, w, h, color, offset):
        GameObject.__init__(self, x, y, w, h)
        self.color = color
        self.offset = offset
        self.moving_left = False
        self.moving_right = False

    ...

    def update(self):
        if self.moving_left:
            dx = -(min(self.offset, self.left))
        elif self.moving_right:
            dx = min(self.offset, c.screen_width - self.right)
        else:
            return

        self.move(dx, 0)
```

Moving ball

The ball simply uses the functionality of the base class `GameObject`, which moves objects based on their speed (its horizontal and vertical components). As we will soon see, the speed of a ball is determined by many factors in the Breakout class. Since the movement consists simply of adding speed to the current position, the direction in which the ball moves is completely determined by the speed along the horizontal and vertical axes.

Setting the initial speed of the ball

The Breakout ball comes out of nowhere at the very beginning of the game every time a player loses his life. It simply materializes from the ether and begins to fall either exactly down or at a slight angle. When the ball is created in the method create_ball(), it gets the speed with a random horizontal component in the range from - 2 to 2 and the vertical component specified in the config.py module (the default value is 3).

```
def create_ball (self):
    speed = (random.randint (-2, 2), c.ball_speed)
    self.ball = Ball (c.screen_width // 2,
                     c.screen_height // 2,
                     c.ball_radius,
                     c.ball_color,
                     speed)
    self.objects.append (self.ball)
```

Summarize

In this part, we looked at handling events such as keystrokes, mouse movements, and mouse clicks. We also examined some elements of Breakout gameplay: moving the racket, moving the ball, and controlling the speed of the ball.

In the fourth part, we will consider the important topic of collision recognition and see what happens when the ball hits different game objects: a racket, bricks, walls, ceiling, and floor. Then we will pay attention to the game menu. We will create our buttons, which we use as a menu, and will be able to show and hide if necessary.

CREATING GAMES ON THE PYGAME FRAMEWORK | PART 2

This is the Second of a Thired-part tutorial on the creating games using Python 3 and Pygame. In the third part, we delved to the heart of Breakout, and learned how to handle events, got acquainted within the main Breakout class and saw how to move different game objects.

In this part, we will learn the how to recognize collisions and what happens to when a ball hits different object: a racket, bricks, walls, ceiling, and floor. Finally, we will look at the important topic of the user interface, and in particular, how to create the menu from your buttons.

Collision Recognition

In games, the objects collide with each other, and Breakout is no exception. The ball is collides with objects. The main method `handle_ball_collisions()` has a built-in function is called `intersect()` that is used to the check whether the ball hit the object and where it collided with the object. It returns 'left,' 'right,' 'top,' 'bottom,' or None if the ball does not collide with an object.

```
def handle_ball_collisions (self):
    def intersect (obj, ball):
        edges = dict (
            left = Rect (obj.left, obj.top, 1, obj.height),
            right = Rect (obj.right, obj.top, 1, obj.height),
            top = Rect (obj.left, obj.top, obj.width, 1),
            bottom = Rect (obj.left, obj.bottom, obj.width, 1))
        collisions = set (edge for edge, rect in edges.items () if
                ball.bounds.colliderect (rect))
        if not collisions:
            return none

        if len (collisions) == 1:
            return list (collisions) [0]

        if 'top' in collisions:
            if ball.centery> = obj.top:
                return 'top'
            if ball.centerx <obj.left:
                return 'left'
            else:
                return 'right'

        if 'bottom' in collisions:
            if ball.centery> = obj.bottom:
                return 'bottom'
            if ball.centerx <obj.left:
                return 'left'
            else:
                return 'right'
```

Collision of a ball with a racket.

When the ball hit the racket, it bounces. If it hit the top of the racket, it bounces back up, but retains same components horizontal fast speed.

But if he hit the side of the racket, it bounces to the opposite side (right or left) and continues to move down until it hits the floor. The code uses a function intersect().

```
# Kick on the racket
s = self.ball.speed
edge = intersect (self.paddle, self.ball)
if edge is not None:
    self.sound_effects ['paddle_hit'].play ()
    if edge == 'top':
        speed_x = s [0]
        speed_y = -s [1]
        if self.paddle.moving_left:
            speed_x -= 1
        elif self.paddle.moving_left:
            speed_x += 1
        self.ball.speed = speed_x, speed_y
    elif edge in ('left', 'right'):
        self.ball.speed = (-s [0], s [1])
```

Collision with the floor.

The ball hits to the racket from the side, the ball continues fall and then hits the floor. At this moment, the player to loses his life and the ball is recreated so that game can continue. The game ends when player runs out of life.

```
# Hit the floor
if self.ball.top > c.screen_height:
    self.lives -= 1
    if self.lives == 0:
        self.game_over = True
    else:
        self.create_ball ()
```

Collision with ceiling and walls

When a ball hits the wall or ceiling, it simply bounces off them.

```
# Hit the ceiling
if self.ball.top < 0:
    self.ball.speed = (s [0], -s [1])

# Kick against the wall
if self.ball.left < 0 or self.ball.right > c.screen_width:
    self.ball.speed = (-s [0], s [1])
```

Collision with bricks

When ball hits a brick, this is the main event the Breakout game - the brick disappeared, the player receives a point, the ball bounce back, and several more events occur (sound effect, and sometimes a special effect), which we will consider later.

To determine that the ball has hit a brick, the code will check if any of the bricks intersects with the ball:

```
#Bump on a brick
for brick in self.bricks:
    edge = intersect (brick, self.ball)
    if not edge:
        continue

    self.bricks.remove (brick)
    self.objects.remove (brick)
    self.score + = self.points_per_brick

    if edge in ('top', 'bottom'):
        self.ball.speed = (s [0], -s [1])
    else:
        self.ball.speed = (-s [0], s [1])
```

Game Menu Design Program

Most games have some kind of U.I. Breakout has simple menu with two buttons, 'PLAY' and 'QUIT.' The menu is display at the beginning of the game and disappears when the player clicks on 'PLAY.'

Let's see how the button and menu are implemented, as well as how they integrate into the game.

Button Creation

Pygame has no built-in UI library. The third-party extensions, but for the menu, we decided to create our buttons. that has three states: normal, highlighted, and press. The normal state when the mouse is not above the buttons, and the highlight state is when the mouse is above the button, the left mouse button not yet press. The press state is when the mouse is above the button, and the player pressed the left mouse button.

The buttons implement as a rectangle with a back ground color and text display on top of it. The button also receive the (onclick function), which is called when the button is clicked.

```
import pygame

from game_object import GameObject
from text_object import TextObject
import config as c

class Button (GameObject):
    def __init__ (self,
                  x,
                  y,
                  w,
                  h,
                  text,
                  on_click = lambda x: None,
                  padding = 0):
        super().__init__(x, y, w, h)
        self.state = 'normal'
        self.on_click = on_click

        self.text = TextObject (x + padding,
                    y + padding, lambda: text,
                    c.button_text_color,
                    c.font_name,
                    c.font_size)

    def draw (self, surface):
        pygame.draw.rect (surface,
                    self.back_color,
                    self.bounds)
        self.text.draw (surface)
```

The button process its own mouse events and changes its internal state based on these events. When the button is in the press state and receives the event MOUSE BUTTONUP, this means that the player has press the button and the function is called on_click().

```
def handle_mouse_event (self, type, pos):
    if type == pygame.MOUSEMOTION:
        self.handle_mouse_move (pos)
    elif type == pygame.MOUSEBUTTONDOWN:
        self.handle_mouse_down (pos)
    elif type == pygame.MOUSEBUTTONUP:
        self.handle_mouse_up (pos)

def handle_mouse_move (self, pos):
    if self.bounds.collidepoint (pos):
        if self.state != 'pressed':
            self.state = 'hover'
    else:
        self.state = 'normal'

def handle_mouse_down (self, pos):
    if self.bounds.collidepoint (pos):
        self.state = 'pressed'

def handle_mouse_up (self, pos):
    if self.state == 'pressed':
        self.on_click (self)
        self.state = 'hover'
```

The property back_color used to draw on the background rectangle to always returns the color corresponding to current form of the button, so that it is clear to the player that the button is active:

```
@property
def back_color (self):
    return dict (normal = c.button_normal_back_color,
                 hover = c.button_hover_back_color,
                 pressed = c.button_pressed_back_color) [self.state]
```

Menu Design

The function create_menu() create a menu with two buttons with the text 'PLAY' and 'QUIT.' It has two built-in function, on_play() and on_quit() which it pass to the correspond button. Each button is add to the list objects (for rendering), as well as in the field menu_buttons.

```
def create_menu (self):
    for i, (text, handler) in enumerate ((('PLAY', on_play),
                                          ('QUIT', on_quit))):
        b = Button (c.menu_offset_x,
            c.menu_offset_y + (c.menu_button_h + 5) * i,
            c.menu_button_w,
            c.menu_button_h,
            text
            handler
            padding = 5)
        self.objects.append (b)
        self.menu_buttons.append (b)
        self.mouse_handlers.append (b.handle_mouse_event)
```

When PLAY the button is prese onplay(), a function is called that removes the button from the list object so that the no longer drawn. In adding, the values of the Boolean field that trigger the starting of the game - is_gamerunningand startlevel- Thats OK

When the button is press, QUIT is _ game_ runningtakes on value (False)(in fact, pausing the game), it set game_ over to True, which triggers the sequence of completion of the game.

```
def on_play (button):
    for b in self.menu_buttons:
        self.objects.remove (b)

    self.is_game_running = True
    self.start_level = True

def on_quit (button):
    self.game_over = True
    self.is_game_running = False
```

Show and hide GameMenu

The display and hiding the menu are performed implicitly. When the buttons are in the list object, the menu is visible : when they removed, it is hidden. Everything is very simple.

Create built-in menu with its surface that renders its subcomponents (buttons and other objects) and then simply add or remove these menu components, but this is not required for such a simple menu.

To summarize

We examined the collision recognition and what happens when the ball is collides with the different objects: a racket, bricks, walls, floor, and ceiling. We also created a menu with our buttons, which can be hidden and displayed on command.

In last part of the series, we will consider completion of the game, tracking points, and lives, sound effects, and music.

We develop complex system of special effects that add few spices to game. Finally, we will the discuss further development and possible improvements.

CREATING GAMES ON THE PYGAME FRAMEWORK| PART 3

This is the last of the Thired parts of the tutorial on creating games using Python 3 and PyGame. In the fourth part, we learned to recognize collisions, respond to the fact that the ball collides with different game objects, and created a game menu with its buttons.

In last part, we will look at various topics: the end of the game, managing lives and points, sound effects, music, and even a flexible system of special effects. For dessert, we will consider possible improvements and directions for further development.

End of the game

Sooner or later, the game should end. In this form of Breakout, the game ends in one of two ways: the player either loses all his life or destroys all the bricks. There is no next level in the game (but it can easily be added).

Game over!

The game_overclass of the Game class is set to False in the method init ()of the Game class. The main loop continues until the variable game_overchanges to True :

```
class Game:
    def __init__ (self,
                  caption
                  width
                  height
                  back_image_filename,
                  frame_rate):

        self.game_over = False
        ...

def run (self):
    while not self.game_over:
        self.surface.blit (self.background_image, (0, 0))

        self.handle_events ()
        self.update ()
        self.draw ()

        pygame.display.update ()
        self.clock.tick (self.frame_rate)
```

All this happens in the Breakout class in the following cases:

- The player presses the QUIT button in the menu.
- The player loses his last life.
- The player destroys all bricks.

```
def on_quit (button):
    self.game_over = True
    self.is_game_running = False

def handle_ball_collisions (self):
    ...
    # Hit the floor
    if self.ball.top > c.screen_height:
        self.lives -= 1
        if self.lives == 0:
            self.game_over = True

            if not self.bricks:
                self.show_message ('YOU WIN !!!', centralized = True)
                self.is_game_running = False
                self.game_over = True
                return

def update (self):

    if not self.bricks:
        self.show_message ('YOU WIN !!!', centralized = True)
        self.is_game_running = False
        self.game_over = True
        return
```

Game End Message Display

Usually, at the end of the game, we do not want the game window to disappear silently. An exception is a case when we click on the QUIT button in the menu. When a player loses their last life, Breakout displays the traditional message 'GAME OVER!', And when the player wins, it shows the message 'YOU WIN!'

In both cases, the function is used show_message(). It displays text on top of the current screen (the game pauses) and waits a few seconds to before returning. The next iteration of the game loop, checking the field game_overwill determine that it is True, after which the program will end.

This is what the function looks like show_message():

```
def show_message (self,
        text
        color = colors.WHITE,
        font_name = 'Arial',
        font_size = 20,
        centralized = False):
    message = TextObject (c.screen_width // 2,
            c.screen_height // 2,
            lambda: text,
            color
            font_name
            font_size)
    self.draw ()
    message.draw (self.surface, centralized)
    pygame.display.update ()
    time.sleep (c.message_duration)
```

Saving records between games

In this version of the game, we do not save records, because there is only one level in it, and the results of all players after the destruction of the bricks will be the same. In general, saving records can be implemented locally, saving records to a file and displaying another message if a player breaks a record.

Adding Sound Effects and Music

Games are an audiovisual process. Many games have sound effects - short audio clips that are played when a player kills monsters finds a treasure, or a terrible death. Some games also have background music that contributes to the atmosphere. There are only sound effects in Breakout, but we will show you how to play music in your games.

Sound effects

To play sound effects, we need sound files (as is the case with image files). These files can be.wav, .mp3, or .ogg format. Breakout stores its sound effects in a folder sound_effects:

```
~/ git / pygame-breakout> tree sound_effects /
sound_effects /
+ - -  brick_hit.wav
+ - -  effect_done.wav
+ - -  level_complete.wav
+ - -  paddle_hit.wav
```

Let's see how these sound effects load and play at the right time. First, play sound effects (or background music), we need to initialize the Pygame sound system. This is done in the Game class:pygame.mixer.pre_init(44100, 16, 2, 4096)

Then, in the Breakout class, all sound effects are loaded from config into the object pygame mixer Soundand stored in the dictionary:

```
# In config.py
sounds_effects = dict (
    brick_hit = 'sound_effects / brick_hit.wav',
    effect_done = 'sound_effects / effect_done.wav',
    paddle_hit = 'sound_effects / paddle_hit.wav',
    level_complete = 'sound_effects / level_complete.wav',
)

# In breakout.py
class Breakout (Game):
    def __init__(self):
        ...
        self.sound_effects = {
            name: pygame.mixer.Sound (sound)
            for name, sound in c.sounds_effects.items ()}
        ...
```

Now we can play sound effects when something interesting happens. For example, when a ball hits a brick:

```
#Bump on a brick
for brick in self.bricks:
    edge = intersect (brick, self.ball)
    if not edge:
        continue

    self.sound_effects ['brick_hit']. play ()
```

The sound effect is played asynchronously: that is, the game does not stop while it is playing. Several sound effects can be played at the same time.

Record your sound effects and messages

Recording your sound effects can be a simple and fun experience. Unlike creating visual resources, it does not require much talent. Anyone can say "Boom!" or "Jump," or shout, "They killed you. Get lucky another time! "

Playing background music

Background music should play continuously. Theoretically, a very long sound effect can be created, but the looped background music is most often used. Music files can be in .wav, .mp3, or .midi format. Here's how the music is implemented:

```
music = pygame.mixer.music.load ('background_music.mp3')
pygame.mixer.music.play (-1, 0.0)
```

Only one background music can play at a time. However, several sound effects can be played on top of background music. This is what is called mixing.

Adding Advanced Features

Let's do something curious. It is interesting to destroy bricks with a ball, but it quickly bothers. What about the overall special effects system? We will develop an extensible special effects system associated with some bricks, which is activated when the ball hits the brick.

This is what the plan will be. Effects have a lifetime. The effect begins when the brick collapses and ends when the effect expires. What happens if the ball hits another brick with a special effect? In theory, you can create compatible effects, but to simplify everything in the original implementation, the active effect will stop, and a new effect will take its place.,

Special effects system

In the most general case, a special effect can be defined as two purposes. The first role activates the effect, and the second reset it. We want attach effects to bricks and give the player a clear understanding of which bricks special , so they can try to hit them or avoid them at certain points.

Our special effects are determined by the dictionary from the module breakout.py. Each effect has a name (for example, long_paddle) and a value that consists of a brick color, as well as two functions. Functions are defined a lambda functions that take a Game instance, which includes everything that can change the special effect in Breakout.

```
special_effects = dict (
  long_paddle = (
    colors.ORANGE,
    lambda g: g.paddle.bounds.inflate_ip (
        c.paddle_width // 2, 0),
    lambda g: g.paddle.bounds.inflate_ip (
        -c.paddle_width // 2, 0)),
  slow_ball = (
    colors.AQUAMARINE2,
    lambda g: g.change_ball_speed (-1),
    lambda g: g.change_ball_speed (1)),
  tripple_points = (
    colors.DARKSEAGREEN4,
    lambda g: g.set_points_per_brick (3),
    lambda g: g.set_points_per_brick (1)),
  extra_life = (
    colors.GOLD1,
    lambda g: g.add_life (),
    lambda g: None))
```

When creating bricks, they can be assigned one of the special effects. Here is the code:

```
def create_bricks (self):
    w = c.brick_width
    h = c.brick_height
    brick_count = c.screen_width // (w + 1)
    offset_x = (c.screen_width - brick_count * (w + 1)) // 2

    bricks = []
    for row in range (c.row_count):
        for col in range (brick_count):
            effect = None
            brick_color = c.brick_color
            index = random.randint (0, 10)
            if index <len (special_effects):
                x = list (special_effects.values ()) [index]
                brick_color = x [0]
                effect = x [1:]

            brick = Brick (offset_x + col * (w + 1),
                           c.offset_y + row * (h + 1),
                           w
                           h
                           brick_color,
                           effect)
            bricks.append (brick)
            self.objects.append (brick)
    self.bricks = bricks
```
The Brick class has an

effect field, which usually has the value None, but (with a probability of 30%) may contain one of the special effects defined above. Note that this code does not know what effects exist. He simply receives the effect and color of the brick and, if necessary, assigns them.

In this version of Breakout, we only trigger effects when we hit a brick, but you can come up with other options for triggering events. The previous effect is discarded (if it existed), and then a new effect is launched. The reset function and effect start time are stored for future use.

```
if brick.special_effect is not None:
    # Reset the previous effect, if any
    if self.reset_effect is not None:
        self.reset_effect (self)

    # Triggering a special effect
    self.effect_start_time = datetime.now ()
    brick.special_effect [0] (self)
    # Setting the current effect reset function
    self.reset_effect = brick.special_effect [1]
```

If the new effect is not launched, we still need to reset the current effect after its lifetime. This happens in the method update(). In each frame, a function to reset the current effect is assigned to the field reset_effect. If the time after starting the current effect exceeds the duration of the effect, then the function is called reset_effect(), and the field reset_effecttakes the value None (meaning that there are currently no active effects).

```
# Reset special effect if necessary
if self.reset_effect:
    elapsed = datetime.now() - self.effect_start_time
    if elapsed >= timedelta(seconds = c.effect_duration):
        self.reset_effect(self)
        self.reset_effect = None
```

Racket increase

The effect of a long racket is to increase the racket by 50%. Its reset function returns the racket to its normal size. The brick has the color Orange.:

```
long_paddle = (
    colors.ORANGE,
    lambda g: g.paddle.bounds.inflate_ip(
        c.paddle_width // 2, 0),
    lambda g: g.paddle.bounds.inflate_ip(
        -c.paddle_width // 2, 0)),
```

Ball slowdown

Another effect that helps in chasing the ball is slowing the ball, that is, reducing its speed by one unit. The brick has an Aquamarine color.

```
slow_ball = (colors.AQUAMARINE2,
    lambda g: g.change_ball_speed(-1),
    lambda g: g.change_ball_speed(1)),
```

More points

If you want great results, then you will like the effect of tripling points, giving three points for each destroyed brick instead of the standard one point. The brick is dark green.

```
tripple_points = (colors.DARKSEAGREEN4,
        lambda g: g.set_points_per_brick (3),
        lambda g: g.set_points_per_brick (1)),
```

Extra lives

Finally, a very useful effect will be the effect of extra lives. He just gives you another life. It does not need a reset. The brick has a gold color.

```
extra_life = (colors.GOLD1,
        lambda g: g.add_life (),
        lambda g: None))
```

Future Features

There are several logical directions for expanding Breakout. If you are interested in trying on yourself in adding new features and functions, here are a few ideas.

Go to the next level

To turn Breakout into a serious game, you need levels: one is not enough. At the beginning of each level, we will reset the screen, but save points and lives. To complicate the game, you can slightly increase the speed of the ball at each level or add another layer of bricks.

Second ball

The effect of temporarily adding a second ball will create enormous chaos. The difficulty here is to treat both balls as equal, regardless of which one is the original. When one ball disappears, the game continues with the only remaining. Life is not lost.

Lasting records

When you have levels with increasing difficulty, it is advisable to create a high score table. You can store records in a file so that they are saved after the game. When a player breaks a record, you can add small pizzas or let him write a name (traditionally with only three characters).

Bombs and bonuses

In the current implementation on, all special effects are associated with bricks, but you can add effects (good and bad) falling from the sky, which the player can collect or avoid.

Summarize

Developing Breakout with Python 3 and Pygame has proven to be an enjoyable experience. This is a compelling combination for creating 2D games (and for 3D games too). If you love Python and want to create your games, then do not hesitate to choose Pygame.

8. OBJECT-ORIENTED PROGRAMMING (OOP) IN PYTHON 3

Algorithms and data structures

Hi, Python lover!

Table of contents

- What is object-oriented programming (OOP)?
- Python classes
- Python Object (Instances)
- How to define class in Python Instance Attribute Class Attributes
- Object CreationWhat's it? Exercise Overview (# 1)
- Instance MethodsChanging Attributes
- Python object inheritance Example of a dog park Expansion of parent class functionality Parent and child classes Overriding parent class functionality Exercise overview (# 2)
- Conclusion

you will become familiars with the following basic concepts of OOP in Python:

- Python Classes

- Object Instances
- Definition and work with methods
- OOP Inheritance

What is object-oriented programming (OOP)?

Object-oriented programming, or, in short, OOP, is a programming paradigm that provides a means of structuring programs in such a way that properties and behavior are combined into separate objects.

For example, an object can represent a person with a name, age, address, etc., with behaviors such as walking, talking, breathing, and running. Or an email with properties such as a recipient list, subject, body, etc., as well as with behaviors such as adding attachments and sending.

In other words, object-oriented programming is an approach for modeling specific real things, such as cars, as well as the relationships between things like companies and employees, students and teachers, etc. OOP models real objects as program objects that have some data that are associated with it and can performs certain function.

Another common program para-digm is procedural program, which structure a program like a recipe in the sense that it provides a set of steps in the form of functions and blocks of code that are executed sequentially to complete a task.

The key conclusion is that objects are at the center of the paradigm of object-oriented programming, representing not only data, as in procedural programming, but also in the general structure of the program.

NOTE Since Python is a programming language with many paradigms, you can choose the paradigm that is best suited to the problem in question, mix different para-digms in one program or switching from one para-digm to another as your program develops.

Python classes

Focusing first on the data, each object or thing is an instance of some class.

The primitive data structures available in Python, such as numbers, strings, and lists, are designed to represent simple things, such as the value of something, the name of the poem, and your favorite colors, respectively.

What if you want to imagine something much more complex?

For example, let say you wanted to track several different animals. If you use a list, the first element may be the name of the animal, while the second element may represent its age.

How would you know which element should be? What if you had 100 different animals? Are you sure that every animal has a name, age, and so on? What if you want to add other properties to these animals? This is not enough organization, and this is exactly what you need for classes.

Classes are used to create new user data structure that contain arbitrary informations abouts some thing. In this case of an animal, we could creates an Animal()class to track animal properties such as name and age.

It is importants to note that a class simply provides structure - it is an example of how something should be defined, but in fact, it does not provide any real content. Animal()The class may indicate that the name and age are required to determine the animal, but it will not claim that the name or age of a particular animal is.

This can help present the class as an idea of how something should be defined.

Python Objects (Instances)

While a class is a plan, an instance is a copy of a class with actual values, literally an object belonging to a particular class. This is no longer an idea: it's a real animal, like a dog named Roger, which is eight years old.

In other words, a class is a form or profile. It determines the necessary informations. After you fullfill out the form, your specific copy is an instance of the class: it contains up-to-date information relevant to you.

You can fill out several copies to create many different copies, but without a form, as a guide, you would be lost without knowing what information is required. Thus, before you can create separate instances of an object, we must first specify what you need by defining a class.

How to define a class in Python

Defining a class is simple in Python:

```
class Dog:
    pass
```

You start with a classkeyword to indicate that you are creating a class, then you add the class name (using the CamelCase notation starting with a capital letter).

Also here we used the Python keyword pass. This is huge often used as a placeholder where the code will eventually go. This allows us to run this code without generating an error.

Note: the above code is correct in Python 3. On Python 2.x ("deprecated Python"), you would use a slightly different class definition:

```
# Python 2.x Class Definition
class Dog(object):
    pass
```

Not the (object)parts in parentheses indicate the parent class that you are inheriting from (more on this below). In Python-3, this is no longer necessary because it is implicit by defaulting.

Instance attribute

All class create objects, and all objects contain characteristics called attributes (called properties in the first paragraph). Use the init ()method to initialize (for example, determine) the initial attributes of an object by giving them a default value (state). This method must have atleast one argument, as well as a self variable that refers to the object itself (for example, Dog).

```
class Dog:
    # Initializer / Instance Attributes
    def __init__(self, name, age):
        self.name = name
        self.age = age
```

In our Dog()class, each dog has a specific name and age, which is certainly important to know when you start creating different dogs. Remember: the class is intended only to define a dog, and not to create instances of individual dogs with specific names and ages: we will come back to this soon.

Similarly, a self variable is also an instance of a class. Since class instances have different meanings, we could argue, Dog.name = namenot self.name = name. But since not all dogs have the same name, we must be able to assign different values for different instances. Hence the need for a special self variable that will help track individual instances of each class.

NOTE: you will never have to call a init ()method: it is called automatically when a new instance of Dog is created.

Class attributes

Although instance attributes are specific to each object, class attributes are the same for all instances, in this case, all dogs.

```
class Dog:

    # Class Attribute
    species = 'mammal'

    # Initializer / Instance Attributes
    def __init__(self, name, age):
        self.name = name
        self.age = age
```

Thus, although each dog has a unique name and age, each dog will be a mammal. Let's create some dogs ...

Create Objects

Instantiating is an unusual term for creating a new unique instance of a class.

For example: >>>

```
>>> class Dog:
...    pass
>>> Dog()
<__main__.Dog object at 0x1004ccc50>
>>> Dog()
<__main__.Dog object at 0x1004ccc90>
>>> a = Dog()
>>> b = Dog()
>>> a == b
False
```

We started by definea new Dog()class, then created two new dogs, each of which was assigned to different

objects. So, to create an instance of the class, you use the class name follow by parentheses. Then, to demonstration that each instance is actually different, we created two more dogs, assigning each variable, and then checking to see if these variables are equal.

What do you think is the type of class instance? >>>

```
>>> class Dog:
    pass
>>> a = Dog()
>>> type(a)
<class '__main__.Dog'>
```

Let's look at the more complex example ...

```
class Dog:

    # Class Attribute
    species = 'mammal'

    # Initializer / Instance Attributes
    def __init__(self, name, age):
        self.name = name
        self.age = age

# Instantiate the Dog object
philo = Dog("Philo", 5)
mikey = Dog("Mikey", 6)

# Access the instance attributes
print("{} is {} and {} is {}.".format(
    philo.name, philo.age, mikey.name, mikey.age))

# Is Philo a mammal?
if philo.species == "mammal":
    print("{0} is a {1}!".format(philo.name, philo.species))
```

NOTE Notice how we use point records to access the attributes of each objects. Save as (dog_class.py), then run program. You should see:

```
Philo is 5 and Mikey is 6.
Philo is a mammal!
```

What's the matter?

We create a new instance of the Dog()class and assigned it to a variable Philo. Then we passed him two arguments, "Philo" and 5, which represent the name and age of this dog, respectively.

These attribute are pass to the init method, which is called every time you creates a new attaching, instance the name and age to the object. You may be wondering why we should not have given self arguments.

This is the magic of Python: when you create a new instance of the class, Python automatically determines what selfies (in this case, Dog), and passes it to the init method.

Review of exercises (# 1)

Exercise: "The oldest dog"

Using the same Dogclass, create three new dogs, each with a different age. Then write a function with a name get_biggest_number()that takes any number of ages (*args) and returns the oldest. Then print the age of the oldest dog something like this:

The oldest dog is 7 years old. Solution: "The oldest dog" Solution "The oldest dog."

```
class Dog:

    # Class Attribute
    species = 'mammal'

    # Initializer / Instance Attributes
    def __init__(self, name, age):
        self.name = name
        self.age = age

# Instantiate the Dog object
jake = Dog("Jake", 7)
doug = Dog("Doug", 4)
william = Dog("William", 5)

# Determine the oldest dog
def get_biggest_number(* args):
    return max (args)

# Output
print ("The oldest dog is {} years old.". format (
    get_biggest_number (jake.age, doug.age, william.age)))
```

Instance Methods

Instance methods are defined inside the class and are used to get the contents of the instance. They can also be used to perform operation with the attribute of our objects. Like a init method, the first argument is always self:

```python
class Dog:

    # Class Attribute
    species = 'mammal'

    # Initializer / Instance Attributes
    def __init__(self, name, age):
        self.name = name
        self.age = age

    # instance method
    def description(self):
        return "{} is {} years old".format(self.name, self.age)

    # instance method
    def speak(self, sound):
        return "{} says {}".format(self.name, sound)

# Instantiate the Dog object
mikey = Dog("Mikey", 6)

# call our instance methods
print(mikey.description())
print(mikey.speak("Gruff Gruff"))
```

Save as dog_instance_methods.py , then run it:

```
Mikey is 6 years old
Mikey says Gruff Gruff
```

In the last method, speak()we define the behavior. What other types of behavior can you assign to a dog? Go back to the beginning of the paragraph to see examples of the behavior of other objects.

Attribute Change

You can changes the value of attributes based on some behavior: >>>

```
>>> class Email:
... def __init__(self):
... self.is_sent = False
... def send_email (self):
... self.is_sent = True
...
>>> my_email = Email ()
>>> my_email.is_sent
False
>>> my_email.send_email ()
>>> my_email.is_sent
True
```

Here we added a method for sending an email that updates the is_sentvariable to True.

Python object inheritance

Inheritance is a processing in which one class accepts the attributes and methods of another. Newly created classes are called child classes, and the classes from which the child classes derive are called parent classes.

It is importants to note that child classes override or extend the functionality (for example, attributes and behavior) of parent classes. In other words, child classes inherit all the attributes and behavior of the parent, but can also define other behavior to be followed. The most basic type of class is the class object, which usually all other classes inherit as the parents.

When you defining a new class, Python 3 implicitly uses its object as the parent class. Thus, the following two definitions are equivalent:

```
class Dog (object):
    pass

# In Python 3, this is the same as:

class Dog:
    pass
```

Note. In Python 2.x, there is a difference between the new and old-style classes. I will not go into details, but you will usually want to specify an object as the parent class to make sure that you define a new style class if you are writing Python 2 OOP code.

Dog Park Example

Let's imagine that we are in a dog park. There are several Dog objects involved in Dog behavior, each with different attributes. In ordinary conversation, this means that some dogs are running, and some are stretched, and some are just watching other dogs. Besides, each dog was named its owner, and since each dog lives and breathes, each is aging.

How else can you distinguish one dog from another? How about a dog breed: >>>

```
>>> class Dog:
    def __init__ (self, breed):
        self.breed = breed

>>> spencer = Dog ("German Shepard")
>>> spencer.breed
'German Shepard'
>>> sara = Dog ("Boston Terrier")
>>> sara.breed
'Boston Terrier'
```

Each dog breed has slightly different behaviors. To take this into account, let's create separate classes for each breed. These are child classes of the parent Dogclass.

Extending parent class functionality

Create new file this called dog_inheritance.py :

```python
# Parent class
class Dog:

    # Class attribute
    species = 'mammal'

    # Initializer / Instance attributes
    def __init__(self, name, age):
        self.name = name
        self.age = age

    # instance method
    def description(self):
        return "{} is {} years old".format(self.name, self.age)

    # instance method
    def speak(self, sound):
        return "{} says {}".format(self.name, sound)

# Child class (inherits from Dog class)
class RussellTerrier(Dog):
    def run(self, speed):
        return "{} runs {}".format(self.name, speed)

# Child class (inherits from Dog class)
class Bulldog(Dog):
    def run(self, speed):
        return "{} runs {}".format(self.name, speed)

# Child classes inherit attributes and
# behaviors from the parent class
jim = Bulldog("Jim", 12)
print(jim.description())

# Child classes have specific attributes
# and behaviors as well
print(jim.run("slowly"))
```

Read the comments aloud while you are working with this program to help you understand what is happening, and then, before you run the program, see if you can predict the expected result.

You should see:

```
Jim is 12 years old
Jim runs slowly
```

We did not add any special attributes or methods to distinguish between a RussellTerrier and a Bulldog. Still, since they are now two different classes, we could, for example, give them different class attributes that determine their respective speeds.

Parent and child classes

isinstance()The function is used to determine if the instance is also an instance of a specific parent class. Save this as dog_isinstance.py :

```python
# Parent class
class Dog:

    # Class attribute
    species = 'mammal'

    # Initializer / Instance attributes
    def __init__(self, name, age):
        self.name = name
        self.age = age

    # instance method
    def description(self):
        return "{} is {} years old".format(self.name, self.age)

    # instance method
    def speak(self, sound):
        return "{} says {}".format(self.name, sound)


# Child class (inherits from Dog () class)
class RussellTerrier(Dog):
    def run(self, speed):
        return "{} runs {}".format(self.name, speed)


# Child class (inherits from Dog () class)
class Bulldog(Dog):
    def run(self, speed):
        return "{} runs {}".format(self.name, speed)


# Child classes inherit attributes and
# behaviors from the parent class
jim = Bulldog("Jim", 12)
print(jim.description())

# Child classes have specific attributes
# and behaviors as well
print(jim.run("slowly"))

# Is jim an instance of Dog ()?
print(isinstance(jim, Dog))

# Is julie an instance of Dog ()?
julie = Dog("Julie", 100)
print(isinstance(julie, Dog))

# Is johnny walker an instance of Bulldog ()
johnnywalker = RussellTerrier("Johnny Walker", 4)
print(isinstance(johnnywalker, Bulldog))

# Is julie and instance of jim?
print(isinstance(julie, jim))
```

Conclusion: >>>

```
('Jim', 12)
Jim runs slowly
True
True
False
Traceback (most recent call last):
  File "dog_isinstance.py", line 50, in <module>
    print (isinstance (julie, jim))
TypeError: isinstance () arg 2 must be a class, type, or tuple of classes and types
```

It makes sense? Both jimand julieare instances of the Dog()class and johnnywalkerare not instances of Bulldog()the class. Then, as a health check, we checked juliewhether the instance is an instance jim, which is impossible, since jimit instancedoes not belong to the class itself, but to the class TypeError.

Overriding parent class functionality

Remember that child classes can also override the attributes and behavior of the parent class. For example: >>>

```
>>> class Dog:
... species = 'mammal'
...
>>> class SomeBreed (Dog):
... pass
...
>>> class SomeOtherBreed (Dog):
... species = 'reptile'
...
>>> frank = SomeBreed ()
>>> frank.species 'mammal'
>>> beans = SomeOtherBreed ()
>>> beans.species 'reptile'
```
The SomeBreed()class inherits speciesfrom the parent class, while the SomeOtherBreed()class overrides speciesby setting it reptile.

Review of exercises (# 2)

Exercise: "Legacy of the dogs"

Create a Petsclass that contains dog instances: this class is completely separate from the Dogclass. In other words, a Dogclass is not inherited from the Petsclass. Then assign three instances of the dog to the Petsclass instance. Start with the following code below. Save the file as pets_class.py . Your output should look like this:

```
I have 3 dogs.
Tom is 6.
Fletcher is 7.
Larry is 9.
And they're all mammals, of course.
```

Start Code:

```python
# Parent class
class Dog:

    # Class attribute
    species = 'mammal'

    # Initializer / Instance attributes
    def __init__ (self, name, age):
        self.name = name
        self.age = age

    # instance method
    def description (self):
        return "{} is {} years old". format (self.name, self.age)

    # instance method
    def speak (self, sound):
        return "{} says {}". format (self.name, sound)

# Child class (inherits from Dog class)
class RussellTerrier (Dog):
    def run (self, speed):
        return "{} runs {}". format (self.name, speed)

# Child class (inherits from Dog class)
class Bulldog (Dog):
    def run (self, speed):
        return "{} runs {}". format (self.name, speed)
```

Solution: "Dog Inheritance"

```python
# Parent class
class Pets:

    dogs = []

    def __init__(self, dogs):
        self.dogs = dogs


# Parent class
class Dog:

    # Class attribute
    species = 'mammal'

    # Initializer / Instance attributes
    def __init__(self, name, age):
        self.name = name
        self.age = age

    # Instance method
    def description(self):
        return self.name, self.age

    # Instance method
    def speak(self, sound):
        return "%s says %s" % (self.name, sound)

    # Instance method
    def eat(self):
        self.is_hungry = False


# Child class (inherits from Dog class)
class RussellTerrier(Dog):
    def run(self, speed):
        return "%s runs %s" % (self.name, speed)


# Child class (inherits from Dog class)
class Bulldog(Dog):
    def run(self, speed):
        return "%s runs %s" % (self.name, speed)

# Create instances of dogs
my_dogs = [
    Bulldog("Tom", 6),
    RussellTerrier("Fletcher", 7),
    Dog("Larry", 9)
]

# Instantiate the Pets class
my_pets = Pets(my_dogs)

# Output
print("I have {} dogs.".format(len(my_pets.dogs)))
for dog in my_pets.dogs:
    print("{} is {}.".format(dog.name, dog.age))

print("And they're all {}s, of course.".format(dog.species))
```

Exercise: Hungry Dogs

Use the same files, add an instance attribute is_hungry = Truein the Dogclass. Then add the called method, eat()which when called changes the value is_hungryto False. Find out how best to feed each dog, and then print "My dogs are hungry." if everyone is hungry or "My dogs are not hungry." if everyone is not hungry. The final result should look like this:

```
I have 3 dogs.
Tom is 6.
Fletcher is 7.
Larry is 9.
And they're all mammals, of course.
My dogs are not hungry.
```

Solution: Hungry Dogs

```
# Parent class
class Pets:

    dogs = []

    def __init__(self, dogs):
        self.dogs = dogs

# Parent class

    class Dog.

        * Oass attribute
        sped es = 'mamm d '

        * Initi d i zer ." In stance attributes
        def  iriit   (self name age).
            self.name = name
            self.age = age
            self.is hungo.' = True

    = mist ance method
      def descripti on (self).
          return self.name self.age

    = mist ance method
      def speak (self sound).
          return " °. o s says°. o s" °. o (self.name sound)
```

```
= mist ance method
    def eat (self).
        self.is hungo.' = Fd se


= Oiild class (inherits from Dog cl ass)
  class RussellTerri er (Dog).
    def run (self speed).
        return " °. o s runs°. o s" °. o (self.name speedt


= Oiild class (inherits from Dog cl ass)
  class Bulldog (Dog.
    def run (self speed).
        return " °. o s runs°. o s" °. o (self.name speedt


= Create instances of dogs
  m\' dogs = [
      Bulldog (" Tom" 6)
      Ru ssellTerri er (" FI ct cher" Tt
      Dog ("L are.'" 9)


        stanttate the Pets class
    ate'    ts = Pets (ate' dogs)

= Output
  print (" I have { ) dogs.". format (len (m\'    ets.dogs)))
  for dog in m\'    ets.dogs.
      dog.eat Q
      print (" { ) is { ).". format (dog.name dog.age))

      print ("And the\"'re d1 { ) s of ccxirse." . format (dog.species))

  are m\' dogs hungo.' = Fdse
  for dog in m\'    ets.dogs.
      if dog.i s hungo.'.
        are_my_dogs_hungry = True

if are_my_dogs_hungry:
    print ("My dogs are hungry.")
else.
    print ("My dogs are not hungry.")
```

Exercise: "Dog Walking"

Next, add a walk()method like Petsand Dogclasses, so that when you call a method in the Petsclass, each instance of a dog is assigned to Petsa class walk(). Save this as dog_walking.py . This is a little trickier.

Start by implementing a method just like a speak()method. As for the method in the Petsclass, you will need to iterate over the list of dogs and then call the method itself.

The output should look like this:

```
Tom is walking!
Fletcher is walking!
Larry is walking!
```

Solution: "dog walking"

```python
# Parent class
class Pets:

    dogs = []

    def __init__(self, dogs):
        self.dogs = dogs

    def walk(self):
        for dog in self.dogs:
            print(dog.walk())


# Parent class
class Dog:

    # Class attribute
    species = 'mammal'
    is_hungry = True

    # Initializer / instance attributes
    def __init__(self, name, age):
        self.name = name
        self.age = age

    # Instance method
    def description(self):
        return self.name, self.age

    # Instance method
    def speak(self, sound):
        return "%s says %s" % (self.name, sound)

    # Instance method
    def eat(self):
        self.is_hungry = False
```

```python
    def walk (self):
        return "%s is walking!" % (self.name)


# Child class (inherits from Dog class)
class RussellTerrier (Dog):
    def run (self, speed):
        return "%s runs %s" % (self.name, speed)


# Child class (inherits from Dog class)
class Bulldog (Dog):
    def run (self, speed):
        return "%s runs %s" % (self.name, speed)

# Create instances of dogs
my_dogs = [
    Bulldog ("Tom", 6),
    RussellTerrier ("Fletcher", 7),
    Dog ("Larry", 9)
]

# Instantiate the Pet class
my_pets = Pets (my_dogs)

# Output
my_pets.walk ()
```

Exercise: "Testing Understanding"

Answer the following OOP questions to verify your learning progress:

1. What class?
2. What an example?
3. What is the relationship between class and instance?
4. What Python syntax is used to define a new class?
5. What is the spelling convention for a class name?
6. How do you create or create an instance of a class?
7. How do you access the attributes and behavior of an instance of a class?
8. What kind of method?
9. What is the purpose self?
10. What is the purpose of the init method?

11. Describe how inheritance helps prevent code duplication.
12. Can child classes override the properties of their parents?

Solution: "Test of understanding" Show hide

1. A class mechanism used to create new custom data structures. It contains data, as well as methods used to process this data.
2. An instance is a copy of a class with actual values, literally an object of a particular class.
3. While a class is a plan used to describe how to create something, instances are objects created from these drawings.
4. class PythonClassName:
5. Capitalized CamelCase designation - i.e. PythonClassName()
6. You use the class name followed by parentheses. So if the name of the class Dog(), the instance of the dog will be - my_class = Dog().
7. With dot notation - for example, instance_name.attribute_name
8. A function that defined inside a class.
9. The first argument of each method refers to the current instance of the class, which is called by the convention self. The init method self refers to a newly created object, while in other methods, it a self refers into the instance whose method was called. For more on the init con self, check out this article.

10. init The method initializes an instance of the class.
11. Child classes inherit all the attributes and behavior of the parent.
12. Yes.

CONCLUSION

Now you should know what classes are, why you want or should use them, and how to create parent and child classes to better structure your programs.

Remember that OOP is a programming paradigm, not a Python concept. Most modern programming languages, such as Java, C #, C ++, follow the principles of OOP. So the good news is that learning the basics of object-oriented programming will be useful to you in a variety of circumstances - whether you work in Python or not.

Now the industry does not stand still and there are more and more web sites, services and companies that need specialists.

Demand for developers is growing, but competition among them is growing.

To be the best in your business, you need to be almost an absolutely universal person who can write a website, create a design for it, and promote it yourself.

In this regard, even a person who has never sat at this computer begins to think, but should I try?

But very often it turns out that such enthusiasts burn out at the initial stage, without having tried themselves in this matter.

Or maybe he would become a brilliant creator of code? Would create something new? This we will not know.

Every day, the threshold for entering programming is growing. You can never predict what new language will come out.

Such an abundance breaks all the desire of a newly minted programmer and he is lost in this ocean of information.

All these javascripts of yours ... pythons ... what fear ..

A great misconception is the obligation to know mathematics. Yes, it is needed, but only in a narrow field, but it is also useful for understanding some aspects.

The advice that can be given to people who are just starting their activity is not to chase everything at once. Allow yourself time to think.

What do I want to do? Create a program for everyone to be useful? Create additional services to simplify any tasks? Or do you really have to go make games?

The second advice will be to answer my question how much time am I ready to devote to this? The third point is to think about how fast you want to achieve your intended result.

So, there is no "easy way" to start programming, it all depends on you - your interest, what you want to do and your tasks.

In any case, you need to try and do everything possible in your power. Good luck in your endeavors!

PYTHON FOR DATA SCIENCE

Guide to computer programming and web coding. Learn machine learning, artificial intelligence, NumPy and Pandas packages for data analysis. Step-by-step exercises included.

JASON TEST

INTRODUCTION

Data Science has been very popular over the last couple of years. The main focus of this sector is to incorporate significant data into business and marketing strategies that will help a business expand. And get to a logical solution, the data can be stored and explored. Originally only the leading IT corporations were engaged throughout this field, but today information technology is being used by companies operating in different sectors and fields such as e-commerce, medical care, financial services, and others. Software processing programs such as Hadoop, R code, SAS, SQL, and plenty more are available. Python is, however, the most famous and easiest to use data and analytics tools. It is recognized as the coding world's Swiss Army Knife since it promotes structured coding, object-oriented programming, the operational programming language, and many others. Python is the most widely used programming language in the world and is also recognized as the most high - level language for data science tools and techniques, according to the 2018 Stack Overflow study.

In the Hacker rank 2018 developer poll, which is seen in their love-hate ranking, Python has won the developer's hearts. Experts in data science expect to see an increase in the Python ecosystem, with growing popularity. And although your journey to study Python programming may just start, it's nice to know that there are also plentiful (and increasing) career options.

Data analytics Python programming is extensively used and, along with being a flexible and open-source language, becomes one of the favorite programming languages. Its large libraries are used for data processing, and even for a beginner data analyst, they are very easy to understand. Besides being open-source, it also integrates easily with any infrastructure that can be used to fix the most complicated problems. It is used by most banks for data crunching, organizations for analysis and processing, and weather prediction firms such as Climate monitor analytics often use it. The annual wage for a Computer Scientist is $127,918, according to Indeed. So here's the good news, the figure is likely to increase. IBM's experts forecast a 28 percent increase in data scientists' demands by 2020. For data science, however, the future is bright, and Python is just one slice of the golden pie. Luckily mastering Python and other principles of programming are as practical as ever.

DATA SCIENCE AND ITS SIGNIFICANCE

Data Science has come a long way from the past few years, and thus, it becomes an important factor in understanding the workings of multiple companies. Below are several explanations that prove data science will still be an integral part of the global market.

1. The companies would be able to understand their client in a more efficient and high manner with the help of Data Science. Satisfied customers form the foundation of every company, and they play an important role in their successes or failures. Data Science allows companies to engage with customers in the advance way and thus proves the product's improved performance and strength.

2. Data Science enables brands to deliver powerful and engaging visuals. That's one of the reasons it's famous. When products and companies make inclusive use of this data, they can share their experiences with their audiences and thus create better relations with the item.

3. Perhaps one Data Science's significant characteristics are that its results can be generalized to almost all kinds of industries, such as travel, health care, and education. The companies can quickly determine their problems with the help of Data Science, and can also adequately address them

4. Currently, data science is accessible in almost all industries, and nowadays, there is a huge amount of data existing in the world, and if used adequately, it can lead to victory or failure of any project. If data is used properly, it will be important in the future to achieve the product's goals.

5. Big data is always on the rise and growing. Big data allows the enterprise to address complicated Business, human capital, and capital management problems effectively and quickly using different resources that are built routinely.

6. Data science is gaining rapid popularity in every other sector and therefore plays an important role in every product's functioning and performance. Thus, the data scientist's role is also enhanced as they will conduct an essential function of managing data and providing solutions to particular issues.

7. Computer technology has also affected the supermarket sectors. To understand this, let's take an example the older people had a fantastic interaction with the local seller. Also, the seller was able to meet the customers' requirements in a personalized way. But now this attention was lost due to the emergence and increase of supermarket chains. But the sellers are able to communicate with their customers with the help of data analytics.

8. Data Science helps companies build that customer connection. Companies and their goods will be able to have a better and deeper understanding of how clients can utilize their services with the help of data science.

Data Technology Future: Like other areas are continually evolving, the importance of data technology is increasingly growing as well. Data science impacted different fields. Its influence can be seen in many industries, such as retail, healthcare, and education. New treatments and technologies are being continually identified in the healthcare sector, and there is a need for quality patient care. The healthcare industry can find a solution with the help of data science techniques that helps the patients to take care with. Education is another field where one can clearly see the advantage of data science. Now the new innovations like phones and tablets have become an essential characteristic of the educational system. Also, with the help of data science, the students are creating greater chances, which leads to improving their knowledge.

Data Science Life Cycle:

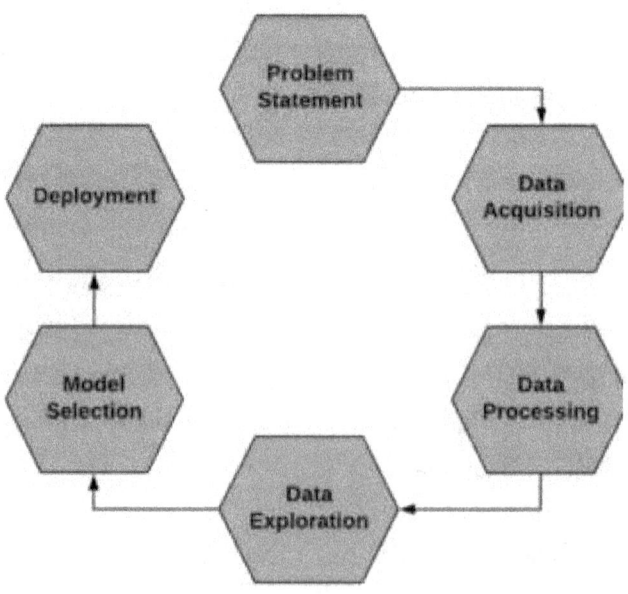

Data Structures

A data structure may be selected in computer programming or designed to store data for the purpose of working with different algorithms on it. Every other data structure includes the data values, data relationships, and functions between the data that can be applied to the data and information.

Features of data structures

Sometimes, data structures are categorized according to their characteristics. Possible functions are:

- Linear or non-linear: This feature defines how the data objects are organized in a sequential series, like a list or in an unordered sequence, like a table.
- Homogeneous or non-homogeneous: This function defines how all data objects in a collection are of the same type or of different kinds.
- Static or dynamic: This technique determines to show to assemble the data structures. Static data structures at compilation time have fixed sizes, structures, and destinations in the memory. Dynamic data types have dimensions, mechanisms, and destinations of memory that may shrink or expand depending on the application.

Data structure Types

Types of the data structure are determined by what sorts of operations will be needed or what kinds of algorithms will be implemented. This includes:

Arrays: An array stores a list of memory items at adjacent locations. Components of the same category are located together since each element's position can be easily calculated or accessed. Arrays can be fixed in size or flexible in length.

Stacks: A stack holds a set of objects in linear order added to operations. This order may be past due in first out (LIFO) or first-out (FIFO).

Queues: A queue stores a stack-like selection of elements; however, the sequence of activity can only be first in the first out. Linked lists: In a linear order, a linked list stores a selection of items. In a linked list, every unit or node includes a data item as well as a reference or relation to the next element in the list.

Trees: A tree stocks an abstract, hierarchical collection of items. Each node is connected to other nodes and can have several sub-values, also known as a child.

Graphs: A graph stores a non-linear design group of items. Graphs consist of a limited set of nodes, also called vertices, and lines connecting them, also known as edges. They are useful for describing processes in real life, such as networked computers.

Tries: A tria or query tree is often a data structure that stores strings as data files, which can be arranged in a visual graph.

Hash tables: A hash table or hash chart is contained in a relational list that labels the keys to variables. A hash table uses a hashing algorithm to transform an index into an array of containers containing the desired item of data. These data systems are called complex because they can contain vast quantities of interconnected data. Examples of primal, or fundamental, data structures are integer, float, boolean, and character.

Utilization of data structures

Data structures are generally used to incorporate the data types in physical forms. This can be interpreted into a wide range of applications, including a binary tree showing a database table. Data structures are used in the programming languages to organize code and information in digital storage. Python databases and dictionaries, or

JavaScript array and objects, are popular coding systems used to gather and analyze data. Also, data structures are a vital part of effective software design. Significance of Databases Data systems is necessary to effectively handle vast volumes of data, such as data stored in libraries, or indexing services.

Accurate data configuration management requires memory allocation identifier, data interconnections, and data processes, all of which support the data structures. In addition, it is important to not only use data structures but also to select the correct data structure for each assignment.

Choosing an unsatisfactory data structure could lead to slow running times or disoriented code. Any considerations that need to be noticed when choosing a data system include what type of information should be processed, where new data will be put, how data will be organized, and how much space will be allocated for the data.

PYTHON BASICS

You can get all the knowledge about the Python programming language in 5 simple steps.

Step 1: Practice Basics in Python

It all starts somewhere. This first step is where the basics of programming Python will be learned. You are always going to want an introduction to data science. Jupyter Notebook, which comes pre-portioned with Python libraries to help you understand these two factors, which make it one of the essential resources which you can start using early on your journey.

Step 2: Try practicing Mini-Python Projects

We strongly believe in learning through shoulders-on. Try programming stuff like internet games, calculators, or software that gets Google weather in your area. Creating these mini-projects can help you understand Python. Projects like these are standard for any coding languages, and a fantastic way to strengthen your working knowledge. You will come up with better and advance API knowledge, and you will continue site scraping with advanced techniques. This will enable you to learn Python programming more effectively, and the web scraping method will be useful to you later when collecting data.

Stage 3: Learn Scientific Libraries on Python

Python can do anything with data. Pandas, Matplotliband, and NumPyare are known to be the three best used and most important Python Libraries for data science. NumPy and Pandas are useful for data creation and development. Matplotlib is a library for analyzing the data, creating flow charts and diagrams as you would like to see in Excel or Google Sheets.

Stage 4: Create a portfolio

A portfolio is an absolute need for professional data scientists. These projects must include numerous data sets and leave important perspectives to readers that you have gleaned. Your portfolio does not have a specific theme; finding datasets that inspire you, and then finding a way to place them together. Showing projects like these provide some collaboration to fellow data scientists, and demonstrates future employers that you have really taken the chance to understand Python and other essential coding skills. Some of the good things about data science are that, while showcasing the skills you've learned, your portfolio serves as a resume, such as Python programming.

Step 5: Apply Advanced Data Science Techniques

Eventually, the target is to strengthen your programming skills. Your data science path will be full of continuous learning, but you can accomplish specialized tutorials to make sure you have specialized in the basic programming of Python. You need to get confident with clustering models of regression, grouping, and k-means. You can also leap into machine learning-using sci-kit lessons to bootstrap models and create neural network models. At this point, developer programming could include creating models using live data sources.

This type of machine learning technique adjusts s its assumptions over time.

How significant is Python for Data Science?

\# Efficient and simple to use – Python is considered a tool for beginners, and any student or researcher with only basic understanding could start working on it. Time and money spent debugging codes and constraints on different project management are also minimized. The time for code implementation is less compared to other programming languages such as C, Java, and C #, which makes developers and software engineers spend far more time working on their algorithms.

\# Library Choice-Python offers a vast library and machine learning and artificial intelligence database. Scikit Learn, TensorFlow, Seaborn, Pytorch, Matplotlib, and many more are among the most popular libraries. There are many online tutorial videos and resources on machine learning and data science, which can be easily obtained.

\# Scalability – Python has proven itself to be a highly scalable and faster language compared to other programming languages such as c++, Java, and R. It gives flexibility in solving problems that can't be solved with other computer languages. Many companies use it to develop all sorts of rapid techniques and systems.

\#Visual Statistics and Graphics-Python provides a number of visualization tools. The Matplotlib library provides a reliable framework on which those libraries such as gg plot, pandas plotting, PyTorch, and others are developed. These services help create graphs, plot lines ready for the Web, visual layouts, etc.

How Python is used for Data Science

#First phase – First of all, we need to learn and understand what form a data takes. If we perceive data to be a huge Excel sheet with columns and crows lakhs, then perhaps you should know what to do about that? You need to gather information into each row as well as column by executing some operations and searching for a specific type of data. Completing this type of computational task can consume a lot of time and hard work. Thus, you can use Python's libraries, such as Pandas and Numpy, that can complete the tasks quickly by using parallel computation.

#Second phase – The next hurdle is to get the data needed. Since data is not always readily accessible to us, we need to dump data from the network as needed. Here the Python Scrap and brilliant Soup libraries can enable us to retrieve data from the internet.

#Third phase – We must get the simulation or visual presentation of the data at this step. Driving perspectives gets difficult when you have too many figures on the board. The correct way to do that is to represent the data in graph form, graphs, and other layouts. The Python Seaborn and Matplotlib libraries are used to execute this operation.

#Fourth phase – The next stage is machine-learning, which is massively complicated computing. It includes mathematical tools such as the probability, calculus, and matrix operations of columns and rows over lakhs. With Python's machine learning library Scikit-Learn, all of this will become very simple and effective.

Standard Library

The Python Standard library consists of Python's precise syntax, token, and semantic. It comes packaged with deployment core Python.

When we started with an introduction, we referenced this. It is written in C and covers features such as I / O and other core components. Together all of the versatility renders makes Python the language it is. At the root of the basic library, there are more than 200 key modules. Python ships that library. But aside from this library, you can also obtain a massive collection of several thousand Python Package Index (PyPI) components.

1. Matplotlib

'Matplotlib' helps to analyze data, and is a library of numerical plots. For Data Science, we discussed in Python.

2. Pandas

'Pandas' is a must for data-science as we have said before. It provides easy, descriptive, and versatile data structures to deal with organized (tabulated, multilayered, presumably heterogeneous) and series data with ease (and fluidly).

3. Requests

'Requests' is a Python library that allows users to upload HTTP/1.1 requests, add headers, form data, multipart files, and simple Python dictionary parameters. In the same way, it also helps you to access the response data.

4. NumPy

It has basic arithmetic features and a rudimentary collection of scientific computing.

5. SQLAlchemy

It has sophisticated mathematical features, and SQLAlchemy is a basic mathematical programming library with well-known trends at a corporate level. It was created to make database availability efficient and high-performance.

6. BeautifulSoup

This may be a bit on the slow side. BeautifulSoup seems to have a superb library for beginner XML- and HTML- parsing.

7. Pyglet

Pyglet is an outstanding choice when designing games with an object-oriented programming language interface. It also sees use in the development of other visually rich programs for Mac OS X, Windows, and Linux in particular. In the 90s, they turned to play Minecraft on their PCs whenever people were bored. Pyglet is the mechanism powering Minecraft.

8. SciPy

Next available is SciPy, one of the libraries we spoke about so often. It does have a range of numerical routines that are user-friendly and effective. Those provide optimization routines and numerical integration procedures.

9. Scrapy

If your objective is quick, scraping at the high-level monitor and crawling the network, go for Scrapy. It can be used for data gathering activities for monitoring and test automation.

10. PyGame

PyGame offers an incredibly basic interface to the system-independent graphics, audio, and input libraries of the Popular Direct Media Library (SDL).

11. Python Twisted

Twisted is an event-driven networking library used in Python and authorized under the MIT open-source license.

12. Pillow

Pillow is a PIL (Python Imaging Library) friendly fork but is more user efficient. Pillow is your best friend when you're working with pictures.

13. pywin32

As the name suggests, this gives useful methods and classes for interacting with Windows.

14. wxPython

For Python, it's a wrapper around wxWidgets.

15. iPython

iPython Python Library provides a parallel distributed computing architecture. You will use it to create, run, test, and track parallel and distributed programming.

16. Nose

The nose provides alternate test exploration and test automation running processes. This intends to mimic the behavior of the py.test as much as possible.

17. Flask

Flask is a web framework, with a small core and several extensions.

18. SymPy

It is a library of open-source symbolic mathematics. SymPy is a full-fledged Computer Algebra System (CAS) with a very simple and easily understood code that is highly expandable. It is implemented in python, and therefore, external libraries are not required.

19. Fabric

As well as being a library, Fabric is a command-line tool to simplify the use of SSH for installation programs or network management activities. You can run local or remote command line, upload/download files, and even request input user going, or abort activity with it.

20. PyGTK

PyGTK allows you to create programs easily using a Python GUI (Graphical User Interface).

Operators and Expressions

Operators

In Python, operators are special symbols that perform mathematical operation computation. The value in which the operator is running on is called the operand.

Arithmetic operators

It is used by arithmetic operators to perform mathematical operations such as addition, subtraction, multiplying, etc.

Comparison operators

Comparison operators can be used for value comparisons. Depending on the condition, it returns either True or False.

Logical operators

Logical operators are and, or, not.

Operator	Meaning	Example
And	True if both operands are true	x and y
Or	True if either of the operands is true	x or y
Not	True if the operand is false (complements the operand)	not x

Bitwise operators

Bitwise operators operate as if they became binary-digit strings on operands. Bit by bit they work, and therefore the name. For example, in binary two is 10, and in binary seven is 111.

Assignment operators

Python language's assignment operators are used to assign values to the variables. a = 5 is a simple task operator assigning 'a' value of 5 to the right of the variable 'a' to the left. In Python, there are various compound operators such as a + = 5, which adds to the variable as well as assigns the same later. This equals a= a + 5.

Special operators

Python language gives other different types of operators, such as the operator of the identity or the operator of membership. Examples of these are mentioned below.

Identity operators

'Is' and 'is not' are Python Identity Operators. They are used to test if there are two values or variables in the same memory section. Two equal variables do not mean they are equivalent.

Membership operator

The operators that are used to check whether or not there exists a value/variable in the sequence such as string, list, tuples, sets, and dictionary. These operators return either True or False if a variable is found in the list, it returns True, or else it returns False

Expressions

An expression is a mix of values, variables, operators, and function calls. There must be an evaluation of the expressions. When you ask Python to print a phrase, the interpreter will evaluate the expression and show the output.

Arithmetic conversions

Whenever an arithmetic operator interpretation below uses the phrase "the numeric arguments are converted to a common type," this means the execution of the operator for the built-in modes operates as follows

If one argument is a complex quantity, then the other is converted to a complex number; If another argument is a floating-point number, the other argument is transformed to a floating-point; Or else both will be integers with no need for conversion.

Atoms

Atoms are the most important expressional components. The smallest atoms are literals or abstract identities. Forms contained in parentheses, brackets, or braces are also syntactically known as atoms. Atoms syntax is:

atom ::= identifier | enclosure| literal

enclosure ::= list_display| parenth_form| dict_display | set_display

Identifiers (Names)

A name is an identifier that occurs as an atom. See section Lexical Description Identifiers and Keywords and group Naming and binding for naming and binding documents. Whenever the name is connected to an entity, it yields the entity by evaluating the atom. When a name is not connected, an attempt to assess it elevates the exception for NameError.

Literals

Python provides logical string and bytes and numerical literals of different types:

literal::= string literal | bytes literal

| integer | float number | image number

Assessment of a literal yield with the predicted set an object of that type (bytes, integer, floating-point number, string, complex number). In the scenario of floating-point and imaginary (complex) literals, the value can be approximated.

Parenthesized forms

A parenthesized type is an available set of parentheses for the expression:

parenth_form ::= "(" [starred_expression] ")"

A list of parenthesized expressions yields whatever the list of expressions produces: if the list includes at least one comma, it produces a tuple. If not, it yields the sole expression that forms up the list of expressions. A null pair of parentheses generates an incomplete object of tuples. As all tuples are immutable, the same rules would apply as for literals (i.e., two empty tuple occurrences does or doesn't yield the same entity).

Displays for lists, sets, and dictionaries

For the construction of a list, Python uses a series or dictionary with a particular syntax called "displays," each in complementary strands: The contents of the container are listed explicitly, or They are calculated using a series of instructions for looping and filtering, named a 'comprehension.' Common features of syntax for comprehensions are:

comprehension ::= assignment_expressioncomp_for

comp_for   ::= ["async"] "for" target_list "in" or_test [comp_iter] comp_iter   ::= comp_for | comp_if

comp_if   ::= "if" expression_nocond [comp_iter]

A comprehension contains one single sentence ready for at least one expression for clause, and zero or more for or if clauses. Throughout this situation, the components of the container are those that will be generated by assuming each of the for or if clauses as a block, nesting from left to right, and determining the phase for creating an entity each time the inner core block is approached.

List displays

A list view is a probably empty sequence of square brackets including expressions:

list_display ::= "[" [starred_list | comprehension] "]"

A list display generates a new column object, with either a list of expressions or a comprehension specifying the items. When a comma-separated database of expressions is provided, its elements are assessed from left to right and positioned in that order in the category entity. When Comprehension is provided, the list shall be built from the comprehension components.

Set displays

Curly braces denote a set display and can be distinguished from dictionary displays by the lack of colons dividing data types:

set_display ::= "{" (starred_list | comprehension) "}"

A set show offers a new, mutable set entity, with either a series of expressions or a comprehension defining the contents. When supplied with a comma-separated list of expressions, its elements are evaluated from left to right and assigned to the set entity. Whenever a comprehension is provided, the set is formed from the comprehension-derived elements. Unable to build an empty set with this {}; literal forms a blank dictionary.

Dictionary displays

A dictionary view is a potentially empty sequence of key pairs limited to curly braces:

dict_display ::= "{" [key_datum_list | dict_comprehension] "}"

key_datum_list ::= key_datum ("," key_datum)* [","]

key_datum ::= expression ":" expression | "**" or_expr

dict_comprehension ::= expression ":" expression comp_for

The dictionary view shows a new object in the dictionary. When a comma-separated series of key / datum pairs is provided, they are analyzed from left to right to identify dictionary entries: each key entity is often used as a key to hold the respective datum in the dictionary. This implies you can clearly state the very same key numerous times in the key /datum catalog, but the last one given will become the final dictionary's value for that key.

Generator expressions

A generator expression is the compressed syntax of a generator in the parenthesis :

generator_expression ::= "(" expression comp_for ")"

An expression generator produces an entity that is a new generator. Its syntax will be the same as for comprehensions, except for being enclosed in brackets or curly braces rather than parentheses. Variables being used generator expression are assessed sloppily when the generator object (in the same style as standard generators) is called by the __next__() method. Conversely, the iterate-able expression in the leftmost part of the clause is evaluated immediately, such that an error that it produces is transmitted at the level where the expression of the generator is characterized, rather than at the level where the first value is recovered.

For instance: (x*y for x in range(10) for y in range(x, x+10)).

Yield expressions

yield_atom   ::= "(" yield_expression ")"

yield_expression ::= "yield" [expression_list | "from" expression]

The produced expression is used to define a generator function or async generator function, and can therefore only be used in the function definition body. Using an expression of yield in the body of a function tends to cause that function to be a generator, and to use it in the body of an asynchronous def function induces that co-routine function to become an async generator. For example:

def gen(): # defines a generator function

yield 123

asyncdefagen(): # defines an asynchronous generator function

yield 123

Because of their adverse effects on the carrying scope, yield expressions are not allowed as part of the impliedly defined scopes used to enforce comprehensions and expressions of generators.

Input and Output of Data in Python

Python Output Using print() function

To display data into the standard display system (screen), we use the print() function. We may issue data to a server as well, but that will be addressed later. Below is an example of its use.

>>>>print('This sentence is output to the screen')

Output:

This sentence is output to the screen

Another example is given:

a = 5

print('The value of a is,' a)

Output:

The value of a is 5

Within the second declaration of print(), we will note that space has been inserted between the string and the variable value a. By default, it contains this syntax, but we can change it.

The actual syntax of the print() function will be:

print(*objects, sep=' ', end='\n', file=sys.stdout, flush=False)

Here, the object is the value(s) that will be printed. The sep separator between values is used. This switches into a character in space. Upon printing all the values, the finish is printed. It moves into a new section by design. The file is the object that prints the values, and its default value is sys.stdout (screen). Below is an example of this.

print(1, 2, 3, 4)

print(1, 2, 3, 4, sep='*')

print(1, 2, 3, 4, sep='#', end='&')

Run code

Output:

1 2 3 4

1*2*3*4

1#2#3#4&

Output formatting

Often we want to style our production, so it looks appealing. It can be done using the method str.format(). This technique is visible for any object with a string.

>>> x = 5; y = 10

>>>print('The value of x is {} and y is {}'.format(x,y))

Here the value of x is five and y is 10

Here, they use the curly braces{} as stand-ins. Using numbers (tuple index), we may specify the order in which they have been printed.

print('I love {0} and {1}'.format('bread','butter'))

print('I love {1} and {0}'.format('bread','butter'))

Run Code

Output:

I love bread and butter

I love butter and bread

People can also use arguments with keyword to format the string.

>>>print('Hello {name}, {greeting}'.format(greeting = 'Goodmorning', name = 'John'))

Hello John, Goodmorning

Unlike the old sprint() style used in the C programming language, we can also format strings. To accomplish this, we use the '%' operator.

>>> x = 12.3456789

>>>print('The value of x is %3.2f' %x)

The value of x is 12.35

>>>print('The value of x is %3.4f' %x)

The value of x is 12.3457

Python Indentation

Indentation applies to the spaces at the start of a line of the compiler. Whereas indentation in code is for readability only in other programming languages, but the indentation in Python is very important. Python supports the indent to denote a code block.

Example

if 5 > 2:

print("Five is greater than two!")

Python will generate an error message if you skip the indentation:

Example

Syntax Error:

if 5 > 2:

print("Five is greater than two!")

Python Input

Our programs have been static. Variables were described or hard-coded in the source code. We would want to take the feedback from the user to allow flexibility. We have the input() function in Python to enable this. input() is syntax as:

input([prompt])

While prompt is the string we want to show on the computer, this is optional.

```
>>>num = input('Enter a number: ')
```

Enter a number: 10

```
>>>num
```

'10'

Below, we can see how the value 10 entered is a string and not a number. To transform this to a number we may use the functions int() or float().

```
>>>int('10')
```

10

```
>>>float('10')
```

10.0

The same method can be done with the feature eval(). Although it takes eval much further. It can even quantify expressions, provided that the input is a string

```
>>>int('2+3')
```

Traceback (most recent call last):

  File "<string>", line 301, in runcode

  File "<interactive input>", line 1, in <module>

ValueError: int() base 10 invalid literal: '2+3'

```
>>>eval('2+3')
```

5

Python Import

As our software gets larger, splitting it up into separate modules is a smart idea. A module is a file that contains definitions and statements from Python. Python packages have a filename, and the .py extension begins with it. Definitions may be loaded into another module or to the integrated Python interpreter within a module. To do this, we use the keyword on import.

For instance, by writing the line below, we can import the math module:

import math

We will use the module as follows:

import math

print(math.pi)

Run Code

Output

3.141592653589793

So far, all concepts are included in our framework within the math module. Developers can also only import certain particular attributes and functions, using the keyword.

For instance:

>>>from math import pi

>>>pi

3.141592653589793

Python looks at multiple positions specified in sys.path during the import of a module. It is a list of positions in a directory.

>>> import sys

>>>sys.path

['',

'C:\\Python33\\Lib\\idlelib',

'C:\\Windows\\system32\\python33.zip',

'C:\\Python33\\DLLs',

'C:\\Python33\\lib',

'C:\\Python33',

'C:\\Python33\\lib\\site-packages']

We can insert our own destination to that list as well.

FUNCTIONS

You utilize programming functions to combine a list of instructions that you're constantly using or that are better self-contained in sub-program complexity and are called upon when required. Which means a function is a type of code written to accomplish a given purpose. The function may or may not need various inputs to accomplish that particular task. Whenever the task is executed, one or even more values can or could not be returned by the function. Basically there exist three types of functions in Python language:

1. Built-in functions, including help() to ask for help, min() to just get the minimum amount, print() to print an attribute to the terminal. More of these functions can be found here.
2. User-Defined Functions (UDFs) that are functions created by users to assist and support them out;
3. Anonymous functions, also labeled lambda functions since they are not defined with the default keyword.

Defining A Function: User Defined Functions (UDFs)

The following four steps are for defining a function in Python:

1. Keyword def can be used to declare the function and then use the function name to backtrack.
2. Add function parameters: They must be within the function parentheses. Finish off your line with a colon.
3. Add statements which should be implemented by the functions.

When the function should output something, end your function with a return statement. Your task must return an object None without return declaration. Example:

1. def hello():

2. print("Hello World")

3. return

It is obvious as you move forward, the functions will become more complex: you can include for loops, flow control, and more to make things more fine-grained:

def hello():

name = str(input("Enter your name: "))

if name:

print ("Hello " + str(name))

else:

print("Hello World")

return

hello()

In the feature above, you are asking the user to give a name. When no name is provided, the 'Hello World' function will be printed. Otherwise, the user will receive a custom "Hello" phrase. Also, consider you can specify one or more parameters for your UDFs function. When you discuss the segment Feature Statements, you will hear more about this. Consequently, as a result of your function, you may or may not return one or more values.

The return Statement

Note that since you're going to print something like that in your hello) (UDF, you don't really have to return it. There'll be no distinction between the above function and this one:

Example:

1. defhello_noreturn():

2. print("Hello World")

Even so, if you'd like to keep working with the result of your function and try a few other functions on it, you'll need to use the return statement to simply return a value, like a string, an integer. Check out the following scenario in which hello() returns a "hello" string while the hello_noreturn() function returns None:

1.   def hello():

2.   print("Hello World")

3.   return("hello")

4.   defhello_noreturn():

5.   print("Hello World")

6.   # Multiply the output of `hello()` with 2

7.   hello() * 2

8. # (Try to) multiply the output of `hello_noreturn()` with 2

9. hello_noreturn() * 2

The secondary part gives you an error because, with a None, you cannot perform any operations. You will get a TypeError that appears to say that NoneType (the None, which is the outcome of hello_noreturn()) and int (2) cannot do the multiplication operation. Tip functions leave instantly when a return statement is found, even though that means they will not return any result:

1. def run():

2. for x in range(10):

3. if x == 2:

4. return

5. print("Run!")

6. run()

Another factor worth noting when dealing with the 'return expression' is many values can be returned using it. You consider making use of tuples for this. Recall that this data structure is very comparable to a list's: it can contain different values. Even so, tuples are immutable, meaning you can't alter any amounts stored in it! You build it with the aid of dual parentheses). With the assistance of the comma and the assignment operator, you can disassemble tuples into different variables.

Read the example below to understand how multiple values can be returned by your function:

1. # Define `plus()`

2.   def plus(a,b):

3.sum = a + b

4.return (sum, a)

5. # Call `plus()` and unpack variables

6.   sum, a = plus(3,4)

7.   # Print `sum()`

8.   print(sum)

Notice that the return statement sum, 'a' will result in just the same as the return (sum, a): the earlier simply packs total and an in a tuple it under hood!

How To Call A Function

You've already seen a lot of examples in previous sections of how one can call a function. Trying to call a function means executing the function you have described-either directly from the Python prompt, or by a different function (as you have seen in the "Nested Functions" portion). Call your new added hello() function essentially by implementing hello() as in the DataCamp Light chunk as follows:

1.   hello()

Adding Docstrings to Python Functions

Further valuable points of Python's writing functions: docstrings. Docstrings define what your function does, like the algorithms it conducts or the values it returns. These definitions act as metadata for your function such that anybody who reads the docstring of your feature can understand what your feature is doing, without having to follow all the code in the function specification. Task docstrings are placed right after the feature header in the subsequent line and are set in triple quote marks. For your hello() function, a suitable docstring is 'Hello World prints.'

def hello():

"""Prints "Hello World".

Returns:

    None

"""

print("Hello World")

return

Notice that you can extend docstrings more than the one provided here as an example. If you want to study docstrings in more depth information, you should try checking out some Python library Github repositories like scikit-learn or pandas, in which you'll find lots of good examples!

Function Arguments in Python

You probably learned the distinction between definitions and statements earlier. In simple terms, arguments are the aspects that are given to any function or method call, while their parameter identities respond to the arguments in the function or method code. Python UDFs can take up four types of arguments:

1. Default arguments
2. Required arguments
3. Keyword arguments
4. Variable number of arguments

Default Arguments

Default arguments would be those who take default data if no value of the argument is delivered during the call function. With the assignment operator =, as in the following case, you may assign this default value:

1. #Define `plus()` function

2. def plus(a,b = 2):

3.return a + b

4. # Call `plus()` with only `a` parameter

5. plus(a=1)

6. # Call `plus()` with `a` and `b` parameters

7. plus(a=1, b=3)

Required Arguments

Because the name sort of brings out, the claims a UDF needs are those that will be in there. Such statements must be transferred during the function call and are absolutely the right order, such as in the example below:

1. # Define `plus()` with required arguments

2. def plus(a,b):

3. return a + b

Calling the functions without getting any additional errors, you need arguments that map to 'a' as well as the 'b' parameters. The result will not be unique if you swap round the 'a' and 'b,' but it could be if you modify plus() to the following:

1. # Define `plus()` with required arguments

2. def plus(a,b):

3.return a/b

Keyword Arguments

You will use keyword arguments in your function call if you'd like to make sure you list all the parameters in the correct order. You use this to define the statements by the name of the function. Let's take an example above to make it a little simpler:

1. # Define `plus()` function

2. def plus(a,b):

3.return a + b

4. # Call `plus()` function with parameters

5. plus(2,3)

6. # Call `plus()` function with keyword arguments

7. plus(a=1, b=2)

Notice that you can also alter the sequence of the parameters utilizing keywords arguments and still get the same outcome when executing the function:

1. # Define `plus()` function

2. def plus(a,b):

3. return a + b

4. # Call `plus()` function with keyword arguments

5. plus(b=2, a=1)

Global vs. Local Variables

Variables identified within a function structure usually have a local scope, and those specified outside have a global scope. This shows that the local variables are specified within a function block and can only be retrieved through that function, while global variables can be retrieved from all the functions in the coding:

1. # Global variable `init`

2. init = 1

3. # Define `plus()` function to accept a variable number of arguments

4. def plus(*args):

5. # Local variable `sum()`

6. total = 0

7. for i in args:

8. total += i

9. return total

10. # Access the global variable

11. print("this is the initialized value " + str(init))

12. # (Try to) access the local variable

13. print("this is the sum " + str(total))

You will find that you can get a NameError that means the name 'total' is not specified as you attempt to print out the total local variable that was specified within the body of the feature. In comparison, the init attribute can be written out without any complications.

Anonymous Functions in Python

Anonymous functions are often termed lambda functions in Python since you are using the lambda keyword rather than naming it with the standard-def keyword.

1. double = lambda x: x*2

2. double(5)

The anonymous or lambda feature in the DataCamp Light chunk above is lambda x: x*2. X is the argument, and x*2 is the interpretation or instruction that is analyzed and given back. What is unique about this function, and it has no tag, like the examples you saw in the first section of the lecture for this function. When you had to write the above function in a UDF, you would get the following result:

def double(x):

return x*2

Let us see another example of a lambda function where two arguments are used:

1. # `sum()` lambda function

2. sum = lambda x, y: x + y;

3. # Call the `sum()` anonymous function

4. sum(4,5)

5. # "Translate" to a UDF

6. def sum(x, y):

7. returnx+y

When you need a function with no name for a short interval of time, you utilize anonymous functions and this is generated at runtime. Special contexts where this is important are when operating with filter(), map() and redu():

1. from functools import reduce

2. my_list = [1,2,3,4,5,6,7,8,9,10]

3. # Use lambda function with `filter()`

4. filtered_list = list(filter(lambda x: (x*2 > 10), my_list))

5. # Use lambda function with `map()`

6. mapped_list = list(map(lambda x: x*2, my_list))

7. # Use lambda function with `reduce()`

8. reduced_list = reduce(lambda x, y: x+y, my_list)

9. print(filtered_list)

10. print(mapped_list)

11. print(reduced_list)

As the name states the filter() function it help filters the original list of inputs my_list based on a criterion > 10.By contrast, with map(), you implement a function to every components in the my_listlist. You multiply all of the components with two in this scenario. Remember that the function reduce() is a portion of the functools library. You cumulatively are using this function to the components in the my_list() list, from left to right, and in this situation decrease the sequence to a single value 55.

Using main() as a Function

If you have got any knowledge with other programming languages like java, you'll notice that executing functions requires the main feature. As you've known in the above examples, Python doesn't really require this. However, it can be helpful to logically organize your code along with a main() function in your python code- - all of the most important components are contained within this main() function.

You could even simply achieve and call a main() function the same as you did with all of those above functions:

1. # Define `main()` function

2. def main():

3. hello()

4. print("This is the main function")

5. main()

After all, as it now appears, when you load it as a module, the script of your main ( ) function will indeed be called. You invoke the main() function whenever name == ' main ' to ensure this does not happen.

That implies the source above code script becomes:

1.# Define `main()` function

2.def main():

3.hello()

4.print("This is a main function")

5.# Execute `main()` function

6. if __name__ == '__main__':

7. main()

Remember that in addition to the main function, you too have a init function, which validates a class or object instance. Plainly defined, it operates as a constructor or initializer, and is termed automatically when you start a new class instance. With such a function, the freshly formed object is assigned to the self-parameter that you've seen in this guide earlier.

Consider the following example:

class Dog:

"""

Requires:

legs – legs for a dog to walk.

color – Fur color.

"""

def __init__(self, legs, color):

self.legs = legs

self.color = color

def bark(self):

bark = "bark" * 2

return bark

```python
if __name__ == "__main__":

    dog = Dog(4, "brown")

    bark = dog.bark()

    print(bark)
```

LISTS AND LOOPS

Lists

A list is often a data structure in Python, which is an ordered list of elements that is mutable or modifiable. An item is named for each element or value inside a list. Just like strings are defined like characters between quotations, lists are specified by square brackets '[ ]' having values.

Lists are nice to have because you have other similar principles to deal with. They help you to hold data that are relevant intact, compress the code, and run the same numerous-value methods and processes at once.

It could be helpful to get all the several lists you have on your computer when beginning to think about Python lists as well as other data structures that are types of collections: Your assemblage of files, song playlists, browser bookmarks, emails, video collections that you can access through a streaming platform and much more.

We must function with this data table, taken from data collection of the Mobile App Store (RamanathanPerumal):

Name	price	currency	rating_count	rating
Instagram	0.0	USD	2161558	4.5
Clash of Clans	0.0	USD	2130805	4.5

Temple Run	0.0	USD	1724546	4.5
Pandora – Music & Radio	0.0	USD	1126879	4.0
Facebook	0.0	USD	2974676	3.5

Every value is a data point in the table. The first row (just after titles of the columns) for example has 5 data points:

- Facebook
- 0.0
- USD
- 2974676
- 3.5

Dataset consists of a collection of data points. We can consider the above table as a list of data points. Therefore we consider the entire list a dataset. We can see there are five rows and five columns to our data set.

Utilizing our insight of the Python types, we could perhaps consider we can store each data point in their own variable — for example, here's how we can store the data points of the first row:

```
script.py
track_name_row1 = 'Facebook'
price_row1 = 0.0
currency_row1 = 'USD'
rating_count_tot_row1 = 2974676
user_rating_row1 = 3.5
```

Above, we stored:

- Text for the string as "Facebook."
- Float 0.0 as a price
- Text for the string as "USD."
- Integer 2,974,676 as a rating count
- Float 3.5 for user rating

A complicated process would be to create a variable for every data point in our data set. Luckily we can use lists to store data more effectively. So in the first row, we can draw up a list of data points:

```
script.py
row_1 = ['Facebook', 0.0, 'USD', 2974676, 3.5]
print(row_1)
type(row_1)
```

```
Output
['Facebook', 0.0, 'USD', 2974676, 3.5]
list
```

For list creation, we:

- Separating each with a comma while typing out a sequence of data points: 'Facebook,' 0.0, 'USD,' 2974676, 3.5
- Closing the list with square brackets: ['Facebook', 0.0, 'USD', 2974676, 3.5]
- After the list is created, we assign it to a variable named row_1and the list is stored in the computer's memory.

For creating data points list, we only need to:

- Add comma to the data points for separation.
- Closing the list with brackets.

See below as we create five lists, in the dataset each row with one list:

row_1 =]['FACEBOOK', 0.0, 'usd', 2974676, 3.5]

row_2 = ['INSTAGRAM', 0.0, 'usd', 2161558, 4.5

row_3 = ['CLASH OF CLANS', 0.0, 'usd', 2130805, 4.5]

row_4 = ['TEMPLE RUN', 0.0, 'usd', 1724546, 4.5]

row_5 =['PANDORA', 0.0, 'usd', 1126879, 4.0]

Index of Python Lists

A list could include a broader array of data types. A list containing [4, 5, 6] includes the same types of data (only integers), while the list ['Facebook', 0.0, 'USD,' 2974676, 3.5] contains many types of data:

- Consisting Two types of floats (0.0, 3.5)
- Consisting One type of integer (2974676)
- Consisting two types of strings ('Facebook,' 'USD')

['FACEBOOK', 0.0, 'usd', 2974676, 3.5] list got 5 data points. For the length of a list, len() command can be used:

```
script.py
row_1 = ['Facebook', 0.0, 'USD', 2974676, 3.5]
print(len(row_1))

list_1 = [1, 6, 0]
print(len(list_1))

list_2 = []
print(len(list_2))

Output
5
3
0
```

For smaller lists, we can simply count the data points on our displays to figure the length, but perhaps the len() command will claim to be very useful anytime you function with lists containing many components, or just need to compose data code where you really don't know the length in advance.

Every other component (data point) in a list is linked to a particular number, termed the index number. The indexing also begins at 0, which means that the first element should have the index number 0, the 2nd element the index number 1, etc.

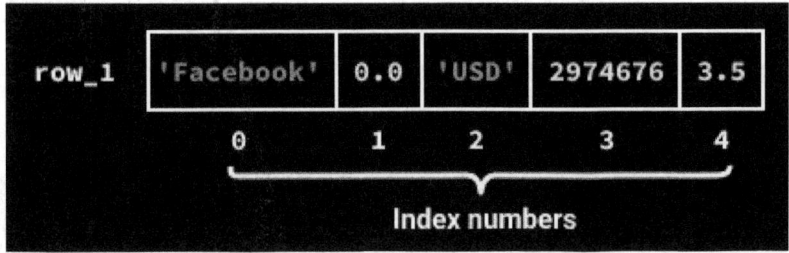

To locate a list element index rapidly, determine its location number in the list and then subtract it by 1. The string 'USD,' for instance, is the third item in the list (stance number 3), well its index number must be two because $3 - 1 = 2$.

The index numbers enable us to locate a single item from a list. Going backward through the list row 1 from the example above, by executing code row 1[0], we can obtain the first node (the string 'Facebook') of index number 0.

```
script.py
row_1 = ['Facebook', 0.0, 'USD', 2974676, 3.5]
row_1[0]
```

```
Output
'Facebook'
```

The Model list_name[index number] follows the syntax for locating specific list components. For example, the title of our list above is row_1 and the index number of a first element is 0, we get row_1[0] continuing to follow the list_name[index number] model, in which the index number 0 is in square brackets just after the name of the variable row_1.

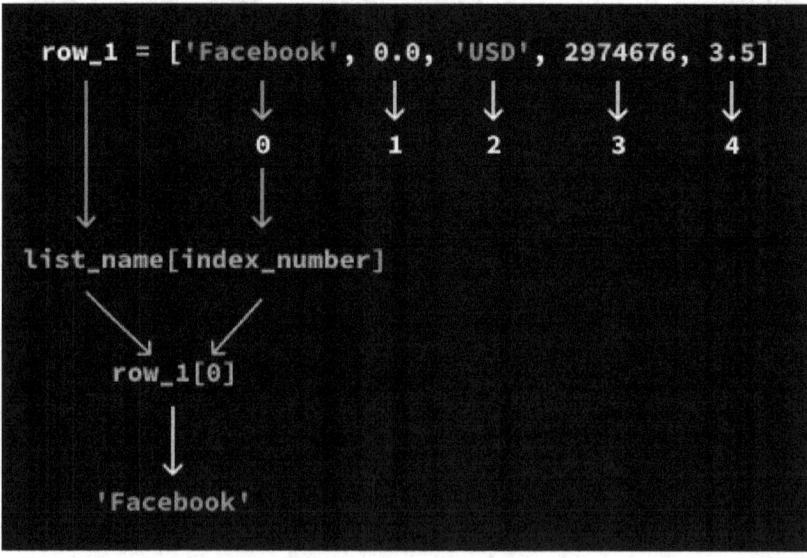

The method to retrieve each element in row_1:

```
script.py
row_1 = ['Facebook', 0.0, 'USD', 2974676, 3.5]
            0         1      2       3      4
                    Index numbers
print(row_1[0])
print(row_1[1])
print(row_1[2])
print(row_1[3])
print(row_1[4])
```
```
Output
Facebook
0.0
USD
2974676
3.5
```

Retrieval of list elements makes processes easier to execute. For example, Facebook and Instagram ratings can be selected, and the aggregate or distinction between the two can be found:

```
script.py
row_1 = ['Facebook', 0.0, 'USD', 2974676, 3.5]
row_2 = ['Instagram', 0.0, 'USD', 2161558, 4.5]

difference = row_2[4] - row_1[4]
average_rating = (row_1[4] + row_2[4]) / 2

print(difference)
print(average_rating)
```
```
Output
1.0
4.0
```

Try Using list indexing to retrieve and then average the number of ratings with the first 3 rows:

ratings_1 = row_1[3]

ratings_2 = row_2[3]

ratings_3 = row_3[3]

total = ratings_1 + ratings_2 + ratings_3

average = total / 3

print(average)

2422346.3333333335

Using Negative Indexing with Lists

There are two indexing systems for lists in Python:

1. Positive indexing: The index number of the first element is 0; the index number of the second element is 1 and furthermore.
2. Negative indexing: The index number of the last element is -1; the index number of the second element is -2 and furthermore.

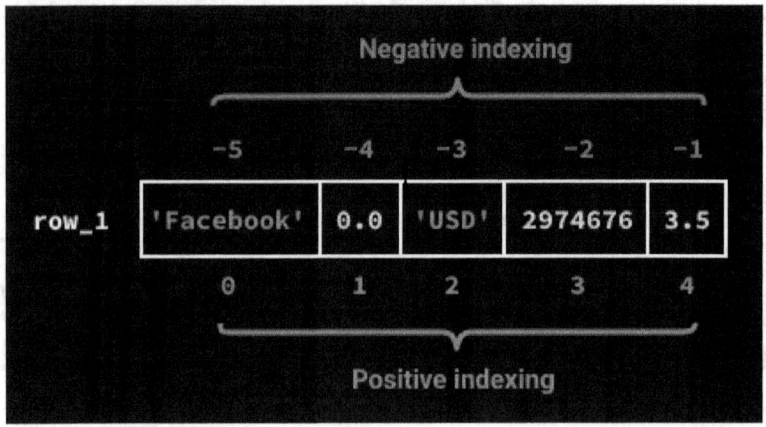

In exercise, we mostly use positive indexing to obtain elements of the list. Negative indexing is helpful whenever we want to pick the last element in such a list, mostly if the list is lengthy, and by calculating, we cannot figure out the length.

```
script.py
row_1 = ['Facebook', 0.0, 'USD', 2974676, 3.5]
print(row_1[-1])
print(row_1[4])
```
```
Output
3.5
3.5
```

Note that when we use an index number just outside of the scope of the two indexing schemes, we are going to have an IndexError.

```
script.py
row_1 = ['Facebook', 0.0, 'USD', 2974676, 3.5]
row_1[6]
```
```
Output
IndexError: list index out of range
```

```
script.py
row_1 = ['Facebook', 0.0, 'USD', 2974676, 3.5]
row_1[-7]
```
```
Output
IndexError: list index out of range
```

How about using negative indexing to remove from each of the top 3 rows the user rating (the very last value) and afterwards average it.

row_1 [-1]=rating_1

row_2[-1]=rating_2

row_3[-1]=rating_3

rating_1 + rating_2 + rating_3=total_rating

total_rating / 3= average_rating

print(average)

2422346.33333

Slice Python Lists

Rather than selecting the list elements separately, we can pick two consecutive elements using a syntax shortcut:

```
script.py
row_3 = ['Clash of Clans', 0.0, 'USD', 2130805, 4.5]
cc_pricing_data = row_3[0:3]   ← syntax shortcut
print(cc_pricing_data)

Output
['Clash of Clans', 0.0, 'USD']
```

While selecting the first n elements from a list called a list (n stands for a number), we can use the list syntax shortcut [0: n]. In the above example, we had to choose from the list row 3 the first three elements, so we will use row 3[0:3].

When the first three items were chosen, we sliced a portion of the set. For this function, the collection method for a section of a list is known as list slicing.

List slice can be done in many ways:

```
                        Slice 3
                     ┌──────────────────┐
['Clash of Clans', 0.0, 'USD', 2130805, 4.5]
 └──────────────────────┘  └──────────────┘
         Slice 1                Slice 2


Slice 1: ['Clash of Clans', 0.0, 'USD']

Slice 2: [2130805, 4.5]

Slice 3: [0.0, 'USD', 2130805]
```

Retrieving any list slice we need:

- Firstly identify the first and last elements of the slice.
- The index numbers of the first and last element of the slice must then be defined.
- Lastly, we can use the syntax a list[m: n] to extract the list slice we require, while:

'm' means the index number of both the slice's 1st element; and 'n' symbolizes the index number of the slice's last element in addition to one (if the last element seems to have index number 2, after which n is 3, if the last element seems to have index number 4, after which n is 5, and so on).

```
                                    The slice we want
                              ┌──────────────────────┐
row_3 = ['Clash of Clans', 0.0, 'USD', 2130805, 4.5]
```

(Step 1) Identify the first and the last element of the slice: `0.0` is the first element, and `2130805` is the last.

(Step 2) Identify the index numbers of the first and the last element of the slice: `0.0` has the index number 1, and `2130805` has the index number 3.

(Step 3) Retrieve the list slice by using `a_list[m:n]`: `row_3[1:4]` — remember that n is the index number of the last element plus one (3 + 1, in this case)

When we want to choose the 1st or last 'x' elements (x represents a number), we may use even less complex shortcuts for syntax:

a_list[:x] when we need to choose the first x elements.

a_list[-x:] when we need to choose the last x elements.

```
script.py
row_3 = ['Clash of Clans', 0.0, 'USD', 2130805, 4.5]

first_3 = row_3[:3]
last_3 = row_3[-3:]

print(first_3)
print(last_3)
```

```
Output
['Clash of Clans', 0.0, 'USD']
['USD', 2130805, 4.5]
```

See how we retrieve from the first row the first four elements (with Facebook data):

first_4_fb = row_1[:4]

print(first_4_fb)

['Facebook', 0.0, 'USD', 2974676]

From the same row, the last three elements are:

last_3_fb = row_1[-3:]

print(last_3_fb)

['USD', 2974676, 3.5]

In the fifth row (data in the row for Pandora) with elements third and fourth are:

pandora_3_4 = row_5[2:4]

print(pandora_3_4)

['USD', 1126879]

Python List of Lists

Lists were previously introduced as a viable approach to using one variable per data point. Rather than having a different variable for any of the five 'Facebook' data points, 0.0, 'USD,' 2974676, 3.5, we can connect the data points into a list together and then save the list in a variable.

We have worked with a data set of five rows since then and have stored each row as a collection in each different variable (row 1, row 2, row 3, row 4, and row 5 variables). Even so, if we had a data set of 5,000 rows, we would probably have ended up with 5,000 variables that will create our code messy and nearly difficult to work with.

To fix this issue, we may store our five variables in a unified list:

```
script.py
row_1 = ['Facebook', 0.0, 'USD', 2974676, 3.5]
row_2 = ['Instagram', 0.0, 'USD', 2161558, 4.5]
row_3 = ['Clash of Clans', 0.0, 'USD', 2130805, 4.5]
row_4 = ['Temple Run', 0.0, 'USD', 1724546, 4.5]
row_5 = ['Pandora - Music & Radio', 0.0, 'USD', 1126879, 4.0]

data_set = [row_1, row_2, row_3, row_4, row_5]
data_set
```

```
Output      ── Notice the double brackets
    ↓
[['Facebook', 0.0, 'USD', 2974676, 3.5],  ──→ Notice the commas
['Instagram', 0.0, 'USD', 2161558, 4.5],
['Clash of Clans', 0.0, 'USD', 2130805, 4.5],
['Temple Run', 0.0, 'USD', 1724546, 4.5],
['Pandora - Music & Radio', 0.0, 'USD', 1126879, 4.0]]
```

As we're seeing, the data set is a list of five additional columns (row 1, row 2, row 3, row 4, and row 5). A list containing other lists is termed a set of lists.

The data set variable is already a list, which indicates that we can use the syntax we have learned to retrieve individual list elements and execute list slicing. Under, we have:

- Use datset[0] to locate the first list element (row 1).
- Use datset[-1] to locate the last list element (row 5).
- Obtain the first two list elements (row 1 and row 2) utilizing data set[:2] to execute a list slicing.

```
script.py
data_set = [row_1, row_2, row_3, row_4, row_5]
print(data_set[0])
print(data_set[-1])
print(data_set[:2])
```

```
Output

['Facebook', 0.0, 'USD', 2974676, 3.5]
['Pandora - Music & Radio', 0.0, 'USD', 1126879, 4.0]
[['Facebook', 0.0, 'USD', 2974676, 3.5],
['Instagram', 0.0, 'USD', 2161558, 4.5]]
```

Often, we will need to obtain individual elements from a list that is a portion of a list of lists — for example; we might need to obtain the rating of 3.5 from the data row ['FACEBOOK', 0.0, 'USD', 2974676, 3.5], which is a portion of the list of data sets. We retrieve 3.5 from data set below utilizing what we have learnt:

- Using data set[0], we locate row_1, and allocate the output to a variable named fb_row.
- fb_row ['Facebook', 0.0, 'USD', 2974676, 3.5] outputs, which we printed.
- Using fb_row[-1], we locate the final element from fb_row (because fb row is a list), and appoint the output to a variable called fb_rating.
- Print fb_rating, outputting 3.5

```
script.py
data_set = [row_1, row_2, row_3, row_4, row_5]
fb_row = data_set[0]
print(fb_row)

fb_rating = fb_row[-1]
print(fb_rating)

Output
['Facebook', 0.0, 'USD', 2974676, 3.5]
3.5
```

Earlier in this example, we obtained 3.5 in two steps: data_set[0] was first retrieved, and fb_row[-1] was then retrieved. There is also an easy way to get the same 3.5 output by attaching the two indices ([0] and [-1]); the code data_set[0][-1] gets 3.5.:

```
script.py
data_set = [row_1, row_2, row_3, row_4, row_5]
print(data_set[0][-1])
            ⎵⎵⎵⎵⎵⎵
             row_1
            ⎵⎵⎵⎵⎵⎵
   ['Facebook', 0.0, 'USD', 2974676, 3.5]

Output
3.5
```

Earlier in this example, we have seen two ways to get the 3.5 value back. Both methods lead to the same performance (3.5), but the second approach requires fewer coding, as the steps we see from the example are elegantly integrated. As you can select an alternative, people generally prefer the latter.

Let's turn our five independent lists in to the list of lists:

app_data_set = [row_1, row_2, row_3, row_4, row_5]

then use:

print(app_data_set)

```
[
  ['FACEBOOK', 0.0, 'usd', 2974676, 3.5]
  ['INSTAGRAM', 0.0, 'usd', 2161558, 4.5
  ['CLASH OF CLANS', 0.0, 'usd', 2130805, 4.5]
  ['TEMPLE RUN', 0.0, 'usd', 1724546, 4.5]
  ['PANDORA', 0.0, 'usd', 1126879, 4.0]
]
```

List Processes by Repetitive method

Earlier, we had an interest in measuring an app's average ranking in this project. It was a feasible task while we were attempting to work only for three rows, but the tougher it becomes, the further rows we add. Utilizing our tactic from the beginning, we will:

1. Obtain each individual rating.
2. Take the sum of the ratings.
3. Dividing by the total number of ratings.

```
script.py
row_1 = ['Facebook', 0.0, 'USD', 2974676, 3.5]
row_2 = ['Instagram', 0.0, 'USD', 2161558, 4.5]
row_3 = ['Clash of Clans', 0.0, 'USD', 2130805, 4.5]
row_4 = ['Temple Run', 0.0, 'USD', 1724546, 4.5]
row_5 = ['Pandora - Music & Radio', 0.0, 'USD', 1126879, 4.0]

app_data_set = [row_1, row_2, row_3, row_4, row_5]
avg_rating = (app_data_set[0][-1] + app_data_set[1][-1] +
              app_data_set[2][-1] + app_data_set[3][-1] +
              app_data_set[4][-1]) / 5

avg_rating
```
```
Output
4.2
```

As you have seen that it becomes complicated with five ratings. Unless we were dealing with data that includes thousands of rows, an unimaginable amount of code would be needed! We ought to find a quick way to get lots of ratings back.

Taking a look at the code example earlier in this thread, we see that a procedure continues to reiterate: within app_data_set, we select the last list element for every list. What if we can just directly ask Python we would like to repeat this process in app_data_set for every list?

Luckily we can use it — Python gives us a simple route to repeat a plan that helps us tremendously when we have to reiterate a process tens of thousands or even millions of times.

Let's assume we have a list [3, 5, 1, 2] allocated to a variable rating, and we need to replicate the following procedure: display the element for each element in the ratings. And this is how we can turn it into syntax with Python:

```
script.py

ratings = [3, 5, 1, 2]

for element in ratings:
    print(element)
```
```
Output
3
5
1
2
```

The procedure that we decided to replicate in our first example above was "generate the last item for each list in the app_data_set." Here's how we can transform that operation into syntax with Python:

```
script.py

app_data_set = [row_1, row_2, row_3, row_4, row_5]

for each_list in app_data_set:
    rating = each_list[-1]
    print(rating)
```
```
Output
3.5
4.5
4.5
4.5
4.0
```

Let's attempt and then get a good idea of what's going on above. Python differentiates each list item from app_data_set, each at a time, and assign it to each_list (which essentially becomes a vector that holds a list — we'll address this further):

```
script.py
app_data_set = [row_1, row_2, row_3, row_4, row_5]

for each_list in app_data_set:
    print(each_list)
```
```
Output
['Facebook', 0.0, 'USD', 2974676, 3.5]
['Instagram', 0.0, 'USD', 2161558, 4.5]
['Clash of Clans', 0.0, 'USD', 2130805, 4.5]
['Temple Run', 0.0, 'USD', 1724546, 4.5]
['Pandora - Music & Radio', 0.0, 'USD', 1126879, 4.0]
```

In the last figure earlier in this thread, the code is a much simpler and much more conceptual edition of the code below:

```
script.py
app_data_set = [row_1, row_2, row_3, row_4, row_5]

print(app_data_set[0])  ⎫
print(app_data_set[1])  ⎪
print(app_data_set[2])  ⎬  for each_list in app_data_set:
print(app_data_set[3])  ⎪      print(each_list)
print(app_data_set[4])  ⎭
```
```
Output
['Facebook', 0.0, 'USD', 2974676, 3.5]
['Instagram', 0.0, 'USD', 2161558, 4.5]
['Clash of Clans', 0.0, 'USD', 2130805, 4.5]
['Temple Run', 0.0, 'USD', 1724546, 4.5]
['Pandora - Music & Radio', 0.0, 'USD', 1126879, 4.0]
```

Utilizing the above technique requires that we consider writing a line of code for each row in the data set. But by using the app_data_set methodology for each list involves that we write only two lines of code irrespective of the number of rows in the data set — the data set may have five rows or a hundred thousand.

Our transitional goal is to use this special method to calculate the average rating of our five rows above, in which our ultimate goal is to calculate the average rating of 7,197 rows for our data set. We're going to get exactly that within the next few displays of this task, but we're going to concentrate for now on practicing this method to get a strong grasp of it.

We ought to indent the space characters four times to the right before we want to write the code:

```
script.py
app_data_set = [row_1, row_2, row_3, row_4, row_5]
for each_list in app_data_set:
    print(each_list)
```

We need to indent the code we want repeated four space characters to the right

Theoretically, we would only have to indent the code to the right with at least one space character, but in the Python language, the declaration is to use four space characters. This assists with readability — reading your code will be fairly easy for other individuals who watch this convention, and you will find it easier to follow theirs.

Now use this technique to print each app's name and rating:

foreach_list in app_data_set:

name = each_list[0]

rating = each_list[-1]

print(name, rating)

Facebook 3.5

Instagram 4.5

Clash of Clans 4.5

Temple Run 4.5

Pandora - Music & Radio 4.0

Loops

A loop is frequently used to iterate over a series of statements. We have two kinds of loops, 'for loop' and 'while loop' in Python. We will study 'for loop' and 'while loop' in the following scenario.

For Loop

Python's for loop is used to iterate over a sequence (list, tuple, string) or just about any iterate-able object. It is called traversal to iterate over a sequence.

Syntax of For loop in Python

for<variable> in <sequence>:

  # body_of_loop that has set of statements

  # which requires repeated execution

In this case < variable > is often a variable used to iterate over a < sequence >. Around each iteration the next value is taken from < sequence > to approach the end of the sequence.

Python – For loop example

The example below illustrates the use of a loop to iterate over a list array. We calculate the square of each number present in the list and show the same with the body of for loop.

#Printing squares of all numbers program

List of integer numbers

numbers = [1, 2, 4, 6, 11, 20]

#variable to store each number's square temporary

sq = 0

#iterating over the given list

forval in numbers:

   # calculating square of each number

sq = val * val

   # displaying the squares

print(sq)

Output:

1

4

16

36

121

400

For loop with else block

Excluding Java, we can have the loop linked with an optional 'else' block in Python. The 'else' block only runs after all the iterations are finished by the loop. Let's see one example:

For val in range(5):

    print(val)

else:

    print("The loop has completed execution")

Output:

0

1

2

3

4

The loop has completed execution

Note: else block is executed when the loop is completed.

Nested For loop in Python

If there is a loop within another for loop, then it will be termed a nested for loop. Let's take a nested for loop example.

for num1 in range(3):

    for num2 in range(10, 14):

        print(num1, ",", num2)

Output:

0 , 10

0 , 11

0 , 12

0 , 13

1 , 10

1 , 11

1 , 12

1 , 13

2 , 10

2 , 11

2 , 12

2 , 13

While Loop

While loop is also used to continuously iterate over a block of code until a specified statement returns false, we have seen in many for loop in Python in the last guide, which is used for a similar intent. The biggest distinction is that we use for looping when we are not sure how many times the loop needs execution, yet on the other side when we realize exactly how many times we have to execute the loop, we need for a loop.

Syntax of while loop

while conditioning:

   #body_of_while

The body of the while is a series of statements from Python which require repetitive implementation. These claims are consistently executed until the specified condition returns false.

while loop flow

1. Firstly given condition is inspected, the loop is canceled if the condition returns false, and also the control moves towards the next statement in the compiler after the loop.

2. When the condition returns true, the set of statements within the loop will be performed, and the power will then switch to the loop start for the next execution.

Those two measures continuously occur as long as the condition defined in the loop stands true.

While loop example

This is an example of a while loop. We have a variable number in this case, and we show the value of the number in a loop, the loop will have an incremental operation where we increase the number value. It is a very crucial component, while the loop should have an operation of increase or decrease. Otherwise, the loop will operate indefinitely.

```
num = 1

#loop will repeat itself as long as it can

#num< 10 remains true

whilenum< 10:`

print(num)

    #incrementing the value of num

num = num + 3
```

Output:

1

4

7

Infinite while loop

Example 1:

This will endlessly print the word 'hello' since this situation will always be true.

```
while True:

    print("hello")
```

Example 2:

```
num = 1

whilenum<5:

    print(num)
```

This will endlessly print '1' since we do not update the number value inside the loop, so the number value would always remain one, and the condition number<5 would always give back true.

Nested while loop in Python

While inside another while loop a while loop is present, then it will be considered nested while loop. To understand this concept, let us take an example.

```
i = 1

j = 5

while i< 4:

    while j < 8:

        print(i, ",", j)

        j = j + 1

    i = i + 1
```

Output:

1 , 5

2 , 6

3 , 7

Python – while loop with else block

We may add an 'else' block to a while loop. The section 'else' is possible. It executes only when the processing of the loop has ended.

num = 10

whilenum> 6:

print(num)

num = num-1

else:

print("loop is finished")

Output:

10

9

8

7

Loop is finished

ADDING MULTIPLE VALUED DATA IN PYTHON

Often the creator wants users to input multiple values or inputs in a line. In Python, users could use two techniques to take multiple values or inputs in one line.

1. Use of split() method
2. Use of List comprehension

Use of split() method :

This feature helps to receive many user inputs. It splits the defined separator to the given input. If no separator is given, then a separator is blank space. Users generally use a split() method to separate a Python string, but it can be used when multiple inputs are taken.

Syntax:

input().split(separator, maxsplit)

Example:

```
filter_none
edit
play_arrow
brightness_4
#Python program showing how to add
#multiple input using split
#taking two inputs each time
x, y = input("Enter a two value: ").split()
print("Number of boys: ", x)
print("Number of girls: ", y)
print()
# taking three inputs at a time
x, y, z = input("Enter a three value: ").split()
print("Total number of students: ", x)
print("Number of boys is : ", y)
print("Number of girls is : ", z)
print()
# taking two inputs at a time
a, b = input("Enter a two value: ").split()
print("First number is {} and second number is {}".format(a, b))
print()
# taking multiple inputs at a time
# and type casting using list() function
x = list(map(int, input("Enter a multiple value: ").split()))
print("List of students: ", x)
```

Output:

```
Enter a two value: 5 10
Number of boys:  5
Number of girls:  10

Enter a three value: 30 10 20
Total number of students:  30
Number of boys is :  10
Number of girls is :  20

Enter a four value: 20 30
First number is 20 and second number is 30

Enter a multiple value: 20 30 10 22 23 26
List of students:  [20, 30, 10, 22, 23, 26]
```

Using List comprehension:

Comprehension of lists is an easy way of describing and building a list in Python. Just like mathematical statements, we can generate lists within each line only. It is often used when collecting multiple device inputs.

Example:

```
filter_none
edit
play_arrow
brightness_4
# Python program showing
# how to take multiple input
# using List comprehension
# taking two input at a time
x, y = [int(x) for x in input("Enter two value: ").split()]
print("First Number is: ", x)
print("Second Number is: ", y)
print()
# taking three input at a time
x, y, z = [int(x) for x in input("Enter three value: ").split()]
print("First Number is: ", x)
print("Second Number is: ", y)
print("Third Number is: ", z)
print()
# taking two inputs at a time
x, y = [int(x) for x in input("Enter two value: ").split()]
print("First number is {} and second number is {}".format(x, y))
print()
# taking multiple inputs at a time
x = [int(x) for x in input("Enter multiple value: ").split()]
print("Number of list is: ", x)
```

Output:

```
Enter two value: 2 5
First Number is:   2
Second Number is:  5

Enter three value: 2 4 5
First Number is:   2
Second Number is:  4
Third Number is:   5

Enter two value: 2 10
First number is 2 and second number is 10

Enter multiple value: 1 2 3 4 5
Number of list is:  [1, 2, 3, 4, 5]
```

Note: The definitions above take inputs divided by spaces. If we prefer to pursue different input by comma (","), we can just use the below:

taking multiple inputs divided by comma at a time

x = [int(x) for x in input("Enter multiple value: ").split(",")]

print("Number of list is: ", x)

Assign multiple values to multiple variables

By separating the variables and values with commas, you can allocate multiple values to different variables.

a, b = 100, 200

print(a)

100

print(b)

200

You have more than three variables to delegate. In addition, various types can be assigned, as well.

a, b, c = 0.1, 100, 'string'

print(a)

0.1

print(b)

100

print(c)

#string

Assign the same value to multiple variables

Using = consecutively, you could even appoint multiple variables with the same value. For instance, this is helpful when you initialize multiple variables to almost the same value.

a = b = 100

print(a)

100

print(b)

100

Upon defining the same value, another value may also be converted into one. As explained later, when allocating mutable objects such as lists or dictionaries, care should be taken.

a = 200

print(a)

200

print(b)

100

It can be written three or more in the same way.

a = b = c = 'string'

print(a)

string

print(b)

string

print(c)

string

Instead of immutable objects like int, float, and str, be careful when appointing mutable objects like list and dict.

When you use = consecutively, all variables are assigned the same object, so if you modify the element value or create a new element, then the other object will also modify.

a = b = [0, 1, 2]

print(a is b)

True

a[0] = 100

print(a)

[100, 1, 2]

print(b)

[100, 1, 2]

Same as below.

b = [0, 1, 2]

a = b

print(a is b)

True

a[0] = 100

print(a)

[100, 1, 2]

print(b)

[100, 1, 2]

If you would like to independently manage them you need to allocate them separately.

after c = []; d = [], c and d are guaranteed to link to two unique, newly created empty,different lists. (Note that c = d = [] assigns the same object to both c and d.)

Here is another example:

a = [0, 1, 2]

b = [0, 1, 2]

print(a is b)

False

a[0] = 100

print(a)

[100, 1, 2]

print(b)

[0, 1, 2]

ADDING STRING DATA IN PYTHON

What is String in Python?

A string is a Character set. A character is just a symbol. The English language, for instance, has 26 characters. Operating systems do not handle characters they handle the (binary) numbers. And if you may see characters on your computer, it is represented internally as a mixture of 0s and 1s and is manipulated. The transformation of character to a number is known as encoding, and probably decoding is the reverse process. ASCII and Unicode are two of the widely used encodings. A string in Python is a series of characters in Unicode. Unicode was incorporated to provide all characters in all languages and to carry encoding uniformity. Python Unicode allows you to learn regarding Unicode.

How to create a string in Python?

Strings may be formed by encapsulating characters or even double quotes inside a single quotation. In Python, even triple quotes may be used but commonly used to portray multiline strings and docstrings.

```
# defining strings in Python
# all of the following are equivalent
my_string = 'Hello'
print(my_string)
my_string = "Hello"
print(my_string)
my_string = '''Hello'''
print(my_string)
# triple quotes string can extend multiple lines
my_string = """Hello, welcome to the world of Python"""
print(my_string)
```

When the program is executed, the output becomes:

```
Hello

Hello

Hello

Hello, welcome to the world of Python
```

Accessing the characters in a string?

By indexing and using slicing, we can obtain individual characters and scope of characters. The index commences at 0. Attempting to obtain a character from index range will cause an IndexError to increase. The index has to be integral. We cannot use floats or other types, and this will lead to TypeError. Python lets its sequences be indexed negatively. The -1 index corresponds to the last object, -2 to the second object, and so forth. Using the slicing operator '(colon),' we can access a range of items within a string.

#Python string characters access:

```
str = 'programiz'
print('str = ', str)
#first character
print('str[0] = ', str[0])
#last character
print('str[-1] = ', str[-1])
#slicing 2nd to 5th character
print('str[1:5] = ', str[1:5])
#slicing 6th to 2nd last character
print('str[5:-2] = ', str[5:-2])
If we execute the code above we have the following results:
str = programiz
str[0] = p
str[-1] = z
str[1:5] = rogr
str[5:-2] = am
```

When we attempt to access an index out of the range, or if we are using numbers other than an integer, errors will arise.

index must be in the range

```
>>>my_string[15]

...

IndexError: string index out of range

# index must be an integer

>>>my_string[1.5]

...
```

TypeError: Define string indices as integers only

By analyzing the index between the elements as seen below, slicing can best be visualized. Whenever we want to obtain a range, we need the index that slices the part of the string from it.

How to change or delete a string?

Strings are unchangeable. This means elements of a list cannot be modified until allocated. We will easily reassign various strings of the same term.

```
>>>my_string = 'programiz'
>>>my_string[5] = 'a'
...
TypeError: 'str' object does not support item assignment
>>>my_string = 'Python'
>>>my_string
'Python'
```

We cannot erase characters from a string, or remove them. But it's easy to erase the string completely by using del keyword.

```
>>>delmy_string[1]
...
TypeError: 'str' object doesn't support item deletion
>>>delmy_string
>>>my_string
...
NameError: name 'my_string' is not defined
```

Python String Operations

There are many methods that can be used with string making it one of the most commonly used Python data types. See Python Data Types for more information on the types of data used in Python coding

Concatenation of Two or More Strings

The combination of two or even more strings into one is termed concatenation. In Python, the + operator does that. They are likewise concatenated by actually typing two string literals together. For a specified number of times, the * operator could be used to reiterate the string.

```
# Python String Operations
str1 = 'Hello'
str2 ='World!'
# using +
print('str1 + str2 = ', str1 + str2)
# using *
print('str1 * 3 =', str1 * 3)
Once we execute the program above we get the following results:
str1 + str2 = HelloWorld!
str1 * 3 = HelloHelloHello
Using two literal strings together would therefore concatenate them like + operator.
We might use parentheses if we wish to concatenate strings in various lines.
>>> # two string literals together
>>> 'Hello ' 'World!'
'Hello World!'
>>> # using parentheses
>>> s = ('Hello '
...      'World')
>>>s
'Hello World'
```

Iterating Through a string

With a for loop, we can iterate through a string. This is an example of counting the number of 'l's in a string function.

```
#Iterating through a string
count = 0
for letter in 'Hello World':
if(letter == 'l'):
count += 1
print(count,'letters found')
```

If we execute the code above, we have the following results:

'3 letters found.'

String Membership Test

We can check whether or not there is a substring within a string by using keyword in.

>>> 'a' in 'program'

True

>>> 'at' not in 'battle'

False

Built-in functions to Work with Python

Different built-in functions which can also be work with strings in series. A few other commonly used types are len() and enumerate(). The function enumerate() returns an enumerate object. It includes the index and value as combinations of all elements in the string. This may be of use to iteration. Comparably, len() returns the string length (characters number).

```
str = 'cold'
# enumerate()
list_enumerate = list(enumerate(str))
print('list(enumerate(str) = ', list_enumerate)
#character count
print('len(str) = ', len(str))
```

Once we execute the code above we have the following results:

```
list(enumerate(str) =  [(0, 'c'), (1, 'o'), (2, 'l'), (3, 'd')]
len(str) =  4
```

Formats for Python String

Sequence for escaping

We can't use single quotes or double quotes if we want to print a text like He said, "What's there?" This would result in a Syntax Error because there are single and double quotations in the text alone.

>>>print("He said, "What's there?"")

...

SyntaxError: invalid syntax

>>>print('He said, "What's there?"')

...

SyntaxError: invalid syntax

Triple quotes are one way to get round the problem. We might use escape sequences as a solution. A series of escape starts with a backslash, which is represented differently. If we are using a single quote to describe a string, it is important to escape all single quotes within the string. The case with double quotes is closely related. This is how the above text can be represented.

```
# using triple quotes
print('''He said, "What's there?"''')
# escaping single quotes
print('He said, "What\'s there?"')
# escaping double quotes
print("He said, \"What's there?\"")
```

Once we execute the code above, we have the following results:

He said, "What's there?"

He said, "What's there?"

He said, "What's there?"

Raw String to ignore escape sequence

Quite often inside a string, we might want to reject the escape sequences. To use it, we can set r or R before the string. Which means it's a raw string, and it will neglect any escape sequence inside.

>>>print("This is \x61 \ngood example")

This is a

good example

>>> print(r"This is \x61 \ngood example")

This is \x61 \ngood example

The format() Method for Formatting Strings

The format() sources available and make with the string object is very flexible and potent in string formatting. Style strings contain curly braces{} as placeholders or fields of substitution, which are substituted.

To specify the sequence, we may use positional arguments or keyword arguments.

```
# Python string format() method
# default(implicit) order
default_order = "{}, {} and {}".format('John','Bill','Sean')
print('\n--- Default Order ---')
print(default_order)
# order using positional argument
positional_order = "{1}, {0} and {2}".format('John','Bill','Sean')
print('\n--- Positional Order ---')
print(positional_order)
# order using keyword argument
keyword_order = "{s}, {b} and {j}".format(j='John',b='Bill',s='Sean')
print('\n--- Keyword Order ---')
print(keyword_order)
Once we execute the code above we have the following results:
--- Default Order ---
John, Bill and Sean
--- Positional Order ---
Bill, John and Sean
--- Keyword Order ---
Sean, Bill and John
```

The format() technique can have requirements in optional format. Using colon, they are divided from the name of the field. For example, a string in the given space may be left-justified <, right-justified >, or based ^.

Even we can format integers as binary, hexadecimal, etc. and floats can be rounded or shown in the style of the exponent. You can use tons of compiling there. For all string formatting available using the format() method, see below example:

```
>>> # formatting integers
>>> "Binary representation of {0} is {0:b}".format(12)
'Binary representation of 12 is 1100'
>>> # formatting floats
>>> "Exponent representation: {0:e}".format(1566.345)
'Exponent representation: 1.566345e+03'
>>> # round off
>>> "One third is: {0:.3f}".format(1/3)
'One third is: 0.333'
>>> # string alignment
>>> "|{:<10}|{:^10}|{:>10}|".format('butter','bread','ham')
'|butter    |   bread  |       ham|'
```

Old style formatting

We even can code strings such as the old sprint() style in the programming language used in C. To accomplish this; we use the '%' operator.

```
>>> x = 12.3456789
>>>print('The value of x is %3.2f' %x)
The value of x is 12.35
>>>print('The value of x is %3.4f' %x)
The value of x is 12.3457
```

String common Methods for Python

The string object comes with various methods. One of them is the format() method we described above. A few other frequently used technique include lower(), upper(), join(), split(), find(), substitute() etc. Here is a wide-range list of several of the built-in methodologies in Python for working with strings.

```
>>> "PrOgRaMiZ".lower()
'programiz'
>>> "PrOgRaMiZ".upper()
'PROGRAMIZ'
>>> "This will split all words into a list".split()
['This', 'will', 'split', 'all', 'words', 'into', 'a', 'list']
>>> ' '.join(['This', 'will', 'join', 'all', 'words', 'into', 'a', 'string'])
'This will join all words into a string'
>>> 'Happy New Year'.find('ew')
7
>>> 'Happy New Year'.replace('Happy','Brilliant')
'Brilliant New Year'
```

Inserting values into strings

Method 1 - the string format method

The string method format method can be used to create new strings with the values inserted. That method works for all of Python's recent releases. That is where we put a string in another string:

```
>>>shepherd = "Mary"
>>>string_in_string = "Shepherd {} is on duty.".format(shepherd)
>>>print(string_in_string)
```

Shepherd Mary is on duty.

The curved braces indicate where the inserted value will be going.

You can insert a value greater than one. The values should not have to be strings; numbers and other Python entities may be strings.

```
>>>shepherd = "Mary"
>>>age = 32
>>>stuff_in_string = "Shepherd {} is {} years old.".format(shepherd, age)
>>>print(stuff_in_string)
Shepherd Mary is 32 years old.
>>> 'Here is a {} floating point number'.format(3.33333)
'Here is a 3.33333 floating point number'
```

Using the formatting options within curly brackets, you can do more complex formatting of numbers and strings — see the information on curly brace string layout.

This process allows us to give instructions for formatting things such as numbers, using either: inside the curly braces, led by guidance for formatting. Here we request you to print in integer (d) in which the number is 0 to cover the field size of 3:

```
>>>print("Number {:03d} is here.".format(11))
Number 011 is here.
This prints a floating point value (f) with exactly 4 digits after the decimal point:
>>> 'A formatted number - {:.4f}'.format(.2)
'A formatted number - 0.2000'
```

Method 2 - f-strings in Python >= 3.6

When you can rely on having Python > = version 3.6, you will have another appealing place to use the new literal (f-string) formatted string to input variable values. Just at the start of the string, an f informs Python to permit any presently valid variable names inside the string as column names. So here's an example such as the one above, for instance using the f-string syntax:

```
>>>shepherd = "Martha"
>>>age = 34
>>> # Note f before first quote of string
>>>stuff_in_string = f"Shepherd {shepherd} is {age} years old."
>>>print(stuff_in_string)
```

Shepherd Martha is 34 years old.

Method 3 - old school % formatting

There seems to be an older string formatting tool, which uses the percent operator. It is a touch less versatile than the other two choices, but you can still see it in use in older coding, where it is more straightforward to use '%' formatting. For formatting the '%' operator, you demonstrate where the encoded values should go using a '%' character preceded by a format identifier to tell how to add the value.

So here's the example earlier in this thread, using formatting by '%.' Note that '%s' marker for a string to be inserted, and the '%d' marker for an integer.

```
>>>stuff_in_string = "Shepherd %s is %d years old." % (shepherd, age)
>>>print(stuff_in_string)
Shepherd Martha is 34 years old.
```

MODULE DATA

What are the modules in Python?

Whenever you leave and re-enter the Python interpreter, the definitions you have created (functions and variables) will get lost. Consequently, if you'd like to develop a code a little longer, it's better to use a text editor to plan the input for the interpreter and execute it with that file as input conversely. This is defined as script formation. As the software gets bigger, you may want to break it into different files to make maintenance simpler. You might also like to use a handy function that you wrote in many other programs without having to replicate its definition inside each program. To assist this, Python has the option of putting definitions into a file and using them in the interpreter's code or interactive instances. This very file is considered a module; module descriptions can be loaded into certain modules or into the main module (the list of variables you have exposure to in a high-level script and in converter mode).

A module is a file that contains definitions and statements from Python. The name of the file is the name of the module with the .py suffix attached. The name of the module (only as string) inside a module is available as the value, including its global variable __name__. For example, use your preferred text editor to build a file named fibo.py with the following contents in the current working directory:

```python
# Python Module example
def add(a, b):
   """This program adds two numbers and return the result"""
   result = a + b
   return result
```

In this, we defined an add() function within an example titled "module." The function requires two numbers and returns a total of them.

How to import modules in Python?

Within a module, we can import the definitions to some other module or even to the interactive Python interpreter. To do something like this, we use the keyword import. To load our recently specified example module, please enter in the Python prompt.

>>> import example

This should not import the identities of the functions directly in the existing symbol table, as defined in the example. It just imports an example of the module name there.

Using the name of the module, we can use the dot(.) operator to access the function. For instance:

>>>example.add(4,5.5)

9.5

Python comes with lots of regular modules. Check out the complete list of regular Python modules and their usage scenarios. These directories are within the destination where you've installed Python in the Lib directory. Normal modules could be imported just the same as our user-defined modules are imported.

There are different ways of importing the modules. You'll find them below:

Python import statement

Using the import statement, we can extract a module by using the dot operator, as explained in the previous section and access the definitions within it. Here is another example.

```
# import statement example
# to import standard module math
import math
print("The value of pi is", math.pi)
```

Once we execute the code above, we have the following results:

The value of pi is 3.141592653589793

Import with renaming

We can load a module in the following way by changing the name of it:

```
# import module by renaming it

import math as m

print("The value of pi is", m.pi)
```

We called the module Math as m. In certain instances, this will save us time to type. Remember that in our scope, the name math is not identified. Therefore math.pi is incorrect, and m.pi is correctly implemented.

Python from...import statement

We can import individual names from such a module without having to import the entire module. Here is another example.

```
# import only pi from math module

from math import pi

print("The value of pi is", pi)
```

In this, only the pi parameter was imported from the math module. We don't utilize the dot operator in certain cases. We can likewise import different modules:

>>>from math import pi, e

>>>pi

3.141592653589793

>>>e

2.718281828459045

Import all names

With the following form, we can import all terms (definitions) from a module:

\# import all names from standard module math

from math import *

print("The value of pi is," pi)

Above, we have added all of the math module descriptions. This covers all names that are available in our scope except those that start with an underscore. It is not a good programming technique to import something with the asterisk (*) key. This will lead to a replication of an attribute's meaning. This also restricts our code's readability.

Python Module Search Path

Python looks at many locations when importing a module. Interpreter searches for a built-in module instead. So if not included in the built-in module, Python searches at a collection of directories specified in sys.path. The exploration is in this sequence:

PYTHONPATH (list of directories environment variable)

The installation-dependent default directory

```
>>> import sys

>>>sys.path

['',

'C:\\Python33\\Lib\\idlelib',

'C:\\Windows\\system32\\python33.zip',

'C:\\Python33\\DLLs',

'C:\\Python33\\lib',

'C:\\Python33',

'C:\\Python33\\lib\\site-packages']
```

We can insert that list and customize it to insert our own location.

Reloading a module

During a session, the Python interpreter needs to import one module only once. This makes matters more productive. Here is an example showing how that operates.

Assume we get the code below in a module called my_module:

```
# This module shows the effect of
#  multiple imports and reload
print("This code got executed")
```

Now we suspect that multiple imports have an impact.

>>> import my_module

This code was executed:

>>> import my_module

>>> import my_module

We have seen our code was only executed once. This means that our module has only been imported once.

Also, if during the process of the test our module modified, we will have to restart it. The way to do so is to reload the interpreter. But that doesn't massively help. Python offers an effective way to do so. Within the imp module, we may use the reload() function to restart a module. Here are some ways to do it:

>>> import imp

>>> import my_module

This code executes

>>> import my_module

>>>imp.reload(my_module)

This code executes

<module 'my_module' from '.\\my_module.py'>

The dir() built-in function

We may use the dir() function to locate names specified within a module. For such cases, in the example of the module that we had in the early part, we described a function add().

In example module, we can use dir in the following scenario:

```
>>>dir(example)
['__builtins__',
'__cached__',
'__doc__',
'__file__',
'__initializing__',
'__loader__',
'__name__',
'__package__',
'add']
```

Now we'll see a list of the names sorted (alongside add). Many other names that start with an underscore are module-associated (not user-defined) default Python attributes. For instance, the attribute name contains module __name__.

```
>>> import example
>>>example.__name__
'example'
```

You can find out all names identified in our existing namespace by using dir() function with no arguments.

```
>>> a = 1
>>> b = "hello"
>>> import math
>>>dir()
['__name__', '__doc__','__builtins__ ', 'a', 'b', 'math', 'pyscripter']
```

Executing modules as scripts

Python module running with python fibo.py <arguments>the program will be running in such a way, just like it was being imported, but including the __name__ set to "__main__." That implies this program is inserted at the end of the module:

If __name__ == "__main__": import sys fib(int(sys.argv[1]))

You could even create the file usable both as a script and as an importable module since this code parsing the command - line interface runs only when the module is performed as the "main" file:

$ python fibo.py 50

0 1 1 2 3 5 8 13

When the module is imported, the code will not be executed:

>>>

>>> import fibo

>>>

It is most often used whether to get an efficient user interface to a module or for test purposes (the module runs a test suite as a script).

"Compiled" Python files

To speed up loading modules, Python caches the compiled version of each module in the __pycache__ directory with the name module.version.pyc, in which the version encapsulates the assembled file format; it normally includes the firmware version of Python. For instance, the compiled edition of spam.py in CPython launch 3.3 will be cached as __pycache__/spam.cpython-33.pyc. This naming convention enables the coexistence of compiled modules from various updates and separate versions of Python.

Python tests the source change schedule against the compiled edition to see if it is out-of-date and needs recompilation. That's a fully automated system. Even the assembled modules become platform-independent, so different algorithms will use the same library between systems. In two situations Pythoniswill not check the cache:

➢ First, it often recompiles the output for the module, which is loaded explicitly from the command line but does not store it.
➢ Second, when there is no root module, it will not search the cache. The compiled module must be in the source directory to facilitate a non-source (compiled only) release, and a source module should not be installed.

Some tips for users:

- To minimize the size of a compiled file, you can use the -O or -OO switches in the Python order. The -O switch erases statements of assert, the -OO switch removes statements of assert as well as strings of doc. Although some codes may

support getting these options available, this method should only be used if you are aware of what you are doing. "Optimized" modules usually have such an opt-tag and are tinier. Future releases may modify the optimal control implications.
- A project run no faster once it is read from a.pyc file than how it was read from a.py file; just one thing about.pyc files that are faster in the speed with which they will be loaded.
- A compile all modules can generate .pyc files in a directory for all of the other modules.
- More details on this process are given in PEP 3147, along with a flow chart of the decision making.

Standard Modules

Python has a standard modules library, mentioned in a separate section, the Python Library allusion (hereafter "Library Reference"). A few modules are incorporated into the interpreter; that provide direct exposure to processes that are not component of the language's base but are nonetheless built-in, whether for effectiveness or to supply access to primitive operating systems such as source code calls. The collection of these modules is an alternative to customize and also relies on the framework underlying it. The winreg module, for instance, is only available on Microsoft windows. One particular module is worthy of certain interest: sys, which is integrated into every Python interpreter. The sys.ps1 and sys.ps2 variables classify strings which are used as primary and secondary instructions:

```
>>>

>>> import sys

>>> sys.ps1
```

'>>> '

>>> sys.ps2

'... '

>>> sys.ps1 = 'C> '

C>print('Yuck!')

Yuck!

C>

Only when the interpreter is in interactive mode are those two variables defined. The sys.path variable is a collection of strings that defines the search path for modules used by the interpreter. When PYTHONPATH is not a part of the set, then it will be defined to a predefined path taken from either the PYTHONPATH environment variable or through a built-in default. You can change it with regular list procedures:

>>>

>>> import sys

>>>sys.path.append('/python/ufs/guido/lib/')

Packages

Packages are indeed a way to construct the namespace of the Python module by using "pointed names of the module." For instance, in a package called A., the module title A.B specifies a submodule named B. Even as the use of modules prevents the writers of various modules from stopping to know about the global variable names of one another, any use of dotted module names prevents the developers of multi-module bundles like NumPy or Pillow from needing to worry more about module names of one another. Consider making a series of lists of modules (a "package") to handle sound files and sound data in an even manner.

There are several various programs of sound files usually familiar with their extension, for example: 'wav,.aiff,.au,' though you'll need to build and maintain a massive collection of modules to convert between some of the multiple formats of files. There are several other different operations that you may like to run on sound data (such as blending, adding echo, implementing an equalizer function, producing an optical stereo effect), and you'll just be writing an infinite series of modules to execute those interventions. Here is another feasible package layout (described in terms of a hierarchical file system):

```
sound/                          Top level package
    __init__.py                 sound package initialization
    formats/                    Subpackage for conversions of file format
            __init__.py
            wavread.py
            wavwrite.py
            aiffread.py
            aiffwrite.py
            auread.py
            auwrite.py
            ...
    effects/                    Sound effectssubpackage
            __init__.py
            echo.py
            surround.py
            reverse.py
            ...
    filters/                    Filterssubpackage
            __init__.py
            equalizer.py
            vocoder.py
            karaoke.py
            ...
```

While loading the bundle, Python checks for the packet subdirectory via the folders on sys.path. To allow Python view directories that hold the file as packages, the __init__.py files are needed. This protects directories with a common name, including string, from accidentally hiding valid modules, which later appear mostly on the search path of the module. In the correct order; __init__.py can only be a blank file, but it could also implement the package preprocessing code or establish the variable __all__ described below

o   Package users could even upload individual modules from the package, such as: 'import sound.effects.echo'
o   This loads the 'sound.effects.echo' sub-module. Its full name must be mentioned: 'sound.effects.echo.echofilter(input, output, atten=4, delay=0.7)'
o   Another way to import the submodule is: 'fromsound.effects import echo'

- o It, therefore, launches the sub-module echo and provides access but without package prefix: 'echo.echofilter(input, output, atten=4, delay=0.7)'
- o And just another option is to explicitly import the desired function or attribute: 'fromsound.effects.echo import echofilter'
- o This again activates the echo sub-module however this enables its echofilter() feature explicitly accessible: 'echofilter(input, output, delay=0.7, atten=4)'

So it heaps the sub-module echo; however this tends to make its function; remember that the object will either be a sub-module (or sub-package)of the package or any other name described in the package, such as a function, class or variable while using from package import object. Initially, the import statement analyses if the object is characterized in the package; otherwise, it supposes that it is a module and makes an attempt to load it. Once it fails to reach it, an exception to 'ImportError' will be promoted.

Referring to this, while using syntax such as import 'item.subitem.subsubitem', each item has to be a package, but the last one; the last item could be a module or package, but this cannot be a class or function or variable identified in the previous item.

CONCLUSION

Research across almost all fields has become more data-oriented, impacting both the job opportunities and the required skills. While more data and methods of evaluating them are becoming obtainable, more data-dependent aspects of the economy, society, and daily life are becoming. Whenever it comes to data science, Python is a tool necessary with all sorts of advantages. It is flexible and continually improving because it is open-source. Python already has a number of valuable libraries, and it cannot be ignored that it can be combined with other languages (like Java) and current frameworks. Long story short -Python is an amazing method for data science.

"A BIG BUSINESS STARTS SMALL"

RICHARD BRANSON

OPTIONS TRADING

FOR BEGINNERS

Trade for a living and earn extra passive income. Invest from home, learn how to swing trade stocks. Tips on risk management. Get financial freedom with a positive ROI in 7 days

---

MARK BROKER

© Copyright 2020 - All rights reserved.

The content contained within this book may not be reproduced, duplicated or transmitted without direct written permission from the author or the publisher.

Under no circumstances will any blame or legal responsibility be held against the publisher, or author, for any damages, reparation, or monetary loss due to the information contained within this book. Either directly or indirectly.

Legal Notice:

This book is copyright protected. This book is only for personal use. You cannot amend, distribute, sell, use, quote or paraphrase any part, or the content within this book, without the consent of the author or publisher.

Disclaimer Notice:

Please note the information contained within this document is for educational and entertainment purposes only. All effort has been executed to present accurate, up to date, and reliable, complete information. No warranties of any kind are declared or implied. Readers acknowledge that the author is not engaging in the rendering of legal, financial, medical or professional advice. The content within this book has been derived from various sources. Please consult a licensed professional before attempting any techniques outlined in this book.

By reading this document, the reader agrees that under no circumstances is the author responsible for any losses, direct or indirect, which are incurred as a result of the use of information contained within this document, including, but not limited to, — errors, omissions, or inaccuracies.

INTRODUCTION

Out of many misconceptions, one that surrounds many markets is options are risky. Well, if you ask an options trader, he won't agree to this. The reason is if options trading were risky, it would have been an obsolete concept in the market. Why are more and more traders and investors jumping into this business?

There is just fear that makes people think that options are not profitable. All you need to do is grab all the concepts carefully and apply them when needed. Moreover, make sure you pick the right strategy and at the right time.

"Investing should be more like watching paint dry or watching grass grow. If you want excitement, take $800 and go to Las Vegas." - Paul Samuelson

Have some patience since investment is no joke! According to a ballpark estimate, a beginner needs at least one to two years to become a highly successful trader.

You can rely on this beginners' guide book on options trading that contains all the basic concepts, tips, techniques, solutions related to options trading. Read the theory carefully and then implement the concepts given in it one by one. Here is an authentic mantra to options trading:

Whenever you make a trading strategy, think it through at least three times before your final call – this is the real recipe to success!

1. OPTIONS TRADING BASICS

"Never invest in a business you cannot understand," says Warren Buffett, the famous American Investor, and we agree to him! That's why we shall start from scratch for you in this book.

In this chapter, you will learn the basics of Options Trading with examples. We suggest you take notes of the new concepts you come across in here so you could absorb more than expected.

Here is a Pro Tip: Focus on the concepts and terms given in this. This will help you grab the basics really well. So, shall we start?

What Options Trading is?

At first, options trading looks overpowering, but it is very easy to understand if you start from scratch. By that we mean if you start from concept to concept.

Basically, traders' portfolios are created with different asset categories. For instance, they may be ETFs, stocks, mutual funds, and bonds, etcetera. Options are sort of an asset category with many frills. Meaning, they can give you more benefits than ETFs and stocks.

Uses of Options

Options can make a trader powerful. It is because they can add to a trader's income, leverage, and protection. For every investor, there is an option scenario present. For instance, one can use options as a beneficial hedge against a falling stock market in order to limit the losses. They can also be utilized to make recurring earnings. Besides, options are also used for 'speculative purposes' like betting on the movement of stocks, etcetera.

With bonds and stocks, there isn't anything such as free lunch. Options are also not different. It involves risk, and investors should be well-aware of this.

Derivatives

Derivatives are considered as a 'bigger' group of securities – and options belong to them. A derivative's price is 'derived' from something else. For instance, ketchup is the derivate of tomatoes, and fries are the derivative of potatoes. Similarly, a stock option is the derivate of stocks, while options are derived from financial securities.

Some of the examples of derivate include puts, calls, mortgage-backed securities, futures, swaps, forwards, and more.

So, what you understand by options?

- Options are basically contracts. They allow buyers the rights (not obligations) to purchase or sell (in case of a call or put) a specific asset at a certain price or before specified expiry date.

- Investors use them for generating income, hedging risks, or speculating.

- They are called derivatives. The reason is options derive their value from underlying assets.

- A (stock option) contract typically has 100 shares of (an underlying) stock, but they may be written on any type of underlying asset from currencies, bonds to commodities.

Options Trading Characteristics

All Options Expire

Remember, all options expire one day. This means they 'DIE' after the expiration day. This expiry could be after two days or two years. Meaning, traders need to think about the expiry time before buying an option.

Stocks can be held for life, on the other hand.

All Options Have a Strike Price

There is a 'strike price' for every option. This is the prince in which an option can be converted into 'shares of stock.' For instance, if there is a strike price set for an option at $109. You can use the option to buy/sell shares of stock at this strike price.

Option Contract Multiplier

Let us suppose there is a share of stock with a price of $105. It can be purchased at $105. When an option is $6.00, It CANNOT be purchased at $6.00. you would rather need $600 to buy this.

The reason is options can be traded with 100 shares of stock. Meaning, you need to multiply an option price with 100 to attain its 'premium.'

Types of Options

Options trading has immense upward potential with limited risk. There are two main types of Options.

- Call Options

Call option price shows an upward movement when the stock price increases, and it starts to go down when the stock price goes down. Meaning, you can say that it is directly proportional to stock prices.

Call Option Price moves with the Stock price!

One can share 100 shares of stock with the strike price of a Call Option. Let us suppose that there is a rental apartment, and its price is $200,000. You want to purchase this apartment, thinking that its value will be doubled after some time. However, you do not want to pay the full price of this apartment.

What to do?

You can purchase a 'Call Option' for this apartment. This option will allow you to make this purchase (of amount $200,000) in 24 months. But this process will involve a contract, and you will have to pay for that contract.

This financial contract is known as 'Option.'

So, the strike price of this option will be $200,000 with the expiration date of 24 months. The advantage of this is if the apartment price rises during this period, it won't affect you (you will not have to pay extra on that).

Now, let us imagine that the opposite happens. The price of the apartment does not increase in value. Rather it decreases after 24 months to $150,000.

In this case, you are not forced to buy the apartment because you have the option not to buy it. With the decreased price of $150,000 in mind, you will not opt to purchase it at the strike price of $200,000.

Since you paid for the contract at a minimal price (the contract), you only lose that. Now compare this loss with the option to buy the house by paying the full price at once. You would have lost $200,000 or (at least $50,000), wouldn't you?

What is Call? What is Put?

A call option allows an investor the right to purchase stock, while the put option allows him to sell it. Here is an example of the Call option. A person may be interested in purchasing a new apartment in a new building under construction near his locality. However, he would only want to pay for it once the construction work is complete.

That person can take advantage of his purchase option. Through option, he can purchase it from the owner in the next four years at (let us say) $400,000 as a down payment. This cost will be called "premium."

Here is a put example. Suppose you buy a home, and with that, you also purchase a homeowner's insurance policy. This policy helps to protect your property against damage. You have to pay a premium for this for a fixed period of time. This premium is highly valuable, and it helps to protect the insurance holder in case of a home accident.

Suppose, instead of an apartment, your asset was index investment or stock. So, if a trader wants to buy insurance on his S & P 500 Index, he can buy put options.

Suppose again that you foresee bear market in the future, and you do not want to lose more than 10 or 11 percent in that Index. If the Index trades at $2800 (for instance), you can buy a put option, which will make you eligible to sell the Index at $2550 at any point before the expiration date.

This will help reduce your loss. Even if the market drops at zero, your loss would not be more than 10 percent, in case you hold the put option.

Buying and Selling

Options allow you to do four things:

- Sell Calls
- Sell Puts
- Buy Calls
- Buy Put

Keep these four scenarios in mind because this is important when you enter the trading business. Purchasing stock offers a long position for investors. But buying a call option can extend your position (it can make it even longer). Short selling offers a shorter position. In an underlying stock, selling an uncovered call also gives a short position.

Similarly, buying puts also makes a short position for you in the underlying stocks. While selling naked puts offers you a longer position.

Remember that buyers of options are known as holders, and sellers of options are known as option 'Writers.'

1. There is no obligation on call and put holders to buy or sell. They have their rights. The only risk for them is to spend money on buying premium.

2. However, it is important to call and put writers to buy and sell in case their option expires. This means they can make more, but they also have a higher risk level than holders.

2. WHY TRADE WITH OPTIONS

Options trading first started in 1973. They can give a lot of benefits to individual traders, though they have a reputation for being risky. Well, you must be thinking, what are those benefits, aren't you? Here is the answer to this.

The Benefits of Options Trading

Although options have been around for quite a time now, most investors still 'fear' using them. The reason is less information and incorrect use. Meaning, if you have good knowledge of all the basics of options (like we are providing here), you are more likely to succeed as an investor.

Individual investors should be aware of the correct usage and benefits of options before blindly following the rumors that options are 'risky.'

Options have Low Risk

Some situations call for high risk for buying options than having equities. However, there are also scenarios when using options trading becomes the best strategy. This also depends on how properly you use them. Options need low financial commitment than equities. Moreover, they are impervious, which promises less risk.

Another quality of options is compared with stocks; options are safer. They are protected by stock-loss order. This order helps to halt losses under a predetermined price indicated by the trader. However, the nature of the order also matters a lot.

Let us suppose a trader purchases a stock investing $50. He does not want to lose more than 10 percent; he places a $45 stop order. It becomes a market order when the stock trades below this price. This order can work during the daytime, not during night time.

For instance, stocks close at $51, but the next day, you hear bad news about stocks like the company owner lies about earnings or there is embezzlement noted. Stocks might open down at $20. If this happens, this price would be the first trade below the investor's stop order price. The trader would sell at this price ($20), locking in the loss.

For his protection, if the trader had bought the put, he would not have suffered from that loss. Options do not close when the market goes down and closes. This happens with stop orders. Meaning, stop orders close if the market shuts down.

Options keep the traders covered 24/7. Stop orders cannot provide insurance 24 hours. This is why options are considered as a 'dependable form of hedging.'

Options are More Cost-Effective

With greater leveraging power, options can help save you a lot of money. You can attain an option position the same as you obtain a stock position. To buy 200 shares of a stock worth $80, you have to pay $16,000, for instance. But if you want to buy double calls worth $20 (representing 100 shares contract), the total expenditure would be $4000. How?

Try this formula: 2 contracts multiply by 100 shares divided by contract x $20 price in the market. You will have an additional $12,000 for use at your discretion.

Although this is not so simple, it requires a good understanding and good strategy. You will need to pick the right call at the right time to buy for mimicking the stock position in the correct manner. This strategy is known as Stock Replacement, which is not only viable but also cost-effective and practical.

Let's suppose you want to buy Schlumberger (SLB, thinking that it might increase in value in the next few months. You think you should buy 200 shares and the company is trading at $131. So, your overlay would be $26,200.

Instead of investing such a heavy amount, you could pick options to mimic the stocks and buy a call option called, August – using only a $100 strike price for $34.

If you want to acquire a position equal to the size of 200 shares that are mentioned above, you need to purchase double contracts. Your total investment for this would be $6,800, instead of $26,200. (Here is how: double contacts x 100 shares/contract x market price of $34). You can also get interested on this or use your money for another investment.

Options Offer Higher Returns

Options trading promises higher percentage returns. Traders do not need a calculator to find this. They can invest a low amount and get a higher amount back.

Let us consider the above use case to compare the return on investment. Traders need to purchase stocks for $50 and an option for $6. Suppose options price changes by 80 percent (of the stock price). If stocks move up to $5.5, a trader will get a 10 percent return. But the option would gain 80 percent of the stock price of $4.5. A return of this kind on $6 investment amounts to 67.5 percent, which is much better than a 10 percent profit on stocks.

More Alternatives with Options

Traders can find more investing alternatives with options. They are highly flexible. There are many strategies to recreate synthetic option positions.

These positions offer investors a plethora of ways to obtain their investment goals. Besides synthetic positions, options have many other alternatives. For instance, many investors work with brokers who charge a little margin for shorting stocks. Other traders work with them (brokers) who do not wish to short stocks.

The incapability to do the downside when required limits traders and investors. However, no broker can rule against traders for buying puts in order to 'play the downside.' This is a big benefit for investors.

Options also allow traders to trade the 'third dimension' of the market. Interestingly, they can even trade-in 'no direction,' stock movements, and during volatility. Mostly, stocks do not show 'big' moves; but investors have the edge to trade in stagnation too. Thus, options can only offer multiple alternatives that can give them profit in all types of markets.

Why Options are a Better Choice?

Still, if you want to know why options are a better choice, read this out:

Hedging

The main purpose of inventing options was hedging. It helps to reduce risk. So, take options as your insurance policy. Like you insure your car and home, options can ensure your investment in case of a downfall movement.

Suppose a trader wants to buy something related to tech stocks. But he also wants to limit his loss. The trader can do these easy throughput options, which give him two benefits: minimize risk and maximize profit. Short selling can also reduce loss at the time of a downturn.

Speculation

The ability to predict the future price is speculation, as its name hints. You might think that the price of a stock would go down in a day, based on technical or fundamental analysis. He might sell the stock or sell put after the speculation.

This has got an attraction for many investors to call options because it offers leverage. A call option (out of the money) may cost only some cents of a few dollars compared to the $100 stock's full price.

How does Options Trading work?

When weighing option contracts, it is important to determine the future probabilities. Options get costlier when there is higher predictability in the future. For example, when a stock value rises, the call value also increases. This is crucial to understand the value of options.

A shorter expiry means a lower value of an option as the chances of price rise diminish as the expiry comes near. If a trader purchases an out-of-money 1-month option, while stocks do not move, it losses its value. It is because time is money when it comes to options trading. This wasting con of options is called 'time decay.'

Similarly, if a trader buys an option with a longer expiry; the chances of price movement for that option becomes brighter and brighter as there is enough time for the price to get bigger.

The price also goes up with volatility. When the market is uncertain, the odds get higher. If an asset's volatility goes up, price swings maximize the probability of substantial movements both up and downwards.

Higher price swings also up the chances of an occurring event. It means, the higher the volatility, the greater the options price. Volatility and options trading essentially linked to each other in a way.

On many exchanges, a stock option allows you to buy/sell 100 shares. This is why you should multiply your premium with 100 to get the final amount.

Check out this Example of Investment Table:

	June 1	June 21	Expiry Date
Stock Price	$67	$78	$62
Options Price	$3.15	$8.25	No Value
Contract Value	$315	$825	$0
Paper Loss/Gain	$0	$510	-$315

Most of the time, holders make profits by closing out their positions. Meaning, a holder sells their option; while a writer buys his position back for closing. Not more than 10 percent of the options are executed, and 60 percent are closed (traded out), while 30 expire without having value.

In options, fluctuations can be understood by "time value" (intrinsic and extrinsic value). Their premium is the combination of time value and its intrinsic value. Intrinsic value is the sum above the strike price.

Time value indicates the added value a trader needs to pay above the intrinsic value. This is time value or extrinsic value. Therefore, the option price in the above example can be considered as:

Time Value +	Intrinsic =	Premium
$0.25	$8.00	$8.25

In practical life, Options trade at (some level above) the intrinsic value. It is because the chances of an event's happening can never be absolutely zero – even if it is never in the cards!

Types of Options

There are two major types of options: American and European. The first type can be exercised at any time between the purchase date and expiry. Moreover, Us-based options have a higher premium. The early use feature commends this.

But European options can only be exercised on and near their expiry date. Most of the options on the exchanges belong to the second type.

There is also another type called Exotic Options that are actually a variety of payoff profile from vanilla options. Exotic options are typically meant for professional investors. Other types of options include Binary, Asian, Knock-out, Barrier, and Bermudan Options.

Options Liquidity & Expiry Time

There is another way to categorize options – by the time duration. Short term options expire with 12 months. Long term options have a greater expiry time. They are known as LEAPS or Long-term Equity Anticipation Securities. They are like regular options with typically longer time duration.

Options can also be categorized by their expiry time. Many option sets expire on Fridays, every week, every 30th or 31st of a month, and on a daily basis. There are also quarterly based expiries for ETFs and Index Options.

How to Read Options Table?

It is not possible to do options trading and lack the know-how of reading options tables. Here is how you can read the options table without difficulty.

- You will notice a term "Volume (VLM)" in the table. It indicates the total number of contracts traded in the most recent session.
- You will also hear 'Bid' and 'Ask.' A bid is the most recent price at which the traders wish to purchase an option. While an 'ask' is the most recent price at which the market wishes to sell an option.

- Implied Bid Volatility (IMPL BID VOL) refers to uncertainty in speed and direction of price in the future.
- Delta is the predication or probability. For instance, there are 30 percent chances of expiration of a 30-delta.
- Open Interest (OPTN OP) signifies the grand total of contracts for a specific option. OPTN OP reduces when the open trade closes.
- Gamma (GMM) is called the speed of an option. It can also be called the movement of delta or predication.
- Vega and Theta are two Greek values used in Options trading tables. Vega represents the amount at which an option price is likely to change. Theta represents the degree of value downward change in an option price during a passing day.
- The 'strike price' is a term used for price at which someone buys/sells underlying security if wishes to use options.

3. MAJOR OPTION TRADING CONCEPTS

Options trading is a term that is used in stock exchange the simple definition of options trading is that 'it is the contract between two parties in which the stock option buyer(holder) purchases the right but not the obligation to buy or sell shares of the underlying stock at a predetermined price from/to the option seller (writer) within a fixed period.'

Options offer alternative systems that allow the investor to take advantage of the exchange and trading underlying protections. There are different types of procedures, including different mix options, hidden resources, and different derivatives.

A question will come into your mind that why a person needs options trading at all, options trading is the most efficient method used in the stock exchange and it predates the modern stock exchange by a large margin.

So, one must not think that it is just a scam created by some group of people to manipulate minds to earn money because whenever a common person thinks to invest money in the stock exchange he or she is confused by terms like these, so let us tell you that what options trading is.

History of Option Trading

Some believe that it was the Greeks who gave the idea of option trading. Long before the modern world, humans were trying to decide the prices of different goods, and that's how different methods of trading were introduced into the world.

Let us revise from scratch here…

We will give you a simple example to understand what options trading is but for you to understand we want you to focus on the example with an empty mind, for example, you want to buy stocks for $s 4000 and you go to the broker, but the broker gives you an exciting offer that you can buy stocks for $s 4000 now, or you can give a token of 400 and reserve your write to buy it at $s 4000 after a month, And even if stock increases in value at that time. But the token amount will be non-refundable.

Now you think that it is possible that the stock will increase its price to 4020 at that time and you can even buy it after the increase in price, and since you have only paid 400 so you have the rest of the money to use elsewhere. Now you can wait easily for a month and decide by acknowledging the stock prices after a month that if you want to buy the stock or not.

Now, this is what you all an oversimplification, and this is options trading. In the world of trading, options are used as instruments, just like a musician needs a different instrument to get the perfect song; a broker needs options to make a perfect sale. And its price is mostly derived from stocks.

We assure you that if you read the article to the end, you will perfectly know what option trading is, and we will also tell you different strategies used in options trading.

Risks In Options Trading?

Most strategies that are used by options investors have limited risk but also limited profit, so options trading isn't a method that will make you rich overnight.

Options trading may not suit all types of investors, but they are among the most flexible of investment choices.

Options in investment are most likely used to reduce the risk of a drop in stock prices, but a little risk is involved in every type of investment. Returns are never guaranteed investors look for options to manage risks for ways to limit a potential loss.

Investors may choose to take options because the loss is limited to the price you pay for the token money. And in return, they gain the right to buy or sell stock at there at their desirable price, so options in trading benefit a lot to the investors.

Different Strategies Used In Option Trading

Traders often know very little about strategies used in options trading and jump to trading options, knowing the different strategies may lower the risk of potential loss in the market, and traders may also learn to limit the risk and maximize the return. So with a little effort, traders can learn how to take full advantage of the flexibility and power that stock options can provide.

Stock VS Option

One must think that why is there a need to trade in options when someone can trade simply too this thought confuses many of us so here is the answer

The options contract has an expiration date, depending on what type of options you are using. It may be in weeks, months, or even in years unlike stock, because the stock has no expiration date.

Stocks are usually defined by numbers, but on the other hand, there are no numbers in options.

Options drive their value from something else. That's why they fall into the derivative category, unlike stocks.

Stock owners have their right in the company (dividend or voting)on the other hand options have no right in the company

Some people may find it difficult to understand the method of options though they have even followed it in their other transaction, for example (car insurance or mortgages).

Option Trading Platforms

if a person wants to trade options, he or she must have a brokerage account, and for that, he or she will want to understand what they what before they sign up with a broker. Each platform is unique and has its pros and cons. So a person must learn more about the best options trading platform to determine which one may be the best suited for their needs.

If a person wants to find the best trading platform, he or she must review different brokerages and options trading platforms. A person must consider different factors like competitive pricing, high tech experience, good for a variety of trader needs and styles.

Some of the best options trading platforms for 2020 are:

TD Ameritrade: Best Overall

Tastyworks: Runner-Up

Charles Schwab: Best for Beginners

Webull: Best for No Commissions

Interactive Brokers: Best for Expert Traders

Option Practicing Method

1. Stocks are purchased, and the investor sells call options on the same stock which he has purchased. The number of stock shares you have purchased should match the number of call options you have sold.

2. After buying the stock shares, the investor buys put options to gain equal shares. Married acts as an insurance policy against short-term losses call options with a specific strike price. At the same time, you will sell similar call options at a higher strike price.

3. An investor purchases an option with cash from outside, while simultaneously works an out of the cash call choice for a similar stock.

4. The investor purchases a call option and a put choice simultaneously. The two alternatives ought to have a similar strike cost and expiry date.

5. The Investor purchases the call option out of cash and the put choice simultaneously. They have a similar termination date; however, their strike cost is extraordinary. The expense of the information strike ought to be not exactly the expense of the call strike

Strategies for option trading

Options traders use several strategies to make a profit from this business. The different ways of strategies are used to get profit, which involves using the many alternatives and combinations. The most common strategies are covered calls, iron condors, buying calls, and buying puts. Option trading provides advanced strategies.

Buying calls

Buying calls or long call strategy is used when an investor increasingly buys calls and sets an option on the exact underlying asset with fixed date and price. The investor uses this strategy when they are feeling bullish and confident in an increase in some stock price. In this type, the investor increases the risk as he can face a huge profit or loss, but it's always unknown which way the stock goes.

Buying puts

Usually, the investor uses this strategy when they are bearish on some stock; for example, the investor is confident in a particular stock and had a good understanding of stock but doesn't want to take a huge risk, so he uses short selling strategy.

The put option gets an increase in value when the price of the asset falls. As the market falls, the profit increase in short selling. The risk is not confirmed as the trades return with leverage. But on the off chance that the basic Ascent past the option prices, then the option will expire uselessly.

Covered calls

This strategy provides a small change in the price, the profit is not that big, but the risk it involves is less. The covered call buys 100 shares of stock and then sells one call option per 100 shares. Covered call strategy gives a chance of profit to the investor and also reduce the risk. The share is protected by this call when the price of the stock decreases.

Iron condors

In this strategy, the trader sales a put buys another for a low price and uses them to buy a call then sell the call at a high price after some time. If the stock price is kept somewhere between two puts or calls, then we make a profit. The loss comes with possibilities, one if the price increase suddenly and the other is if the price decrease suddenly, it is spread that causes this condition. This strategy is used by neutral traders or in a neutral place.

Several other strategies are used, which are:

- Broken butterfly
- Iron butterfly
- Jade lizard
- Bear call
- Calendar spread
- Protective put

The Worth of Option Trading

When we buy a bike or car, we want to protect them; the insurance is used for the safety of the car. So just like insurance, the option gives us safety. We invest money and buy shares now we want to protect our investment, for this we use options.

The option provides us good protection of our money. For example:

We bought the 100 shares at the rate of 150 dollars, which Worth 15000. We have invested and now have the risk of a decrease in price. We buy the option to remove risk from our shoulders, and the guy gets paid now assume the risk. We buy the put option for 500 dollars. If the stock increases with the rate of 170, we will get the profit, even buying an option of 500.

But if the stock price decreases with the rate of 130, we still are stable, the loss won't affect us as we have the contract on the option which has the same price. We can sell the shares at the same rate we bought, so in that case, by using the option trade, the chance of loss is very low. It provides a lot of ways to gain profit in trading.

Option Trading VS Stock Trading

An option trading is not stock trading. Well, both of them are trading, but they are quite different. Many people don't even know about the options trading; it's just another type of trading. Few things make the difference between the option trading and stock trading, here is these point.

- In options trading, the value is taken by someone else and had a contract with it. It does not get the values on its own. This is completely different from stock trading. Option trading belongs to the derivative category.

- In stock, the numbers are definite, but an option, the numbers are not definite.

- The options trading use the contract, which has the expiration date, the person has no meaning after the expiry date. The date can be in months or years according to the option there are using. Stock trading has no expiration dates.

- In options trading, the owner has no right in the company. They have no affair of any kind related to the company. In stock share, they had the rights to the company.

Risk in Option Trading

The risk involves in option is not as much as people think. Trading does involve risk. Its procedures work along with the risk. In option, the risk can contain only in few things.

- The options trading use many strategies with these strategies. Each has its own risk. The few options work on the spontaneous increase and decrease process. This sometimes gives a big loss to the investor.

- The option involves a lot of complexity. This trading is bot difficult to understand. The strategies its self are complex. Those who are a beginner in option do not understand it well and invest the money with the little knowledge which results in a loss.

- The other problem with the options trading is that it has the expiration date, which can cause you all you invest if the contract expires. This is one big factor in this trading.

Option Account

For option trade, you need an options account. Before you make an account, you need to fill the agreement with your broker. The broker will know your investment and your trade. He will generate the strategy according to the level of trading you want. The broker will guide you about options trading and its policies.

What Is An Option Account?

The account that is used to access the option trade is an options account. The broker gives access to the user for an options account. For all the trading, the brokerage account is used; it does the selling and buying. After giving all details, you will be able to open the account.

The broker tells the two type of account which you want to open, the real money and demo money account. After all the procedures, your account will ready for trading.

The Right Broker

Before choosing your broker, you check in on him. Always choose the one with an authentic source. The information you provide him should be protected. Always check the payment and its cost. Aim for the right option.

The Best Broker

- Schwab Brokerage ($0.65 per options contract)
- E-trade ($0.65 per options contract)

- Ally Invest ($0.5 per contract traded)
- TD Ameritrade ($0.65 fee per contract)

Best platforms

Options trading is a high-level risk. It needs to be protected from fraud. When selecting the platform, you must select the best one. There are many best platforms available in the market; there has a good reputation, such as.

- Charles Schwab, this platform is best for the beginner. If you are a beginner, you should choose this platform. This platform gives more understanding to users.

- TD Ameritrade is the best platform dor the options trading in the world. The cost is low and no account minimum requirements

- Tastyworks provide trading access to different devices. It allows PC, laptops, and mobile phones. It is one of the most high-tech platforms.

Webull platform gives no commission

Options trading is not meant for beginners who have zero ideas about the market. So if you are just starting your journey with the stock market, you may have to spend some time learning the basic concepts of options trading.

When we talk about stocks, it's all about investment and turning that investment into profit. So it requires strong knowledge and experience to make some big profits and avoid loss.

4. OPTIONS TRADING MYTHS AND MISCONCEPTIONS

There are many myths and misconceptions related to the term "Options Trading" not only in the stock market but also for the general public. Options trading is known to be risky; according to Mike Bellafiore, the Co-Founder of CMB trading, "Trading is a sport of survival, reinvention, and perseverance, even for the successful trader."

Indeed, in the stock market or business, there is no such thing as assurance; there is always a risk involved with putting your money into something. The stock market or business is always about numbers and good strategies. If your strategies and numbers are right, you are in it for the long haul; otherwise, you will end up with nothing.

The winner of U.S. Investing Championship in 1984 Martin S. Schwartz says,

"A lot of people get so enmeshed in the markets that they lose their perspective. Working longer does not necessarily equate with working smarter. In fact, sometimes it's the other way around." in a trading business, you can use your shortcomings or failures for your future benefits as well; according to Brett Steenbarger, an active trader and a Ph.D. scholar, "we will never be perfect as traders. That's what keeps us ever-learning, ever-growing. Our main challenge is to use our shortcomings as inspirations, fueling continuous improvement."

There are many myths and misconceptions about trading.

Misconception #1 Trading and Gambling are same

The first and the most common one is trading and gambling are the two sides of the same coin. In trading, a trader goes through all the present, past data, and numbers whether gambling is a game of available odds.

Trading is about technical analysis you look into the details, risks, profit, gain, and the market, whereas gambling is based on fundamental values. You put in your money in what you might think will happen. Also, gambling is an addiction, illegal, and also very toxic for your mental health and behavior.

Misconception #2 Should only invest in Call and Put Option

Options are the type of contract that allows the buyer to purchase or sell the underlying asset. To simplify it, the trader purchases a call option if he is expecting the demand of the underlying asset to rise within a certain deadline, and the trader opts for a put option if he is expecting the demand of the underlying asset to fall within a certain time period.

It is a misconception about the call and put option that it is the only profitable way of trading options, but in reality, the buying of calls and puts is highly risky in trading because you can never be sure about the demand of the underlying asset for that you need the proper analysis of the direction it is moving, its time frame and size of the move. You can analyze the size and the direction right, but if your options have expired before the move happens, then you may lose money.

Misconception #3 Option selling is more profitable

Option selling is basically giving someone the right, but not the obligation, to make you purchase 100 shares of a stock at a strike price before the expiration date. In simpler terms, they are basically paying to increase their flexibility, and you pay to decrease your flexibility. So when you are selling options, you are not only using the money in your brokerage, but you are also in debt. Option selling can be profitable if you play right by the rules, but there is also high risk involved in it.

Misconception #4 Put Option expire worthlessly

Option expiring worthless is when options expire from your trading account and cease to exist. There are a lot of misconceptions about 90 percent of the option expiring, but according to the report by The Chicago Board Options Exchange (CBOE), approximately, only 30% of the options expire worthlessly. 60% of the option positions are closed before their expiration, and 10% of the options are exercised.

Secondly, options expiring worthless, only work against the option buyers, but option writers still get their profit if the put option has expired.

Misconception #5 Option trading is a zero-sum

This is one of the oldest myths about option trading. It says that if a buyer wins, then the seller has to lose. But no, that is not true at all!

Options are given to manage the risk. They do not give you anything of value other than the choice to buy or sell assets. When you use options to hedge your risk, you are transferring your risk to someone else who is willing to hold on to it. So the options trading is not a zero-sum game.

Misconception #6 Options trading is easy

There is another misconception about options trading that people assume it is easy. According to the Charles Faulkner trader and an author he says "After years of studying traders, the best predictor of success is simply whether the person is improving with time and experience" you need years of experience, learning the market and its resources completely and strategies then you can be a successful trader.

Trading is rarely about "luck" its all about good hand-on knowledge. People do not mostly have an in-depth knowledge of the options trading or stock market. It is more than just investing the money. All the experts in trading business have years of experience and knowledge, and they even use their failures as a weapon for their future success.

Misconception #7 Trading in Tax-deferred account

There is a common misconception about using traditional or IRA accounts for the trading option because they both will ease up the tax advantage, and It could be a perfect retirement plan, but there are certain limits to it. You can only invest to a certain limit through your tax-deferred account. You cannot use the money before retirement. After five years, you are only able to withdraw the income.

5. TOP OPTIONS TRADING STRATEGIES

The options trading utilizes a few strategies for financial specialists to benefit from trading. The various methods of strategies are utilized to get profit, which includes utilizing the numerous other options and combinations.

The alternative exchanging gives advance techniques. These systems help financial specialists to increase the most extreme benefits. The top strategy is used for different levels of trading. Many popular trading strategies are used in the market. These strategies are well known in trading and have numbers of users. The following are the top option trading strategies.

Buying calls

Purchasing calls or long call methodology is utilized when a financial specialist progressively purchases calls and sets a choice on the specific hidden resource with fixed date and cost. The investor expects more leverage than just owning the stock. The financial specialist uses this procedure when they are feeling bullish and certain about increment at some stock cost. The confidence of the investor prepares them to pick this option strategy.

In this sort, the speculators increment the hazard as he can confront the gigantic benefit or loss, but it's consistently obscure what direction the stock goes. If the stock goes up, the investor will get the profit, and if the shares price decrease, then the investor will face a big loss. Even the most experienced traders face loss at some point, but that does not mean it will only give loss.

The profit in it usually covers the loss of investors. For example, If the investor wants to buy a developing house, then he will purchase the buy call option by doing this he can pay the same price according to the contract as the cost of a house is 200,000 now as when the development will be complete, the cost of the house will be increased.

Suppose the price of the house incredibly increased after 2,3 years, and now the house is worth 400,000. The investor will pay the same amount, although its price in the market is double because of the option he can pay the same amount of 200,000 as written on the contract. The only thing the investor will be worried about is the expiration date.

Buying puts

In this options trading strategy, the investor has the legal right to sell the shares at the given price. The date is also fixed at a certain time. The buying puts give more authority to the investor.

Normally, the financial specialist utilizes this strategy when they are bearish on some stock; for the model, the speculator is positive about the specific stock and had great comprehension of stock yet wouldn't like to face an immense challenge, so he utilizes short selling procedure.

The put choice gets increment in esteem when the cost of benefit falls. As the market falls, the benefit increment by short selling. The chance isn't affirmed as the trade return with leverage. But if the fundamental Ascent past the choice value, then the alternative will terminate pointlessly.

Mostly the traders are sure that the market will fall. They purchase the share to sell it at a certain time as they have the right to do so, the values of share increase when the stock moves towards the other direction. It is a simple way to gain profit.

If you want the insurance on your shares in stock, you can buy a put option. If the investor has a share of 500 dollars, and he realized the market would lose the value. They can sell there share at a reduced price of about 475 dollars. The loss is reduced in this way.

Covered call

This strategy provides a small change in the price, the profit is not that big, but the risk it involves is less. The covered call buys 100 shares of stock and then sale one call option per 100 shares.

Covered call strategy gives a chance of profit to the investor and also reduce the risk.

The share is protected by this call when the price of the stock decreases. In this strategy, the seller of the call option possesses the related amount of underlying instrument. In the covered call option, you can buy stock and sell the call option on Out of money(OTM).

The term buy-write is referred to when the call been sold at the same time with the purchase of stock. We get a small amount for call sales when we pay for stock shares. We have to sell calls to generate income in it. This option needs direct investment and calls to sell.

The investor uses this option strategy when they think the price will not further increase. We have to hold a long position. The chance of profit is low as the increase in price is not expected.

Suppose, the stock was trading at $200 on May 20th, 2014; The Leg 1 Buy 100 portions of the stock for $ 200 and Leg 2: Sell the 206 strikes June 26th, 2014 Call for $7.30, Lot size – 100 offers

The sum paid to take these two positions approaches - the Stock cost paid less call premium got, for example, $. 20,000 (Stock buy) – $ 730 (Premium got) = $ 19,270

If the stock value ascends over the call strike of 206, it will be worked out, and the stock will be sold. In any case, the methodology will make a benefit since you are secured by the stock you own.

State, the stock cost at termination is $ 210.

In the event that the stock falls beneath the underlying stock price tag, your long position is at a misfortune. However, you have some pad from the call premium got by selling the call.

State, the stock falls and is at $ 190 on the lapse

Iron condors

In this strategy, the trader sales a put buys another for a low price and uses them to buy a call then sell the call at a high price after some time. If the stock price is kept somewhere between two puts or calls, then we make a profit.

The loss comes with possibilities, one if the price increase suddenly and the other is if the price decrease suddenly, it is spread that causes this condition. This strategy is used by neutral traders or in a neutral place. This is a simple options strategy.

The iron condors option does not require a big investment to start a trade; you can start the trade with a minimum amount. The investor relies on the stock to stay at some particular point. It is a small strategy that involves risk, but the investor invests in a small amount to maintain the risk.

Consider the stock is trading at the cost of $120, executing an Iron Condor trading procedure we will: Sell $100 Strike Put for $3.0 Sell $140 Strike Call for $3.0

With an expectation that the cost will stay inside these two strike costs that we booked so, we make a benefit. In any case, because of the danger of boundless misfortune, we would ensure our situations by Buy Strike Put for $90 Buy Strike $160 Call for $ 2.

Bear calls

This option works on the procedure of sale and buy. The investor sells the call option and then purchases the calls at a high strike rate. This option uses the investment of the trader to get the profit income. The procedure works on limited levels. It uses two legs. These work on a 1:1 ratio to make the net credit.

Even though this is not a Bearish Strategy, it is actualized when one is bullish. It is generally set up for a 'net credit,' and the expense of buying call choices is financed by selling an 'in the cash' call choice. For this Options Trading Strategy, one must guarantee the Call alternatives have a place with a similar expiry, the equivalent hidden resource, and the proportion is kept up.

It, for the most part, ensures the drawback of a Call sold by safeguarding it, for example, by purchasing a Call of a higher strike cost. It is fundamental, however, that you execute the system just when you are persuaded that the market would be moving essentially higher.

The investor is expecting a small decrease in the stock. They sell the calls and then purchase the calls at high strike. The option works better when the volatility is high. The expiration date is good enough to handle things. The traders don't waste the expiry date, as it is important for the trading. The investor uses the long term to execute the process.

If the market is expecting the rise in stock, then the traders sell the one strike call and then buy another at the higher strike. The investor gets the profit by the amount of cost.

If the stock is expecting a sudden rise, then they sales the call and then buy the new ones which they even buy at a high rate, but instead of loss they gain profit, and then they buy more calls.

Jade lizard

In this options trading strategy, the traders sell short calls and put, and the underlying assets should not move. The cost collect in the results is great. All the options have the same expiration date. It minimizes the risk and maximizes the reward. Trading options maximize the risk in one direction.

The jade lizards option are a sort of Options Trading Strategy which is rehearsed by Traders to pick up benefit from their exchanges

If there should arise an occurrence of Straddles and Strangles, Lizards diminish the upside hazard. They are most valuable when basic stays or floats toward the strike. High benefits are created in high IV and non-bearish situations. This neutral strategy involves short calls and short put spread. It is a slow strategy; it does not increase suddenly. It uses the call cost and puts the cost at high volatility.

Let's suppose that the investor accepts this trade is a drawback chance. In the event that ABC stock moves above £25 per share, the financial specialist would lose $£1 on the call spread, yet gains £1.10 from the premium gathered for a net addition of £0.10.

The investor benefits from the exchange, except if the cost of ABC moves underneath the strike cost of the bare put by more than the top-notch that is gathered. In this model, the stock cost would need to dip under £18.90.

Collar option

It is similar to the covered call but has extra protective puts to protect the value of security between 2 bounds. The Collar Options Trading Strategy can be built by holding portions of the hidden all the while and purchasing put-call alternatives and selling call choices against the held offers.

One can support the expected drawback in the offers by purchasing the fundamental and, at the same time, purchasing a put alternative beneath the current cost and selling a call choice over the current cost. Buy one put option than lower the limit for protection; sell the call option at the upper limit.

Both must have the same expiration date and the quantity. The call and put options are out of money. The underlying assets price expired at a strike price of the short call option. The instability is surprising when the market is unstable at the point when the cost of an alternative ascent, there is a likelihood that the cost may fall and you may miss out on the benefit.

In such a case, the advantage should be secured. The option protects the losses a lot and decreases the chances of all loss, but with all the protection, sometimes it reduces the profit.

Let us guess that stock value rises to Rs 50In this case; the trader would have understood the estimation of his stock holding rise to (100*50) = Rs 5000.

As he is the seller of the Call option, he anticipated that the cost of the fundamentals should fall. In any case, its cost has, in certainty, risen. The Call option purchaser will practice his privilege and will purchase the Call alternative at the strike cost of 48, which is lower than the cost of the fundamental that is 50. So the option seller got (48*100) = Rs 4800 by selling the Call option.

For a Put alternative purchaser, an option is in the cash if the strike cost is higher than the cost of the hidden. For this situation, as the strike cost of 43 is not exactly the CMP of the hidden, which is 50, and along these lines, the option is rendered useless for him.

Net benefit from the exchange = Rs 5000 – Rs 4800+500 - 300 = 400

Diagonal spread

The diagonal spread option strategy uses many strikes and months. It works with the combined bits of a long call spread and a short call spread. Diagonal spread moves diagonally and also the names.

The option is presented in different rows and columns. In this options trading strategy, the short terms are sold, and long terms are bought. A transient shortcoming or Strength that you think would go up or go down once more, at that point, to the advantage of it.

The system is controlled on the short-side for risk, and if the market plays smoothly, it can become open-finished on the long side.

At the point when executed for cash, it permits edge necessities to be met. The investment is at high risk when it works quickly in our way. The diagonal spread has its setup, which we have to follow.

- The equal number of options is required.

- The options must have the exact underlying security.

- The options in the diagonal spread should have the same class.

- The different expiry dates are used.

- The two different strike prices.

In the diagonal spread, the bullish long call diagonal spread purchases the option with the lower strike rate and longer expiry date then sells the short date option with high strike rates.

Butterfly

The broken wing butterfly option is a bit similar to the butterfly trading strategy, but In this trading strategy, the calls and puts are much similar to directional strategy rather than the butterfly strategy.

Its sides have a different level of risk; the risk is different on each side. Usually, the profit occurs if the underlying expires at the short strike price. The broken wing butterfly option provides more profit than the butterfly option.

Futuresmag merits the credit for begetting the "Broken Wing Butterfly," an amazing option in contrast to the Butterfly, where the objective is starting an exchange at zero expense.

It is an amazing options trading which expands on the positive attributes of a Butterfly Spread. Dissimilar to the Long Butterfly, where one needs to pay another charge, Broken Wing Butterfly Strategy is a net credit procedure, frequently rehearsed to build the likelihood of benefit.

Broken Wing Butterfly Strategy is equivalent to a Butterfly in which the sold spread is regularly more extensive spread than the bought spread. It has the similarity of long butterfly spread having the same strikes that are not much different from the short strike. It works when the option has all the puts or all the calls.

For example, the stock is trading at Rs100. You buy one 120 calls on ABC, you sell two 105 calls in ABC and purchase one 100 calls in ABC, So you get the net credit of Rs. 10.

6. TOP QUALITIES OF A SUCCESSFUL OPTIONS TRADER

'The key to trading success is emotional discipline. If intelligence were the key, there would be a lot more people making trading money' – Victor Sperandeo

To be an options trader, certain qualities are required that are not at all difficult to achieve. To develop those qualities, you have to know about the options trading.

Options Trading

In options trading, the buyer has the right, when he wants to buy (the case of a call) and when he wants to sell (the case of a put) but he is not bound to buy or sell the certain asset at a specific price, as the name 'Options' suggest. The trader is also not bound to trade in some specific time. He has the total choice of what and when he wants to trade.

Why people tend to go for options trading?

Options can provide better income than any other job. It is not much different than the stock exchange. It is just like your own business; all you have to do is predict where the market and stock rates are going. You have to take a risk, but the income will be higher than you have thought. The end results can give a shock as market rates keep on changing every minute.

Top Qualities of a Successful Options Trader

Just like in any other business, there is a huge risk of loss. Every other person cannot be a good businessman. Many people have weak patience level, they lose their heart, and on failure, they leave the business or sell at a low price without giving another try.

The one who buys that at a low price takes it to another level. Similarly, everyone cannot be a good trader. Being a successful trader demands certain qualities. If you achieve those qualities, nothing can stop you from becoming one of the most successful options traders.

1. Control on emotions
2. Record keeping
3. Finding the right strategy for you
4. Consistency
5. Learning from failures
6. News interpretation
7. Being yourself
8. Patience
9. Flexibility
10. Risk management

These are a few qualities to make you a successful trader in options trading, and a positive attitude towards these skills can make you a professional options trader. Let's dig a bit more into these qualities to polish your personality a little more.

Control on Emotions

Mixing your emotions with your business can take you towards destruction. You have to manage your social life along with the real-life without tangling them with each other. You must be able to manage the happening in real life and happenings in the business. You must have total control over your mind and hold your nerves while doing the business.

Records Management

If you keep a record of whatever you do, next time you will be able to avoid the mistake you have made previously, and you will be able to see where you have gone wrong.

This habit will provide you information on your wealth to improving your odds of success. By keeping the records, you will be able to make up your previous losses. Records will also help you keep track of profit/losses for tax purposes, if applicable.

A Good Planner

Everyone has their own strategy (like the way of doing things). Some people tend to go for short sales and make multiple sales in a day. Others hit their luck after a long time and make a large amount by a single sale.

Even if they perform a single sale in a week, they can earn more than the one who makes many sales in a day. Once you find the right strategy for yourself, you have to stick with that strategy. It is crucial which strategy you are choosing for yourself. It is because in options trading, the right strategy and technique to trade will take you to the top, and the wrong will do the opposite.

Consistency

Nothing other than small chunks can be earned without consistency. You have to give a lot to achieve a lot. In the case of options trading, you have to invest your time to achieve experience. The more experience you get, the more you learn.

Like you learn when and where to put your money; and when to draw it out. Many people get back when they see smaller earnings, not knowing that smaller steps lead towards greater steps.

Learning from Failures

Just as most businessmen lose their money, similarly, every trader also faces losses. This is just part of the game! But a successful trader doesn't give up on his loss and try to avoid loss in the future from the experience he gained from his previous loss.

Then a time comes when he has learned every possible reason leading to his loss. In the future, he can cover up his previous losses by avoiding the same mistake.

News Interpretation

The traders must be able to interpret the news. If you are good at interpreting the news, you will have the exact knowledge to predict which is the product will give profit and when. If you can predict the future, you'll be able to raise your income by investing in a certain product.

You'll also be able to predict when to buy or sell the product to maximize your profit. Some news is just the hype; you have to be able to differentiate between the real news and the hype.

Do not Follow What Others are Doing

Everyone has their thinking. But once you come to the trade business, do not rely completely on others' strategies. In order to be a successful trader, you don't have to do what everyone else is doing. You have to be limitless and be yourself. You may come out of your comfort zone, but following your own passion will be the key to success. Your willingness to take risks will benefit you in being yourself.

Patience

Being a successful options trader demands a lot of patience. You have to be able to wait until; it's the right time to perform the action. It means, if you have to put your money into something, you have to wait until you think; it is the lowest price for a certain product. Similarly, while selling, you have to be patient until it reaches the highest amount of profits.

If you are not patient while trading; a huge loss may be on your way!

Flexibility

The rates of market changes every day; you have to be able to learn the changing dimensions of the market. You have to learn about the changing trends of the market and adopt newer strategies.

You have to be well aware of the relevant news and always believe yourself as a learner. You have to accept the losses as loss in any field of work is inevitable. You have to accept wherever the market is going, whether it suits you or not.

Risk Management

In options, you are playing in millions, so there is a huge risk. You have to manage how much risk you can bear at a certain time. Being limitless does not mean you have to forget about what you are risking while putting your money. If you allot a certain capital to an investment, you may be able to avoid a higher risk of loss but, the greater the risk, the greater will be the gains or losses.

Conclusion

If you have these certain skills or qualities, one day, you will be the most successful trader of the options trading. Just be patient and have consistency in your work. The doors of success will keep opening for you. The most important thing is believing in yourself; if you take larger risks and have belief in yourself, there is nothing you cannot do.

7. HOW TO SELECT THE RIGHT OPTION FOR A MAJOR GAIN

Starting from simple purchases to more complicated spreads like butterflies, options have a plethora of strategies. Moreover, they are available for a bigger range of currencies, stocks and commodities, futures contracts, and exchange-traded funds.

Often, there are hundreds of expiries and strike prices for each option. This poses a challenge for the novices to select the best option out of many. Here is how you can do that like a pro.

Look for the Right Option

Imagine, you already have an asset in mind that you wish to trade on, like a commodity. You picked it from stock screener through your insight and the insight of others (e.g. research). Regardless of the selection technique, after identifying your asset for trading, you need to follow these steps to achieve your goal.

- Frame your purpose of investment
- Determine your payoff
- Analyze volatility
- Recognize events

- Make a Strategy
- Launch parameters of options

These steps follow a logical process, which makes it easy to select the right option to trade on. Let us breakdown what these steps reveal.

Frame your Purpose

The base of getting into the trading business is finding the purpose of investment. Why do you want to start options trading? What is the purpose behind this? Do you want to make real money, or is it just a side-business? Ask yourself these questions. Make a notebook and write all the answers that you have.

Now you might be thinking, why so? It is because you need to be clear on this point. Using options to make real money is very different as compared to purchasing them for speculating or hedging.

This is your first step, and it will form the foundation for other steps. So, buckle up!

Trader's Payoff

In the second step, determine your risk and reward payoff. This should be dependent upon your appetite or tolerance for risk. Know your type – like if you are one of the conservative traders, using aggressive strategies for options trading might not be suitable for you. These strategies include purchasing deep out-of-money options in large quantities or writing puts etcetera.

Each strategy has a well-made risk and reward profile. You have got to keep an eye on it. And do not forget to assess your payoff at the end of the day!

Analyze Volatility

It is one of the most crucial steps in options trading. You have got to analyze implied volatility for sure. Compare it to the history of options stock volatility, plus the volatility level in the market.

This allows you to know about the thinking of other traders. Whether they expect the stocks to move fast or up in the future or not, if there is high volatility, there will be a higher premium too. In this case, options writing will be more suitable for you.

A lower rate of implied volatility means there will be lower premium – good for the purchase of options (if you think that the stocks will move more and so their value will increase as well).

Recognize Events

There are two main types of events: stock-specific and market-wide. Stock specific events include types like spin-offs, product launches, and earnings reports, etcetera. Market-wide events, on the other hand, are those that have a huge role in broad markets like economic data releases and Federal Reserve Announcements.

It is important that you know and recognizes each event type. Since they have a huge impact on implied volatility and, thus, can have a great impact on the price when it occurs. Recognizing events before they can help traders to make a bigger profit, determine the right time and the appropriate expiration date for your trade.

Make Your Strategy

The first four steps allow you to see clearly the way to your options trading business. Now you are in a good position to devise your own plan after knowing the events, implied volatility, risk, and reward pay off and your investment goal.

Suppose a conservative trader with a good portfolio wishes to earn premium within some months. He should then use the covered call "writing" technique to achieve his goal. While an aggressive investor who foresees market decline within some months should purchase puts on main stocks so on.

Launch Parameters

After the fifth step is clear on your mind, try to launch parameters. For instance, you should establish the expiration time, option delta, and strike price, etcetera. Let us say a trader wants to buy the longest expiration date call. But he also wants to pay a low premium on it. In this case, the out-of-the-money call is the most appropriate for him. But for a high delta call, focus on in-the-money option.

In short, follow the given steps to make a good profit and establish yourself as a professional options trader in the market. Determine your objective of investment, analyze your risk and reward, assess volatility, think about the happenings, make your strategy, and then tailor your options parameters.

How to make money with Options Trading

An Option trader earns money by buying or selling or by being an option writer.

With options trading, you do not only buy or own stock in a company, but you are also in a position to sell that stock in the future. If you know the right strategies, you can earn above 100,815$ through options trading. Learning the right strategies, knowledge about risks, learning the market, multiplying the profit, and building wealth will help you make more money with options trading.

Earning Money with options trading in 2020

We have enlisted some special Options Trading techniques that could help you understand and earn money better through Options Trading.

Recap

Before really getting into the business, you need to recap what options trading really is, what its terms are, and how it's done with minimum risks involved. In simple terms, options trading is buying and selling options contracts.

Options trading does not allow you to vote or receive dividends or anything else a (partial) owner of the company can do. It is just a contract between you and some other party that grants you the right to purchase (i.e., "call option") or sells (i.e., "put option") stock of a company at a certain price.

It is one of the most basic 'leveraging' tools available to investors who are looking to increase their potential profit by accepting the increase in risk that always comes attached to it.

There are some essential key terms that are normally used in Options Trading:

Stock

A stock option is a contract between the company and the stock option buyer to buy or sell 100 shares of the company at a determined amount within a certain time period.

Expiration

In options trading, there is a contract involved, and each contract has an expiration date. You can buy or sell your options before the expiration date, but once it crosses the expiration date, the contract has no value to it. In that case, only an option writer can earn.

Strike Price

A strike price is a price at which the commodity or asset is to be bought or sold when the option is exercised. For example, if the strike price is XYZ dollars for a call option, then you could exercise your contract by purchasing the identified stock at the strike price.

Premium

Options Premium is the price to be paid by the party who is purchasing the right buy/the right to sell, to the party that is selling the right to buy/the right to sell, as a premium to enter into a contract for the risk of the option being exercised if the contract is in the money, that the writer (seller) of option is bearing while entering into the option contract. It depends on the strike price, the volatility of the underlying, and expiration date.

Call and Put Option

In options trading, there is a call and Put option A call is when you buy or purchase a stock and put is when you sell a stock. You can buy or sell a stock before the expiration date.

Underlying Asset

The underlying asset is reference security (stock, bond, futures contract, etc.) on which the price of derivative security like an option is based. For example, options are derivative instruments, meaning that their prices are derived from the price of another security. More specifically, options prices are derived from the price of an underlying stock.

Option Style

An option contract is made up of two different styles; American style or European style. Options can be practiced in a particular way, and both styles allow you to practice them differently. American style options can be used any time before expiration, whereas European style options can only be used on expiration dates itself.

Contract Multiplier

The contract multiplier states the quantity of the underlying asset that needs to be delivered in the event the option is exercised. For stock options, each contract covers 100 shares.

Relative Value

Selling a commodity at a higher price than the buying price and purchasing at a lower price than the market or what you sold it as.

Making Money with Options Trading in 2020

Option traders use different strategies to evaluate the trade. A list of tools is included in the process of evaluation.

The list might include; analysis, history, statistics, stability, debt, dividends, etc.

With a little reading, a trader can easily minimize his risk of losing his investment. Here are the top 10 strategies of how to make money through options trading:

Naked Call

A naked call is an options strategy in which an investor sells (a call option) without the security of owning the underlying stock.

Covered Put

A covered option is a strategy where the stock is bought or owned, and an option is sold. The underlying stock is bought, and simultaneously writes–or sells–a call option on those same shares. The Covered Put also has a higher profit in case the stock moves down to the strike price of the short puts.

For example, an investor uses his call option (buys) on a stock that represents 100 shares of stock per call option. For every 100 shares of stock that the investor purchases, they will sell one call option against it. This strategy is referred to as a covered call because, in the event that a stock price increases rapidly, this investor's short call is covered by the long stock position.

The formula for calculating maximum profit is:

Max Profit = Premium Received - Commissions Paid

Max Profit Achieved When Price of Underlying <= Strike Price of Short Put

Making most out of options

Options are like a business; not everyone can achieve high wages or income. To be a successful businessman, you need a certain type of mindset, few skills, and a little capital. While discussing how to make money through options, we don't have to only look onto physical strategies but also mental and indirect strategies.

Indirect Strategies:

Record keeping

Keeping proper records of your progress is really helpful for a successful practical life as well as for business. In options, you can track your progress, the weaknesses, and the reasons for these weaknesses. It will help you to learn from your mistakes and avoid them in the future.

Stay aware

Technology keeps on developing every day; each day, we see new innovation. To walk with others and avoid staying behind them, you must have access to the latest news and updates about technology and stay ready for what is coming next.

Stay updated

To be a successful options trader, you have to be updated on what is going on in the stock market and how and when prices are going to change. This way you will be able to predict the prices of the market and plan your move accordingly to avoid losses

Mental strategies:

Managing the risk

It is a famous saying, "Cut your coat according to the cloth." Applying this on options, you have to agree that don't put all your money into one product. Only invest as much amount for which you can bear the risk.

Managing time

No one can force you to put or call the money in a certain product until you yourself want to do so. Look for the perfect time to do so, invest only when you know it is a perfect time. The most important thing is patience. But keep track of the expiration date.

Separate practical and business life

To make progress as an options trader, never mix up your emotions with your business. If you are going through something bad in real life and getting frustrated, mind taking a break. A fresh mind can think well than the mind busy in solving other issues. Options trading is the game of the mind, so take a break and come back when you are relaxed.

These are the few physical, mental, and indirect strategies that we have discussed above. Hope, this will take you to the heights of success and make most out of options.

8. IMPORTANT TIPS & TRICKS ABOUT OPTIONS TRADING

An option trading is a part of trading that allows you to trade your market expectations while also control the risk that you are going to participate in this trading with. Now, if you get a better a clearer idea of how to rightly perform options trading, there are no limitations to it. This means that you can trade various strategies and seek profit in all sorts of market conditions.

However, this options trading doesn't mean that you have to trade the strategies of your complex trading options to seek profit from them. Instead, you can spend your money more effectively to gain profit by simply replacing your regular trading positions with the help of options.

A Little Insight:

With the start of 2020, the options trading activity has achieved a drastic increase. Now, if we calculate the increase in the options contracts in this year up until now, an estimation of a 53% increase has been calculated – in comparison to that of the same time last year. Hence, there can certainly not be a better time to head onto the trading options activity – if you're thinking about it.

However, understanding the trading options strategies and how it can be performed properly is very important. Therefore, even if you're a pro in trading, it's important to know the major and important tips regarding options trading. Now, these strategies and tips may change according to the conditions and criteria of the market.

But to give you a consistent answer of how you can firmly perform options trading, we'll discuss some tips below that might just do the trick. So without further ado, let's go ahead and discover some such tips!

Follow a Well Defined Exit Plan

Controlling your emotions while trading options can be crucial in terms of helping you achieve great profits. This crucial step can be defined by simply having a plan to work and always sticking to it. This way, you are well aware of the outcome you desire when following that plan, and you can surely achieve it. So no matter how much your emotions force you to change your mind and forget our plan while you're on it, make sure you don't!

Now when you make a well-defined plan, you can't miss on the exit planning here too. This exit plan doesn't mean that you are supposed to minimize your loss in terms of facing the downside of options trading. But instead, having a well-defined exit plan and a downside exit plan in advance can help you get out of the trade at the right time – even if the trade is going right according to your plan.

This is very important because options trading is an activity that faces a decay in the rates when the expiration date starts coming closer.

Educate Yourself

Trading options can be a complex activity in comparison to simply buying and selling stocks. And if you don't understand this activity well, there are chances that you might not be able to get anywhere in it. However, if you keep seeking knowledge and experience in this, you'll be better aware of how you can invest here and gain profit.

Now to get started in this, you need to have a proper assessment of your investment plan. This assessment can include your individual goals, the risk constraints, the time horizon, tax constraints, and the liquidity needs you have.

Don't Double Up for Past Losses

If you are thinking of doubling on an options strategy just because you want to cover your past loss, then you're surely not going to get far with this. A simple reason for that is that options in options trading are simply derivatives, and their prices properties aren't the same as the underlying stock holds them.

Therefore, even if it sometimes makes sense to double up just so that you can catch up on the loss you faced earlier (and because you follow this in the stocks), it doesn't mean that it will also serve you with profit when you're in the options galaxy.

Hence, instead of enhancing your risk, you should simply step back and close the trade. This way, you can cut more of your losses that might further come in the same trade, and simply go for a different opportunity. As a result, instead of digging deeper into the specific options category, you will be accepting your loss and saving yourself from a bigger downfall.

Manage Your Risk

Now the most important aspect here is the risk of the options trading. So when you go for options trading, you must understand how much risk you can take. Whether you're a beginner or someone who has been in the options trading for a while, having a certain risk assessment that you can handle is very important.

Once you have that, you can look into the different methods that can help you manage your risks. Now to manage the risks, you can go for different options throughout the life of the options contract – to manage the risks. These different options include:

Closing a Trade: this mainly refers to taking an offsetting position in the trade. So if you have purchased a call option in trading options, you can simply set the call option and close the trade for managing the risk on time.

Allowing an Option to Expire

This can be possible when a contract in trading options has reached its expiration date without being worked on. Here, you can also purchase or sell a call or put, according to the contract.

Roll out an Option

This is mainly the process of managing risk by simply closing an option that is near to the expiration date, and then simultaneously investing in a similar category of trade that has a distant expiration date.

Assignment

Lastly, another strategy of managing the risks in trading options is to simply go for an assignment. This is possible when you sell an option by simply receiving or delivering the shares that lie under the stock of that option.

Finally

Now trading options are quite a familiar trading aspect for many, but most of the new traders aren't very familiar with it. However, achieving great profits and success in trading options is something anyone can achieve. Only if you educate yourself in this, gain some experience, and righty follow efficient tips and tricks (as mentioned above) – you are sure to go far in trading options.

9. IMPORTANT FAQS OF OPTIONS TRADING

We tried to include all the basic and important frequently asked questions regarding options trading. Hope they help you understand the options trading better and if not. You can post your inquiries in the comment section.

Is there any definition of options?

Options are derivatives that are supported on the value of underlying securities such as stocks.

Options are putting down your money for the right to buy a stock at a specific price before its expiration date. There are two types of options; options buy or sell.

When an investor takes part in options, s/he is either buying or selling an options contract and is making a bet that either the underlying share will rise in price or fall in price before the expiration date.

How to gain maximum profit in options trading?

According to Allen Everhart, the best way to maximize profit in options trading is to just keep it simple. In his words, "I have come to appreciate buying deep-in-the-money/deep-in-time call options despite the disparagement this strategy gets."

Purchase a 70 delta call if you think the market is going higher - or put if you think the market is falling. You will not need to worry much about theta decay (there's a little, but not much) and you'll profit 80% of a $1 move on the stock or ETF at a much lower cost than an equivalent number of shares of stock, and there's no risk of being randomly exercised and having the stock (long or short) suddenly appear in your account the next morning!

When you have 200 short option positions on, and a dozen of them get randomly exercised overnight, you will appreciate the 'simple' approach to options trading.

What happens in a case when options contract expires?

In case if the contract reaches its expiration date and you have not yet exercised your right to options, then you will lose your right and premium. The contract becomes invalid.

The only person who will profit from this is the writer of the contract.

What is the difference between strike price and stock price?

A strike price is a price at which the owner of an option can execute the contract, whereas; a stock price is the last transaction price of at least a single share of an underlying.

What is naked call?

It's a strategy in which an investor writes a call option without having a position in the underlying stock itself. To set up a naked call, an investor simply sells a call option without owning the underlying stock. If s/he writes a naked call & the stock goes up 100 or 200%, the writer has to deliver, but it is a high-risk strategy.

What is American contract?

An American option is a version of an options contract that allows holders to exercise the option rights at any time before and including the day of expiration.

What is an European contract?

A European contract only allows you to exercise on the day of expiration.

Which one is more profitable European contract or American contract?

An American contract option allows the investor to exercise any time before the expiration date whereas, in European contract options during their "exercise period" (usually right when they expire, but no earlier).

So an American style contract is exercised more but is it more profitable?

If I exercise my American contract before its expiration date, the investor might get more profit, but he/she might lose money too. Mathematically, there is no advantage, since an investor can make the same amount of profit on exercising its right on the day of its expiration.

When should you start options trading?

You should start options trading when you have enough investment and savings too. You need the proper knowledge, data, and strategies about the market. You should be able to not only predict but also implement the strategies at the right time.

How much should you invest in options trading?

It is advisable to start your investment with 5,000$ to 15,000$. Try not investing all of your savings or income on it since there is a high-risk factor involved in trading options.

When should you exercise your options?

According to Bill Bischoff, you should exercise your options put the very last-minute.

The last-minute is when the stock has risen to the point where you are ready to unload — or just before the option expiration date, whichever comes first. At the last minute or on the date of expiration, you know that there is no going higher than this, so you can easily exercise your options, although, on the last day, the tax cost is usually higher.

Best strategy of options trading?

According to Allen Everhart, there is no such thing is the best strategy. Everyday stock or market rate is different. Even the underlying asset or companies are different from each other too. You cannot apply one strategy to all of your options. However, all options trading strategies are directional.

What is a short put and long call strategy?

A short put and a long call are direction-ally the same. The shot put and the long call makes money when the stock goes up. But short put is known to be a little riskier than the long call strategy.

The short put can be exercised if the stock does not decline, and in that case, you can keep the premium of the option.

How an option writer makes money?

An option writer makes money when the stock or premium that has been bought reaches its expiration date without being exercised. In that case, the option writer gets to keep the entire premium.

How do investors lose money in options trading?

There is no one specific reason why an investor loses his/her money. There are different cases and scenarios. But the most common mistakes people make are they do not gather enough information or their lack of knowledge. Most people assume that it is a short way to become rich or may believe in "luck" too much.

CONCLUSION

Thank you for downloading this book. The objective of writing it was to let amateurs, novices, and even pros understand the tricky and sometimes hard to digest concepts.

The language of this book is, therefore, simple, easy, and user-friendly (in a sense that anyone can grab the meaning). On top of that, we have added as many examples as we could with each new concept so that the reader does not get confused.

In the end, we would wind up from where we began from – 'learning the concepts of options trading might seem difficult – but once you grab them – they are yours!"

So, just remember, you have got to be patient, risk-tolerant, and a mindful planner when it comes to business. Have a great trade. May each of your investments give you more profit than you expected.

JASON TEST

DAY AND SWING
TRADING

Guide for beginners.
Investment strategies in stock, options, and forex. Add up extra income and get your financial freedom

INTRODUCTION

In this book, we will talk about two types of trading: day trading and swing trading. On this extended version we added a part about Options Trading. It is necessary for every beginner to understand all the sections. In order to start your career as a successful trader, you should have some basic knowledge about trading. This book will help you to clarify your doubts regarding day, swing and options trading, how they should invest their money and which trade will give them more profit.

Day trading is defined as the activity of capturing profit from the variation of stock prices during the day. In other words, day trading is about selling and buying stocks in a short time.

On the other side, swing trading is defined as the activity of buying and selling stocks during a time span of more than one day.

"Trading" is intended as the set of actions aimed to making extra-income money through investment strategies. Those who apply trading strategy in the financial market for gaining profit and helding a position in the market are known as "Swing Traders." Swing traders typically focus on getting profit by small gains in a very short time span. Their position in the market may be held for several days or for a week. They buy some stocks on the market and then sell them when they believe they can get a good profit on it. It is a process going on between a buyer and a seller. Swing traders keep their check and balance in the market; then, with the help of technical analysis, they identify the price swings and determine whether buy a stock or not, whether prices are rising, or they can come out with a loss. Swing traders risk 0.5% on each trade; nevertheless they pursue much higher goals in terms of profit by each trade. Most of the traders buy the stock when they prices are low and sell them when the prices are higher in the market. In some cases, this strategy causes losses, because the stock values decrease (this happens in very rare cases, though).

Most people make confusion between swing trading with day trading. In reality, swing trading is far different from day trading because day trading has lower chances of getting losses than swing trading. Also, in day trading, the time of trading is limited (one day), whereas in swing trading there is no time limit: it is indeed an overnight process. The market of swing traders works for 24hours; therefore, the profit/loss chances are higher because the seller can face the downfall anytime. Swing traders are also rewarded by a leverage of 50%. For example, if a trader is allowed to have a margin in his trading, then he only needs to invest $20,000 for a trade rather than investing $40,000. It is a process through which it is possible to helding profit for a long time. This process is not about getting profit in a day, but it could go from a day to many days. There will be more chances of getting profit than loss. For beginners, swing trading is the best option to choose because swing trading is easy and there are more chances of succeed with it. It is, in fact, less stressful for a seller and it is associated to higher success probability with respect to day trading, since time allows to improve accuracy in investment decision. It is well known that swing traders have several opportunities and options to trade. They may get more opportunities to invest their money during the longer investment time-span. It is very important for a trader be concerned in the price variation of their stock and be patient. After all, everything is all about profit and loss.

So far, all the websites or books about day and swing trading that I have been reading were unfit to a clear understanding of how to enter or exit in any trading system. I wrote this book so that it will help the coming generations to understand what day and swing trading are about, and investing their money on the type of trading that suits better to them.

The options are a particular type of derivative instrument that gives the possibility to buy or sell at a set price, a specific underlying asset, which represents the object of the option contract.

The term "option" comes from the word possibility. The options offer the opportunity to buy or sell an asset. It therefore represents a right for the subscriber and not an obligation.

The terms call, put, strike price, at the money and in the money are all connected to the option management operations. Their meaning, as we will see, is much more intuitive and immediate than it might seem.

The recent evolution of financial markets have given great prominence to options and their particular variations such as binary options. They are considered as profitable and versatile financial instruments to trading strategies. They will offer many savers the opportunity to build pay-off portfolios through the aggregation of different tools.

1. DIFFERENCE BETWEEN SWING TRADING AND DAY TRADING

If you are a beginner, then keep your mind open for both types of trading, do not waste your money or time in investing until you do not have enough knowledge about the trading systems. For a beginner, there is always a lot of things to learn about, whatever the field is learning about your interest is very important. Before starting any trading pattern, it is necessary to understand your needs and expectations that you have related to the trading system. First of all, the trader who wants to trade should know how much active trading he wants. Whether he wants a trading system that survives in the market for a longer time, or not. What are his current requirements and expectations related to trading whether he can handle his trading system for a long time, or did he have enough stamina to bear the loss? Once you decide the right path that suits you and that you believe can fulfill your expectation, then you can easily survive in the trading market.

Traders have divided trading into two parts swing trading and day trading. This book will help you to understand the difference between both the trading systems, and it will help you in choosing which trading system is best for you. The main goal of any beginner is to gain profit on their stock, whether it's a day trader or a swing trader; at the end of the day, every trader needs their name in a profit list. Even though both tradings has different tools and technical analysis procedures.

Day trading is about making multiples trades in a day. As the name suggests doing trade on your stock within a day but multiple times is day trading. This trade is all about doing trade within a day or hours. You cannot go beyond that time, and it doesn't matter how many times you trade in a day. The main objective of the day traders is to make money from their preexisting income in a day with their stock. This trade is only about day trading; it does not contain night hours. They do not keep any overnight securities. The biggest advantage of day trading is that the trader has fewer chances of having any kind of loss. For example, if a trader invests their money on any stock and the market rate of that stock goes down in the middle of the night, so in that case, the trader has to face a loss, but because of day trading, the chances of losses are also less as they will not invest their money for overnight.

According to the U.S Securities and Exchange Commission (SEC), "The Day traders typically suffer financial losses in their first months of trading, and many never graduate to profit-making status." After the SEC cautions the day trader, it was easy to understand that the beginner's traders should not take a risk by investing money more than they can afford, they should not go beyond their limitations. Most of the people commit suicide when they face loss because they had borrowed money from their friends and family or from other sources.

The day traders do not need any partner, they usually work alone, and they do not have their flexible schedule, and they do their work according to their mood and needs. They usually work at their places and take off and rap all of their stuff whenever they want. They do not need anyone's instruction because they do their work independently.

Sometimes it becomes difficult for the beginners of day traders to compete in the market because except making money and position in the market they also have to compete with the high-frequency traders, whereas other faces more advantages than the beginners as they become professionals in their work and have more experience than them. Once you start getting profit on your stock, there will be no come back from this earning adventure; you will desire to invest more and earn more.

The day trader has to generate a lot of effort and use his skills to maintain the position in the market. A beginner who wants to have all the luxuries firstly had to quit his job to maintain all his focus on trading because it would not be easy for a day trader to continue his job as it all depends on you to keep check and balance in the market. Because day trading is stressful, and the trader has to keep his self-up-to date with the ongoing situation in the market. He should be aware of multiple screening so it will help him to spot the trading opportunities.

For example

If someone is continuous his job with day trading and on the opposite hand the shares of an organization like Walmart (WMT) or Apple (AAPL) within the forex market are going high, and there's an excellent opportunity for him to trade his currency like euro or U.S. dollar (EUR/USD), so he will miss the prospect due to his job routine.

So it will be better for the future of the trader to just focus on one thing at a time, his job or a business. For trading, there are various markets; the ups and downs in the market make easier for those who cannot afford it. Once the stocks go down, buyers borrow them and sell them when the rate goes high. In the forex market, it is easier for beginners to invest their money as it requires the least capital for trading purposes. You can start from a little amount like $50, but if you can invest a large amount so it will be more useful. To gain a good position in the market, stocks trade requires to be at least $25,000 to make day trade. Day trade stock requires more capital for the better position, but if you do not have $25,000 or can't maintain your account above $25,000 then stocks are not the right place for you to invest money or do not waste your time on it, but if you have crossed $25,000, then stocks are viable day trading market. Long-time day traders love the joys of pitting their wits against the market and other professionals day in and time out. The adrenaline rush from rapid-fire trading are a few things not many traders will admit to, but it's a giant think about their decision to create a living from day trading. It's doubtful these styles of people would be content spending their days selling widgets or perusing numbers in an office cubicle.

Day trading and swing trading each have advantages and downsides. Neither strategy is healthier than the opposite, and traders should choose the approach that works best for his or her skills, preferences, and lifestyle. Day trading is healthier suited to individuals who are smitten by trading full time and possess the three Ds: decisiveness, discipline, and diligence (prerequisites for successful day trading). Swing trading, on the opposite hand, doesn't require such a formidable set of traits. Since swing trading will be undertaken by anyone with some investment capital and doesn't require full-time attention, it's a viable option for traders who want to stay their full-time jobs, but also dabble within the markets. Swing traders should even be able to apply a mixture of fundamental and technical analysis, instead of technical analysis alone.

If we differentiate swing and day trading, then they both are far different from each other, their framing time to trade is different. Swing trading is about selling and buying stock for days and weeks. Swing traders have more time to trade then the day traders. Their trading frame is longer than then day traders as they hold a position overnight. Because of their 24 hours of trading, they cannot avoid the risk that can cause a big problem against them. There will be more chances of losing money in this trade. They have to worry about the stock all the time because it could be different while opening, or it could be different from how it closed before the day. Swing traders need a lot of patience because he had to face many problems. Trades generally need time to figure out. Keeping a trade for an asset open for some days or weeks may lead to higher profits than trading in and out of the identical security multiple times daily. Swing traders know that it will take a long time, but they generally do not make it look like a full-time job. Swing trade may take a few days or maybe a few weeks to work out. Swing traders do not make this trading a full-time job career like day traders. If you have enough knowledge about swing trading and investment capital that you can try swing trading. If you are a beginner in trading and want to invest your money, then swing trading is a perfect choice because it does not require your 24/7 hours' attention, or you do not need to glued yourselves in front of your computers and keeping your eyes and fingers crossed all the time. A swing trader can even do a full-time job if he wants to because swing trading doesn't require checking on the screens all the time. The margin requirements in swing trading are higher, and usually, its maximum leverage is two times one's capital, whereas day trading has four times and one's capitals. It doesn't need constant monitoring like day trading; it can be stopped anytime whenever you feel like there is a risk in executing the trading process.

Like any other trading swing trading can also result in substantial losses. Infect swing traders has to face a larger loss than day traders as swing traders hold their position in the market for a longer time. That's why they run the risk of larger loss than day trading. Swing traders usually do have their regular jobs, and they also have other sources of income from where they can overcome theirs loses. There are more chances of burnout for swing traders due to stress in swing trading since it's seldom a full-time job. Swing traders have more chances through which they can mitigate or offset their losses.

Swing trading can be done by having just one computer, and with conventional trading tools unlike, day trading it does not require the art technology. Swing traders have overnight leverage of 50% as compared to day trading, but this margin can be risky too, particularly if margin calls occur. These trading are not so much about what you want to trade, be it commodities, i.e., oil futures or stock from the CAC 40. Instead of that, it is simply all about timing. So, where it took 4 hours and daily charts of day trading, it will be more concerned about swing trading where it took multi-day charts and candlestick patterns. Moving average crossovers, Head and shoulders patterns, shooting stars, etc. are some of the most popular.

Swing trading can be extremely challenging in two markets, the bear market environment or raging bull market. Here you will see even highly active traders will not display in the same position there will be same up and down oscillation. To invest in the stock market, it's compulsory to have a well-organized method for trading. It is very important to keep things simple, as in the early stages, it will look a bit difficult for the beginners, but instead of getting panic, they should handle them with confidence. Once you learn the rules of swing trading and the discipline, you will make money in a great quantity in the stock market. Swing trading allows you to trade in every situation, whether it is bullish, bearish, or just going sideways. This is another reason why this trade has a distinct advantage over other approaches to invest in a swing trade.

Swing traders use technical analysis indicators to identify the price swings in the market and determine the condition of the market, whether a stock price will drop or rise in the short run. Through this, they invest the capitalize in securities that have momentum and select the best time for buying or selling the stock. These technical analysis indicators help the traders to use the swing charts for their swing trading on the security current situation trend. To analyze the current trading pattern, swing traders use swing trading charts, which help the trader in providing data based on statistical analysis. Unlike day trading, swing trading is not about the long term value of the security; instead of that, they are just concerned about the ups and downs in the stock price. Swing traders can make large returns on the stock that decay in value over time because they are making returns on each small price swing of their stock while the overall trend is downward.

Swing trading and day trading appears similar in some aspects of trading. The main factor of trading is setting the two techniques apart and maintaining the position on time in the market. Unlike day traders, it does not close within minutes or in hours, it takes several weeks and overnight days. They are subjected to the unpredictability of overnight risks that may result in significant price momentum. Swing traders can check their positions in the market periodically and can take action when critical points are reached.

Main differences between swing trading and day trading are:

Trading times:

Both of them have different timings of trading. In day trading, it takes a maximum of two to four hours daily for trading purposes, and in this time, the trader manages to analyze the charts, entering and getting out of the positions, and review different stocks. Whereas the swing trader's minimum needs 45 minutes in a day, update his order and find the new one. Day trading demands more time than swing trading.

Risks:

Day trader experiences more losses than swing traders because day traders may need to carry out six trades per day, whereas swing traders may need to carry out six trades per month to maintain a good position in the market. That's why day traders had to face more struggle in maintaining their position in the market as their risk level is higher than swing traders, and they had to engage their selves more in the market then swing traders.

Stress:

Day traders are more in stress as they have to keep their selves engage all the time with the market situation. They need great knowledge about market movements and had a great level of patience. A day trader needs to be more focused on their work. On the other hand, swing traders do not take that much pressure and can't say that they are much focused than day traders.

2. HOW DOES IT WORK?

What is swing trading?

"Swing trading is a technique used for buying and selling stocks."

How does it work?

Swing trading is one of the most used and common trading strategies used in almost every market, including forex, futures trading, stocks, and much more. Swing trading is about buying and selling the stock, buying it from the market, and selling it for gains. For this purpose, traders mostly rely on technical analysis to spot good selling and buying opportunities.

Subsequently, swing trading mostly relays on fundamental assets since its great determent of significant price movements. Sometimes it will take days and even weeks. It also helps to improve trade analysis. Therefore, a trader can verify where the fundamental assets are favorable or not, or it could potentially improve instead of relying on the bearish patterns. Swing traders use the technical analysis indicator to identify the price of swing trade and determine whether a stock price will rise in the market or drop. By experiencing technical indicators, swing traders are not concerned about the long term value of the stock.

How to make swing trade with trends?

Swing trading is one of the best solid tradings, and it has one of the obvious trends in trading strategies. For beginners, it is necessary to understand its importance in the market that once you get to know how to invest your money, it will offer a lot of high possibility of trading opportunities with a high upside. For a beginner, it is obligatory to have enough knowledge about the market. The initial step that every beginner should take is to identify the market needs, he should know about the market trends.

For getting a good position in the market, every trader should go with the best trends, any trend that goes on the top of the list that if you show them to a child, they would clearly choose the right one whose prices are getting higher or lower.

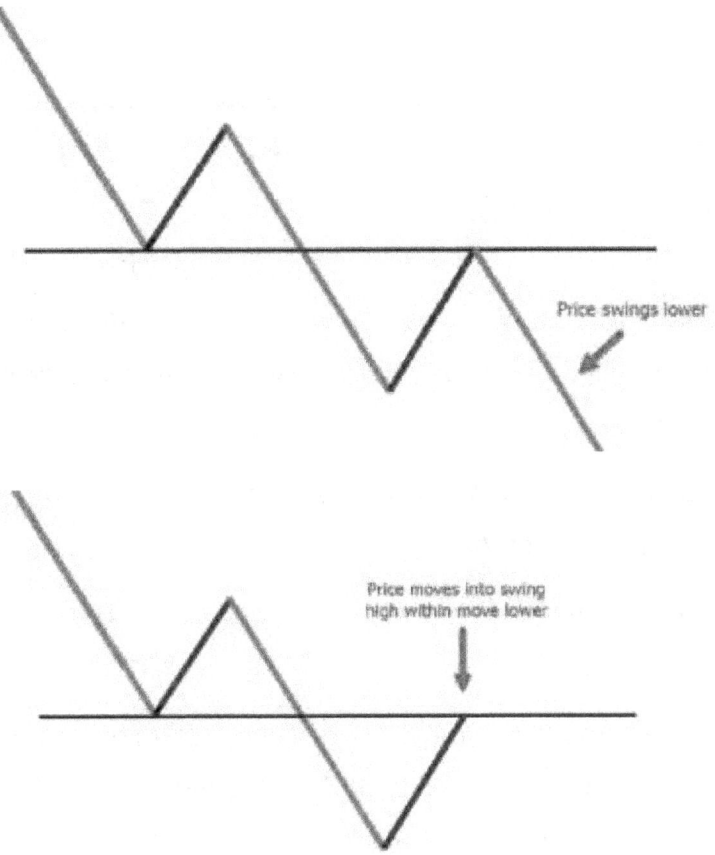

One of the most common mistakes that every beginner makes when looking to swing trade within a trend is not entering with the right swing point.

Tips for Beginners

When you should choose Swing trading:

Swing trading is easier than day trading, but to see whether choosing swing trading is a good decision for you or not, you should enlist all the points and see which one will give you more profit.

- *Make sure that you are ready to spend your days, weeks, and months on this trading as swing trading contains a longer period for trading.*
- *If you already have a job and want to invest your money for extra income, but you do not have enough time to sit in front of a computer, then swing trading is the best option for you.*
- *You do not need to do constant monitoring and keeping an eye on market activities.*
- *Swing trading will give you a less stressful life and will reduce the risk level.*
- *As a beginner, you should always have a plan and stick to it as it's the nature of buying and selling that there will be highs and lows, but you should stick to the plan.*
- *Before you start swing trading, you should practice it by watching markets. Having knowledge about pre-trading will help you in gaining the loss.*
- *Don't expect to have money on a quick note; just focus on your aim and let the process sink in.*
- *Having a good observation will help you in investing money in the right stock, so if you want to gain money on the first stock, then you should know how to use the technical analysis indicators.*

It is important for a beginner to keep in mind while trading the entrance and exit strategy. Before entering a market, we should check everything and keep ourselves update with the study of the charts, noting the price the stock will likely reach in its current swing.

Most of the traders (like partygoers) find it more favorable to choose how to exit before they have entered the trade.

There will be more chances of losing money in the earlier stages of trading, but a good trader should stick to it and should gather basic skills, polish those skills, learn new technical techniques, and improve your knowledge. It's important not to give up in a condition.

He should read books and follow the swing trading tips for beginners.

Trading Platforms

For successful swing trading, the trader should select the right stocks to make a profit in the market. Therefore, traders can also opt for stock with large market capitalization. The most active assets will be among beginners, and they will be the most actively traded ones on top exchange. If we talk about the platforms for swing trading, then, on the one hand, there is a bear market, and on the other is the bull market. Similarly, there is a stable market between both of them. Yet swing trading in a bear or bull market is pretty different from that stable one.

For example, stocks in the market might tend to spike and dump using various patterns in both of these markets, unlike a stable market where a similar pattern could have upheld for weeks or months. In the bear market and bull market, the momentum can cause stocks to trade in a specific way for a long time. In that situation, to gain the maximum profit, a trader should trade in the way of the long term trend. And to experience that profit, a swing trader has to correctly regulate the current market, whether it is bearish or bullish.

The simple moving average (SMA) recommends specific support and resistance stages. It also displays bullish and bearish patterns. When the stock knockouts the support level, it signals a virtuous time to purchase, and once it hits the resistance level, then it's a good time to trade. The bullish and bearish methods also signal entry and exit price points. Therefore, another form of SMA is the exponential moving average (EMA), and it focuses on state-of-the-art data points. The trend signals, as well as entry or exit points presented by the EMA, is quicker compared to the SMA. The 9, 13, and 50 periods EMA can be used to improved time entry points.

For example, when the price of a stock crosses these EMAs, it shows a bullish trend. Therefore, there could probably be a problem with the bearish trend. For instance, when the 9 EMA crosses the 13 EMA, whereas the 13 EMA is above the 50-period EMA, it signals a buying opportunity.

What is day trading?

"Selling and buying a stock multi times in a day."

How does day trading work?

It seems very interesting to trade, and those who wanted to join this trading system may see it with more interest because it seems very easy and interesting, but in reality, the life of a trader is like living a life on the edge. In day trading, we don't have any idea what will happen in the very next moment; unexpected event scan occur at any time. The bitter reality of trading is that most of the days are dry and are quite ordinary, and at the very next moment, you will see your name at the top of the list. In day trading, the high speed of execution is very important as you may see the high numbers of trades you could make in a day to match yourself with the market price you need to match the level of the market. To make your trading work, it is very important to lower the commission rates. It will be more viable day trading as it will have a lower fee rate. Beginners should keep regulatory compliance in their trading. Day traders usually start off with zero positions in their typical portfolios, and day traders trade so frequently that by the end of the day, they have closed all of their trades.

Some day traders work manually, making trade by trade hour by the hour using a chart. Others set up an automatic process that makes orders to purchase and trade for them. Whereas day traders don't actually look at fundamental data, they are concerned in price volatility, liquidity, breaking trends, and trading volume of the day that will change a stock price significantly.

REMINDER:

For day trading, forex is the best platform. For practicing forex and futures trading, a trader should use the Ninja Trader Replay feature. It will help in practicing historical trade days as if you are trading for real.

How to make day trade with trends?

It's very necessary for a trader to follow the market trends for getting a strong position in a market. Trading against the trend and not following it is one of the most common reasons for facing failure in trading. Poor quality of trend and not following a trend is a major reason for not getting the buyer's attention. Those who follow quality and strong trends have more chances of gaining success in trading. In trading, the trend raises the over-all direction of a stock's price. There is another possibility of having traders who are not mentally and physically active all the time to respond to a large number of stocks or price changes. For those who cannot manage things by themselves, they can use a stock screener; it will help the trader to narrow down the number of stocks and decrease the size so that it will make things easier in working for you. If you follow the trending tactics, only trade stocks that have a trending tendency. If you have a stock screener or an assistant, then they can help you isolating stocks that trend so that you will be having a list of stocks, and you can easily apply your day trading strategies through it. Whatever stock you choose to trade represents your trading style, and a good trading style always held a good position in the market.

For stocks, the finest time for day trading is the first one to two hours after the opening, and the last hour before the closing of the market. 9:30 a.m. to 11:30 a.m. The chances of good day trading opportunities usually start a bit earlier than others in the stock market. The forex market trades 24-hours a day throughout the week. The EURUSD is the famous day trading pair. This currency pair usually records better trading volumes between 1 A.M. and 12 P.M. EST. London markets are opened during these hours. Day traders would trade within these hours. The hours from 7 A.M. to 10 A.M. EST typically generate the biggest price changes because both the London and New York markets are opened during this duration. Therefore, this is a very common and active time for day traders.

Tips for Beginners

When you should choose day trading:

For a beginner, it is very important to make a list of all those things that can help him in becoming a good trader and list all those negative points too that can create a problem. Choosing the correct time for trading is very important when you are mentally and physically ready to devote yourself to this path.

Firstly, see whether you are fulfilling all the requirements of SEC and FINRA pattern day trader rule.

- *Give yourself a minute and think that whether you are ready to sit in front of a computer for two to four hours continuously for keeping yourself update from the current situation of the market.*
- *You need a lot of patience to become a good trader; that's why it is very important to keep your patience level up.*
- *A trader does not need a college degree or professional degree for day trading. Neither a trader needs to learn thousands of books.*
- *Discipline is very important for trading; if you start violating everything, then you can never trade your stock in the market.*
- *A day trader should have the ability to take a risk and managing things if he faces the loss.*
- *He should not take stress over things but should control them in a good manner.*
- *You should have a computer for trading, having two monitors is preferable but not necessary. Your computer should have a great memory and fast processer as it can give you a disadvantage if the processer or software is not good.*
- *Having a good internet connection is another most important thing if you lose the connection during a trade than you will also lose the trade too.*
- *To start your trading career, it is necessary to select the right platform. As the beginners do not have enough knowledge about the right platform as you are not aware of a well-developed trading style.*

In day trading, a trader doesn't need to trade all day. You will possibly discover more stability by only trading two to three hours a day.

Make a note about your chart of profits/losses in pips (forex), points (futures), or cents (stocks) on a daily basis because these are scalable figures. Writing down dollar figures can make you confuse because there will be more chances that your account balance may fluctuate by the time, resulting in bigger or smaller trades.

Save all the gathered data with a name, month-day-year.

Make a folder on your computer and store the saved files over there for later reviews.

Each weekend, go through the gathered data from the previous week.

Note where you made a mistake and what you need to improve in yourself.

Day traders should practice all the precise issues in a demo account during non-trading hours.

NOTE:

For having a good position in the market, the trader should find the repeating patterns that are making continually profit in the market.

Trading Platforms

A beginner always has the trading platform in his mind whenever he thinks to start trading where he should trade or not, which platform will be more beneficial for him. The future of trade is more often based on the indexes and commodities. A beginner could trade gold, crude oil, or S&P movements. Not every market is good; it changes and comes down to what you trade and what you can afford by the time. There are a lot of markets for trading that can help beginners in achieving their goals, but finding the right one to invest your money is very important. Day traders are admirable risk-takers. They take risks in that area where they can't afford to take risks. Still, they utilize this trading platform. Day traders must have a fast, reliable platform full of tools and features to ensure an optimal trading experience.

There are thousands of stocks in the market to choose, how do you decide which one will give you more profit or you are going to focus on for day trading? It can be confusing for a beginner trying to figure out the right one. Some day traders find easily new stocks to trade every day or hunt for stocks that are breaking out of patterns. Therefore, others lookout for stocks that breakout of support or resistance levels or are the most volatile. A beginner should keep these things in his mind while choosing a market, that when you have picked up a market for your investment, you should have the proper equipment and software setup, and knowledge about the goods for day trading. When you start thinking about trading, you need to know how to control risk. Day traders may control risk in two ways: trade risk and daily risk. Trade risk is how far you are willing to take the risk on each trade. Ideally, about risk 1% or less of your money on each trade.

A beginner can also start his trade with a little amount of $50, although if he can invest more than starting with more is recommended. Whereas some trading markets required $1,000 to get started. A day trader at least requires $25,000 to trade for his stock. The need for having more capitals to day trade stock will not make it better or worse in the market than the others. It is essential for trading to maintain your position good in the market for that you have to maintain your account up to $25,000, but if you are facing continual failure, then this market is not a good place for you.

3. SWING TRADING AND DAY TRADING: TACTICS AND STRATEGIES

What is strategy?

"Strategy is an action or plan that is used to attain one or more of the organizational aims."

A trading strategy is a procedure through which a trader sells and buys the stock and is based on predefined rules used to make trading decisions. Any type of trading process in the market usually includes a well-considered trading and investing plan that specifies risk tolerance, tax implication, and capitalizing objects. Applying or planning a strategy in trading means that a trader should search and adopt the best practices and ideas and then follows them.

REMINDER:

The strategy includes three stages: Planning a trade, placing a trade, and then executing it.

A trader should understand the level of risk he can take and then decide what is appropriate for him to do. Trading strategies are mainly based on either fundamentals or methodological. To avoid behavioral finance biases and to make sure about consistent results, trading strategies are employed. Even though it is very difficult to develop a trading strategy because there are more chances of having a risk of becoming over-reliant on a strategy.

How many strategies does a trader need?

A trader should use only one or two strategies for successful trading. It is a pattern of buying and selling the stocks every trader uses in their daily routine, which outlines when a trader will enter and exit the market. The trading strategy allows the trader to see the trading opportunities objectively. It also allows the trader to see how the trades and traders have worked out in the past.

Types of strategies:

There are four types of trading styles.

1. Scalping.
2. Day trading.
3. Position trading.
4. Swing trading.

Trading styles, time frame and their time of a period frame are given below:

Trading Style	Time Frame	Time Period of Frame
Scalping	Short-term	Seconds or minutes
Day trading	Short-term	For one day

		(maximum)
Position trading	Long-term	Weeks, months, or years.
Swing Trading	Medium-term	Days or weeks

These trading styles are the four main types of trading mostly use in the forex market.

Day trading strategy

Day trading strategies are important for the trader when he is looking to capitalize on small price movements. A trading strategy helps the trader to understand how from thousands of stocks, a reader can decide or choose the right one. This book will help beginners to understand the market situation and helps in focusing on which strategy will help the trader. Sometimes beginners get confused due to their zero experience in the beginning, and they lose their hopes, but here we will try to end the confusion of the trading beginners before it actually begins in their minds. A consistent, effective strategy in day trading relies on utilizing charts, technical indicators, in-depth technical analysis, and patterns; it helps in predicting future price movements in trading. This book will give you a detailed breakdown of beginners' trading strategies. The fast step of moving investment positions in a single trading day creates a perception that day trading is riskier or extra volatile than other types of trading.

It is essential for a beginner to know the basic concept of trading because it could bog down a trader in a complex world of highly technical indicators, that's why focus and knowledge both are important for a simple day trading strategy. Having patience and control is very important for the day trader because there will be days when it will turn out to be ranging days in trading. One of the most common mistakes that every beginner usually makes is taking the risk of trading too early while knowing it can damage them financially, still trying to get a better price and position in the market and assuming that the trade will trigger them in the future. This is the biggest mistake that every beginner has usually made.

Basic strategic fundamentals every day trader should use:

- *A trader should not expect to make a fortune if he is only allocating an hour or two a day to trading. A trader needs to continuously monitor the markets and keep looking for trading chances.*
- *Before you start doing trading, first, you need to decide how much you're prepared to take a risk. A trader should keep in mind that most successful traders won't put more than 2% of their investment on the line per trade.*
- *A trader should prepare himself for some losses if he wants to be around when the winner's start rolling in.*
- *A trader should make sure that he should stay up to date with the events and market news that will influence your asset, such as a shift in economic policy. A trader can discover a*

wealth of online economic and business resources that will keep them in the know.

For trading, just having the knowledge of the market intricacies isn't enough; a trader should be informed about everything.

The trading market will get volatile when it opens each day and while practiced day traders who are capable of reading the outlines and profit, a trader should bide his time

It's tougher than it looks to keep your emotions at bay when you are five coffees in, and you have been watching at the screen for hours. A trader should let maths, logic, and the trading strategy guide him rather than nerves, fear, or greed.

A trader must have technical tools in the beginning, but also the best place to experiment with new strategies for advanced traders is the demo account. Several demo accounts are unrestricted, so not time restriction.

Important Components for day trading:

Whether it is automated day trading strategies, or advanced tactics and beginner, a trader will need to take three essential components; liquidity, volatility, and volume. If a beginner wants to create money by making tiny price movements, choosing the right stock is vigorous. These three elements will help the trader to make a decision.

1. **Liquidity:**

This enables the trader to suddenly enter and exit trades at an eye-catching and stable price. Liquid commodity strategies, for example, crude oil, focus on gold, and natural gas, etc.

2. Volatility:

Through this, every beginner trader will get to know about their potential profit range. The larger the volatility, the larger profit or loss a trader may make. The cryptocurrency market is an example of high volatility.

3. Volume:

This measurement will help the beginner to know about how many times the stock/asset has been traded within a set period of time. For a day trader beginners, this is known as 'average daily trading volume.' High volume helps in knowing that there's significant interest in the asset or security. Growth in volume is often an indicator a price goes either up or down, is fast approaching.

How much risk is involved in day trading?

According to the experts of (OTA) Online Trading Academy, it is a reality that day trading situations managing in a single day are making it truly safer rather than riskier.

> "One of the best ways to control risk is limiting the length of the trade. The longer you are in a position, the greater the likelihood is that price could move against you. By day trading, you eliminate overnight and weekend risk, especially when you trade markets that close, like stocks."
>
> – Brandon Wendell, CMT

Because it is a fact that day traders don't hold their positions overnight, they usually avoid the probability of a surprise in an overseas market, unfavorable financial news, or an incomes report that comes out once the markets are closed. Even though after-hours trading is offered for numerous securities, the market is high, and it's possible that the position will gap down and open at a dramatically lower price the next day after a negative overnight experience.

In addition, day trading tends to give ease, not increase market volatility. Day traders are usually looking for their earnings in small price movements up or down. Their daily trades offer liquidity, which helps the marketing the running easily, as compared to casually traded markets that are subject to dramatic price swings. Day trading is not a way to become rich instantly. Day trading is a traditional investing approach that is used by many organizations as well by the well-educated institutions who have adopted it as a profession.

In the 1990s, day trading did not have a good reputation, and at that time, many beginners began day trading. They started jumping into different platforms, including online trading platforms, without applying the stock strategies. They believed that they could run the market without having the knowledge about the market and make a fortune in stock trades with their little effort. This proved them wrong.

What do you need to start day trading?

For a day trader beginner, it is important to have technical equipment at your place. Most of the beginners think that daily trading requires heavy and expensive equipment and high investments of capital; that's not the reality.

Here's a list of items usually every trader needs for trading.

Technology:

For trading, traders do not want a supercharged computer with a dozen monitors to trade. They only need one laptop or a computer.

Internet Connection:

It is very important to have a good internet connection; it helps the trader to process his order in a timely manner. Most cables and even satellites suppliers offer sufficient bandwidth to connect to the exchanges. Typical packages of 20mbps of cable internet are enough for this. Most of the traders even use their mobile phone connections of 5mbps to 20mbps, but that is not suggested. The slow mobile phone connection can cause delays in transactions and can cause unexpected loss.

Trading Platform:

Traders should be careful in the trading market because there are many online brokers sitting online to fool the beginners. They offer the beginners their services but route orders over market makers who cost additional money, they often deferral the processing. It is easy to perform trade analysis and place your orders very quickly and properly. The web-based version is less reliable then the downloaded version, the downloaded version offers more features.

Skills

Lots of people are supporters of seeking an education. The main problem is that; education alone is not enough unless it is being utilized rightly in the market. Although having information about the markets, how it will work, and how to read price is essential, and how it will offer an advantage, skill is also necessary to obtain stable results.

Building a skill involves practice and experience, but trying to get trading skills without supervision can be a lengthy, often annoying process. For many traders, working and learning from the experience of a counselor is the best way to improve any of the skills and learn strategies for trading and investing that reduces risk. Even the famous traders like Paul Tudor and Warren Buffett Jones needed mentors. Mr. Buffett worked under Benjamin Graham, and Mr. Jones worked under Eli Tullis.

Day Trading Strategies

Strategies

1. Breakout

In trading breakout strategies center around after the price clears a specified level on the chart, with improved volume. The breakout trader enters into a long situation once the security or asset breaks above resistance. Otherwise, a trader enters a short site after the stock breaks below support.

Once a security or asset trades beyond the quantified amount barrier, volatility frequently increases, and the amount will often trend in the way of the breakout.

A trader needs to catch the right instrument to trade. While doing this, bear in the notice the resistance level and asset's support. The more often the price has hit these facts, the more authenticated and vital they become.

Plan the Entry and Exits Points:

This part of trading is good and direct. Prices set to nearby and above resistance levels want a bearish place. Prices set to nearby and below a maintenance level want a bullish place.

Using the asset's latest performance to establish a sensible price target. Using chart patterns in trading will make this process even more precise. A trader can analyze the average current price swings to generate a target. If the average swings have been 3 points over the last some price swings, this would be a workable target. Once you've got hold of that goal, then you can exit the trade and enjoy the profit.

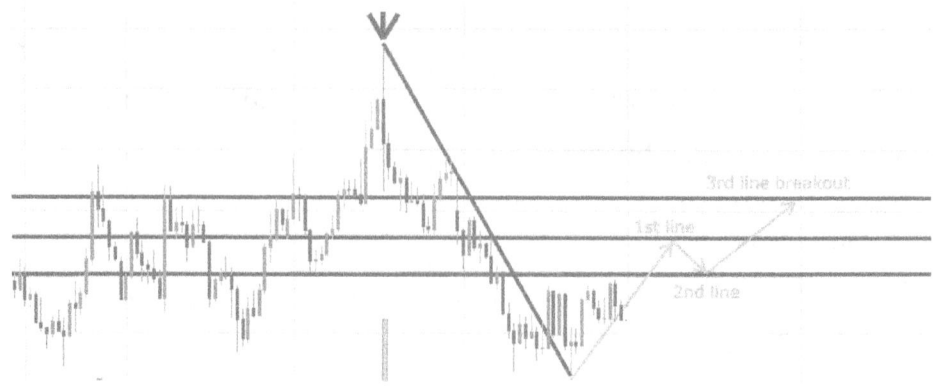

2. Scalping

Scalping is one of the best strategies, mostly used by traders. It is mostly used, and it is popular in the forex market. It looks to capitalize on minute price changes, and its driving force is quantity. You will look to sell the stock as soon as the stock becomes profitable. This is an exciting and fast-paced technique to trade, but then again, it can be risky. You must have a high trading probability to even out the reward ratio vs. low risk. A trader should be on the lookout for volatile tools, attractive liquidity, and be on timing. You cannot wait for the market; you must close losing trades as soon as possible.

3. Momentum:

This strategy is popular among all trading strategies for beginners; this strategy revolves around acting on recognizing large trending moves with the support of high volume and news sources. For the ample opportunity, there is always at least one stock that moves around 20-30% each day. A trader simply holds onto the position until he sees signs of reversal and then gets out. Otherwise, he can disappear the price drop. This way round his price target as soon as volume starts to shrink.

This is the simplest and most effective strategy if used properly. However, a trader must ensure that he is aware of upcoming news and income announcements. Just a small number of seconds on each trade will make all the difference to your end of day profits.

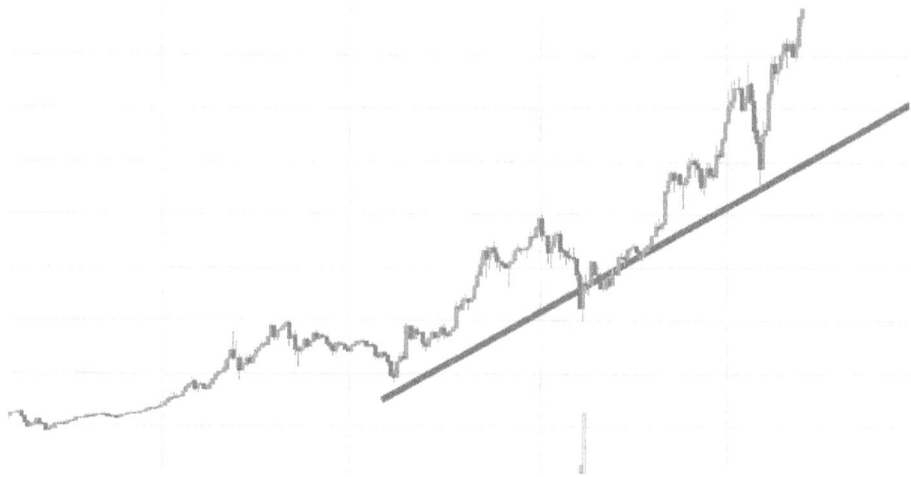

4. Reversal

Though this strategy is hotly debated and potentially unsafe when it comes to using by beginners. Reverse trading is used all over the world. It's also known as pullback trending, trend trading, and a mean reversion strategy. This strategy confronts the basic logic as the trader aims to trade against the trend. A trader must be able to correctly classify possible pullbacks, plus calculate their strength. To do this effectively, a trader must need in-depth market experience and knowledge.

The 'daily pivot' strategy is measured as a unique case of reverse trading, as it centers on selling and buying the daily high and low pullbacks/reverse.

5. Using Pivot Points

A day trading pivot point strategy can be strange or fantastic in trading for acting on critical support and/or resistance levels identifying it. It is mostly useful in the forex market. In addition, pivot points can be used by range-bound traders to recognize points of entry, whereas trend and breakout traders can use pivot points to locate key levels that must break a move to count as a breakout.

Calculating Pivot Points

A pivot point is well-defined as a point of rotation in day trading. A beginner day trader can use the prices of the previous day's low or high and, plus the closing price of a security to analyze the pivot point.

Note that if you analyze a pivot point using price statistics from a quite short time frame, accuracy is often reduced.

So, how does a day trader will analyze/calculate the pivot point?

- Central Pivot Point (P) = (High + Low + Close) / 3

Now day traders can analyze resistance and support levels by using the pivot point. For doing that a trader must use the following formulas:

- First Resistance (R1) = (2*P) – Low
- First Support (S1) = (2*P) – High

The second level of resistance and support is then calculated as follows:

- Second Resistance (R2) = P + (R1-S1)
- Second Support (S2) = P – (R1- S1)

Application

When practically applied in the FX market, for example, a beginner will find the trading range for the session that will frequently take place among the pivot point and the resistance levels and the first support. The reason behind this is having a high number of traders playing this range. It is also worth noting because this is one of the systems &approaches that can be applied to indexes too.

For example, it can help a day trader beginner to form an effective S&P day trading strategy.

Limit Your Losses

This is the most important thing to keep in your mind if you are using a margin is limiting your loss. Requirements are often high for day traders. When a day trader trades on a margin, he will be increasingly susceptible to sharp price movements. This means the potential for a bigger profit, but it also means the probability of substantial losses. Luckily, a trader can employ stop-losses. The stop-loss controls the trade risk for the trader. In a small situation, a trader can place a stop-loss above a recent high; for good big situations, you can place it below a recent low. A trader can also make it dependent on volatility.

For example, if a stock amount moves by £0.05 a minute, so you can place a stop-loss £0.15 away after your entry order, letting it swing (hopefully in the expected direction).

One popular strategy in day trading is to set up two stop-losses. Firstly, a trader places a physical stop-loss order at a precise price level. This will be the maximum capital you can afford to lose. Secondly, you can create a mental stop-loss. Place this, at the point of your entry criteria, are breached. So if the trade makes an unexpected turn, you'll make a swift exit.

Forex Trading Strategies

Forex strategies are risky by nature as a trader must accumulate his profits in a short space of time. A trader can apply any of the strategies in the forex market.

Swing trading strategy

What is a swing trader?

Swing traders are basically those traders that trade for a couple of days or for weeks' time frame. They usually work for four hours (H4) and daily (D1) charts, and they may use a blend of fundamental analysis and technical analysis to monitor trading their decisions. Whether it is a long term trend or whether the market is mainly range-bound, it really does not matter. A Forex swing trader is not going to hold on to a position that is enough for it to count considerably.

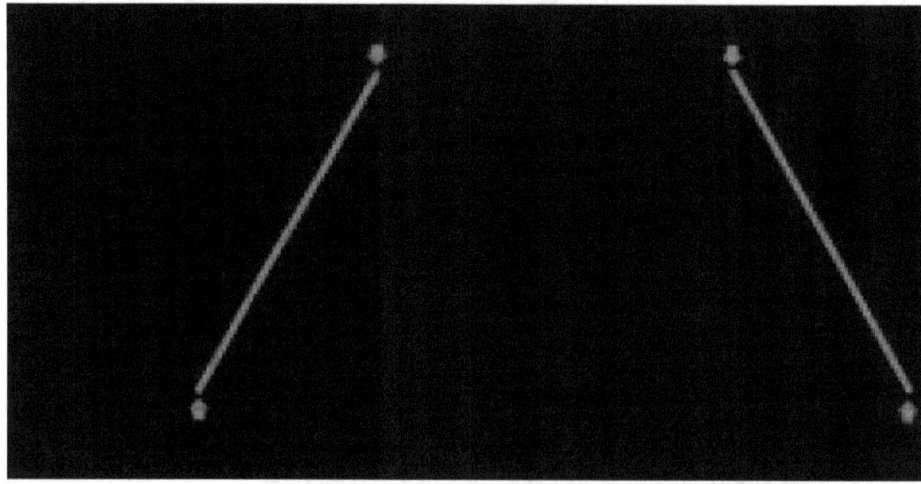

In the trading market, the swing trader is best to be used when markets are going nowhere once indexes rise for multi-days, then decay for the next few days, only to repeat the same over-all patterns again and again. Swing trader has several chances to catch the short-term movements up and down. The problem with swing trading and long-term trend trading is that success is established on correctly recognizing what type of market is presently being practiced. Trend trading might have the perfect strategy for the bull market of the 1990s, while swing trading maybe would have been best for 2000 and 2001.

Simple moving averages (SMAs) offer resistance and support levels, as well as bearish and bullish patterns. Support and resistance levels can help the trader in buying a stock. Bullish and bearish limit patterns signal price ideas where you should enter and exit stocks. The exponential moving average (EMA) is similar to SMA that places extra emphasis on the latest data points. The EMA gives traders clear trend indications, entry, and exit points faster than a simple moving average (SMA). Swing trades can use EMA for entry and exit points.

A swing trader tends to look for multi-day chart outlines. Some of the more common outlines include moving average crossovers, head and shoulders patterns, flags, triangles, and cup-and-handle patterns. Eventually, each swing trader formulates a plan and strategy that gives them an advantage over many trades. This also includes looking for trade arrangements that tend to lead to expectable movements in the asset's price. This is not that easy, and no strategy or any arrangement will work every time. Through a favorable risk or reward, winning every time is not required. The more promising risk or reward of a trading strategy, the fewer times it desires to win in order to produce a complete profit over many trades.

Once it comes to take profits, the swing traders, whether they are beginners or the professionals, they will want to exit the trade as soon as possible to the upper or lower channel line without being too defined, which can cause the risk of missing the finest opportunity.

In the book of Dr. Alexander Elder, "Come Into My Trading Room: A Complete Guide to Trading" (2002), he uses his understanding of a stock's behavior above and below the baseline to define the swing trader's strategy of "buying regularity and selling mania" or "shorting regularity and covering depression." Once the swing trader used the EMA to recognize the typical baseline on the stock chart, the trader goes long at the baseline once the stock is heading up and short at the baseline once the stock is on its way down.

Therefore, swing traders are not looking to smash the home run by a single trade; they are not alarmed with the perfect time to purchase a stock exactly at its bottom and sell exactly at its top. In a perfect trading environment, beginners should wait for the stock to hit its baseline and confirm its way before they make their moves. The story becomes more complex when a tougher uptrend or downtrend is at play. The trader may unexpectedly go long once the stock dips below its EMA and pause for the stock to go back up in an uptrend, or a trader may short a stock that has stuck above the EMA and wait for it to drop if the time-consuming trend is down.

NOTE:

Many traders believe that they cannot make trades by greater as their account is too small.

If a trader is calculating his position before each trade and risking a similar amount in each trade, then a trader ought to be able to play a trade whether the stop is 60 pips or 10.

Popular Swing Trading Strategies:

Swing trading is frequently done within trends, and this is a common way; it can also be successfully carried out in ranging markets. A swing trader analyses the price profit and action from the greater part of the market's next swing. The markets spend far-off extra of their time reaching; then they do create clear trends higher or lower and being capable to successfully trade ranging markets, is critical.

Forex Swing Trading Strategies:

Swing trading is not a strategy; it is a style. The time frame of swing trading describes this style, and within that, there are unlimited strategies that we can use to swing trade. Swing trading is a style that works over short to moderate time frames. Swing trading style lies between the very long time frames of position trading and short time frames of day trading. It is not so short that it requires all your time observing the market, yet it is short enough to offer plenty of trading chances. These strategies are not limited to swing trading; it is the case with most technical strategies, support and resistance are the ideas behind them.

These concepts can give a trader two choices within the swing trading strategy with, following the trend, or trading counter to the trend. Counter trending strategies aim to profit once support and resistance levels hold up. Trend following strategies looks for the chances when support and resistance levels break down.

For trading swing traders can use the following strategies for actionable trading opportunities:

Swing trading strategy 1: Trend trading

When classifying a trend, it's essential to recognize that markets don't tend to move in a straight line. Even while eventually trending, they move up and down in step like moves. A trader should recognize an uptrend by the market, making higher highs and higher lows, and a downtrend by recognizing lower lows and lower highs. Many swing trading strategies of trying to catch and follow a short trend.

Swing trading strategy 2: Counter-trend trading

The next swing trading strategy is counter-trend trading and therefore does the reverse of the first one. We practice the similar principles in terms of trying to spot relatively short-term trends from building, but now try to profit as of the frequency with which these trends tend to break down.

NOTE:

Uptrend = Higher lows and Higher highs

Downtrend = Lower lows and lower highs

A counter-trend trader would effort to catch the swing in this period of reversion. Therefore, the trader would try to identify the break in the trend. In an uptrend, this might be a fresh high was followed by a series of failures to break new highs. Hence we go short in expectation of such a reversion. The reverse is true in a downtrend.

Itis very important to maintain a strong discipline encounter trending if the price travels against you, and if the market resumes its trend against you, then you should be ready to admit that you are wrong, and you had drawn a line under the trade.

Swing trading strategy 3: A versatile swing trading strategy

If a trader would like to take an even deeper dive into swing trading, besides learning a multipurpose strategy that even beginners can use. Being a versatile trader means that a trader is able to trade any instrument, in any timeframe or in any direction.

Improving swing trading strategies for beginners:

What swing can traders do to increase their strategies?

There are numerous things a trader can try. The first thing is to effort to match the trade with the long-term trend. While the hourly chart helps the swing trader to also look at a longer-term chart to get a feel for the long-standing trend. Try and trade merely once your direction matches whatever you see as the long-term trend. Another way to recover your swing trading strategy is to use a technical indicator to confirm your thinking.

A moving average (MA) is one more indicator you can use to help. An MA flattens the prices to give a clearer view of the trend. And because an MA includes older price data, it's an easy way to match how the recent prices compare to older prices.

Managing risk in Forex swing trading:

Have you ever read about trading Forex and that the widely held of traders that lost money because of it? Have you ever understood that this is even true for successful traders?

The reality is that no trader wins 100% of the time. Most of the time it happens that the beginners of the swing trading misjudge the market, sometimes it moves unexpectedly, sometimes the trader might just make a mistake. This is the point where risk management and money management are so important.

In trading, but especially in Forex, a trader should know how to lose before knowing how to get success. And when traders talk about having enough knowledge on how to lose, he should also know how to lose tiny to win big. Basically, if a trader can achieve a swing trading risk, then he can close out losing trades early, which will help to ensure he enjoys extra profits than losses.

Some tips for handling your risk in swing trading include:

1. **Maximum acceptable loss:**

In spite of the fact that a trade clearly wants his next trade to make a profit, it's important to think through the supreme amount you are prepared to lose on a trade. The minute a trader knows this amount can set a stop loss to close his trade spontaneously if it travels too far in the incorrect direction then this will help to protect him when he can't automatically be at your computer observing every trade.

2. Taking a risk on any one trade:

No matter what is the size of your trading account, you must avoid risking your whole balance on a trade. If a trader does not follow that, then he can possibly lose it all. Andover-all rule is not to risk more than 2% of your account balance on any one trade.

3. Increasing account balance to diversify risk:

Despite the fact that a trader might be able to open an account from as little as €300, it is better to start using a larger sum. This means that a trader will have an adequate amount of your account to trade a diversity of assets and expand the risk of swing trading. Swing trading is by description a long-term investment style, so you need extra verge on your places to manage with market explosive nature.

4. Information about your profile:

One of the first and most important things to do when you start trading in the market is to understand your risk aversion and volatility. In other words, at what stage of the loss will a trader starts to panic? If a swing trader has an account balance of €25,000 and he has lost €3,000, then this means that the trader has lost 10% of his capital. In that case, would he be a failure, or would he think through that to be usual? How the trader will respond to this loss will influence the risks he is willing to take in trading.

You can see that this strategy will be easy for a beginner to understand. Therefore, a Swing Trading strategy is an average and long-term trading strategy. This strategy is very dependent on the capital and management of risks. It is most commonly called money management swing trading.

Swing trading money management:

Once a trader understands the big picture of the trading after that, he still has to manage his risk every day in the market. And one way to do trading wisely is by managing your money successfully. It might give the impression like a complex question, but in reality, it doesn't have to be.

For example: If a trader wanted to keep the total risk of 6% of his account balance so he could have six trades opened, each risking 1% of his assets.

For that reason, a trader could lose 1% of his capital in six different trades or a maximum amount of €200 in each trade if you had an account of €20,000. At that point, before taking a position, a trader should be aware of his maximum risk for proper management of his assets in Swing Trading that will be 1% or 200 euros. For that reason, your stop-loss and neutralization position will be determined previously by each position. And from there, you should perform as many actions as you can without overcoming your risk management.

That boundary will then affect your actions, and you will close since the trade is approaching your loss limit, or you will lose the trade because the asset goes up and reaches the target profit. And if a trade passes the breakeven fact, at which point it develops a 'neutral' trade, you can take on a new site, without endangering your risk limit.

The best tools for swing trading:

There is a range of tools a trader can use to improve his chances of success while performing swing trading strategies.

Some ranges that are recommended:

Correlation Matrix: *The relationship between Forex pairs, supplies, or stock guides is one element of analysis that allows sensible trading to trade with self-confidence.*

Mini Charts*:*

A mini charting tool permits the trader to analyze numerous units of time on a single chart. Which means that there is no need for the trader to shift from swing chart W1 to D1 to come to be on the H4 chart to discover his entry point

Symbol Info:

In the same manner, this Forex swing indicator lets traders understand on a single chart the trading signals of the maximum used indicators on eight different interval scales.

Mini Terminal:

The mini terminal tool allows the trader to open a place in Meta Trader in a second, but then again, it also permits the swing trader to open trades regarding the risk in permanent euros or in percentage. In fact, it provides you with diverse information associated with the stock market or the currency pair in which a trader can apply it, including the current trend, the strength of current movements and current momentum

Other useful indicators for swing traders include are:

Exponential Mobile Average

MACD

Overwhelming oscillator

Parabolic SAR

CCI

Admiral Donchian

So here comes the question that troubles the beginners, that from where the beginners of swing trading can access these swing trading tools? It's easy for those who have a demo or a live account with Admiral Markets. And if not, then the good news is that any of the beginners can easily access these totally free with Meta-Trader Supreme Edition.

Meta-Trader Supreme Edition is an absolutely free plugin for MT4 and MT5 that contains a range of unconventional features, such as an indicator package with technical analysis trading ideas provided by Trading Central, and 16 new indicators and mini terminals and mini charts to mark your trading even more effectual.

Top tips for Forex swing trading for beginners:

After knowing the basics of the swing, and after having enough information about the Forex swing trading strategies, here are the top tips that will help you to succeed as a swing trader.

    1. Match your trades by the long-term trend:

Although a trader may always be looking at a time chart of shorter-term (e.g., H1 or H4), it may also comfort the beginner to look at a longer-term chart (D1 or W1) to get the information about the long-term trend. Then you can make sure that you aren't trading beside a larger trend. Swing trading is also much easier when it's been trading by means of the trend, rather than against the trend.

    2. Make the best of Moving Averages (MAs):

The MA indicator may profit the trader to classify trends by moderating shorter-term price differences. Since the MA comprises old data prices, it is the easiest way to associate what way the existing price links with older prices.

3. **Use a little leverage:**

Leverage lets the trader access a larger position than it would usually let your deposit, together with strengthening your profits and losses. Once used wisely, leverage can help the trader to make the most of winning trades.

4. **Trade a wide-ranging portfolio of Forex pair:**

Lookout as several currency pairs as you can to discover the best opportunities. The Forex market will every time offer you trading opportunities you want; you need to look for the ones that match best with your signal. Plus, trading a range of pairs will support to diversify your portfolio, and achieve the risk of having all your eggs in one basket.

5. **Pay attention to swaps:**

Swaps are a cost of trading concern charge ready for positions held overnight. These swaps need to be taken into account in swing trading of the trader in order to be able to manage your money better.

6. **Maintaining a positive profit/loss ratio:**

Whether it is H4 or daily trading, swing trading allows the trader to tap into large market schedules, giving the trader the chance to get larger profit ratios associated with very small losses possible, especially when matched to scalping.

7. **Put a side your sentiments:**

It's better to trade without emotions, but then again, to make swing trades as a part of a fixed Forex trading plan and strategy.

Choose a Broker for Forex Swing:

Before a trader starts trading, a trader needs to choose a broker. Choosing a broker for the Forex market will give a chance to the new traders to access the markets in a way that wants to trade, along with a trading platform to carry out his trades. Though some brokers are better than others, that's why it is essential to keep the following in mind while making a choice.

Check if they are synchronized by the local regulator in your area? Admiral Markets is a Forex and CFD broker that is controlled by the EFSA, ASIC CYSEC, and FCA.

The costs of trading contain the spread, the swap, and orders on trades, which know how to eat into your profits. That's why it is essential to have knowledge about typical trading costs.

A standard Forex share, or trading contract, is value 100,000 of the base currency of the pair before the first currency listed (if one share of the EUR/USD costs EUR 100,000). For new traders, this might be extra than you want to see, so check whether the broker deals micro (0.01) and mini (0.1) lots for trading.

To make knowledgeable trading decisions, it is essential to have the latest market information. Good Forex and CFD brokers will deal with live price facts in their trading platform.

The next point is having knowledge about the market and how much leverage does the broker offer? If you talk about Europe, in Europe, the brokers should offer access to leverage up to 1:500 for Specialized Clients and 1:30 for Retail Customers.

What is the least amount a trader needs to start trading? At Admiral Markets, a trader can supply the trading account with as little as €100. This also allows the trader to start small trade without taking a major risk and add as you learn the market psychology and behavior of self-governing trading.

Admiral Markets can support the trader to decrease his trading risk with volatility defense and negative balance protection.

Will, the broker, let the trader not simply swing trade, but day trade and scalp as well, if that's a part of the strategy?

Does the broker in swing trading provide tools and resources to help the beginner to succeed as a trader? As if we talk about Admiral Markets, for example, it has a library of more than hundreds of Forex articles, free courses like Forex 101, and free trading webinars.

Forex Swing Trading Strategies

A Summary

Swing trading is a style suitable for volatile markets, and it also suggests frequent trading chances. Though the trader will need to capitalize a reasonable amount of time into observing the market with swing trading, the supplies are not as difficult as trading styles with smaller time frames, such as day trading or scalping. In calculation, even if you give favor to day trade or scalping, swing trading will offer you few diversifications in your outcomes as well as additional profits. It is said that swing trading is not for all traders, so it is best to practice it with risk-free first with a demo trading account.

Admiral Markets:

Admiral Markets is a market that has attained many successes in the market due to its multi-award-winning achievement. Forex and CFD broker, providing trading on over 8,000 financial instruments via the world's most popular trading platforms:

1. MetaTrader 4

2. MetaTrader 5

This substantial does not hold and should not be construed as containing asset advice, asset recommendations, an offer of or solicitation for any dealings in financial instruments. A beginner should not forget that such trading analysis is not a trustworthy indicator for any current or future performance, as conditions may change over time. Before making any investment conclusions, he should seek guidance from independent financial advisors to confirm that you understand the risks.

4. SWING AND DAY TRADING INDICATORS

What are the indicators of trading?

"Trading indicators are the mathematical calculations, that are designed to predict what market will do."

Trading indicators are plotted as lines on a price chart and may comfort traders to identify certain signals and trends within the market. The number one indicator could be a forecast signal that calculates future price movements, while a lagging indicator looks at past trends and indicates momentum.

Why Are Technical Indicators Important?

Technical indicators are supported algorithms that practice previous price-data in the calculation. As an outcome, all technical indicators of trading are lagging in their natural surroundings, but that doesn't mean that they can't return useful information once day trading the markets. Deprived of the assistance of indicators, traders would have a tough time calculating this volatility of the markets, the strength of a trend, or whether market conditions are overbought or oversold.

That being said, an entire trading strategy shouldn't be dependent solely on technical indicators. They return the simplest results as a confirmation tool. Don't buy just because the RSI is below 30 or sell because the Stochastics oscillator increases directly above 80. As an alternative, a trader should create a definite trading strategy (built on price-action or the fundamentals, for instance) and using technical indicators simply to substantiate a possible setup and modify your entry levels.

Types of Technical Indicators

Depending on the knowledge that technical indicators provide, they'll be grouped into three main categories:

Trend-following indicators.

Momentum indicators.

Volatility indicators.

1. Trend-following indicators

Trend-following indicators are accustomed to determine trends and to live the strong point of a trending market. While most traders are able to identify a trend just by staring at the value chart, it's often difficult to live its strength or to identify a trend early in its establishment. The common trend-following indicators also contain moving averages, MACD, and also the ADX indicator, to call some.

2. Momentum indicator:

It usually measures the strength of recent price-moves relative to previous periods. They vary in the middle of 0 and 100, on condition of the signals of the indicator of overbought and oversold market circumstances. Momentum indicators return a marketing signal when values begin to maneuver strongly higher, and a buying signal when prices start to maneuver strongly lower. While this will be profitable in ranging markets, momentum indicators usually return false signals during strong trends. Some samples of momentum indicators include the RSI, Stochastics, and CCI.

3. Volatility indicators:

Volatility indicators, as per their name recommends, it measures the volatility of the fundamental instrument. Traders are generally chasing volatility from corner to different corner markets to hunt out profitable trading opportunities, which makes volatility indicators a strong tool for day trading. Samples of volatility indicators include Bollinger Bands and also the ATR indicator, among others.

Every investor has faith in the strategy of buying and holding. The only topic of disputation is how long the holding era should last. For every teenager who started buying unappreciated equity and holds it for eight decades, collecting shares along the way, there are dozens of more risk-takers who dearth to get out of their positions in less than a week. This not only requires a stock to rise quickly but also to go up in price high sufficient to offset any matter costs. Swing trading is for the stockholder who factually can't wait for the weekend.

Swing trading is the most fast-paced trading process that is manageable for everyone, even those beginners who have just jumped into the world of trading. The speed of swing trading is slower than day trading, which also delivers the trader with sufficient time to formulate a practice and execute a little research before building decisions on your trade. Swing trading is also a rare method for those looking to create a foray into day trading to increase their skills before embarking on the extra complex day trading process.

Those technical indicators are the mathematical tools that can give actionable info out of a stock plan that can seem uninformed at times. In the hands of an appropriately lucky risk-taker, the right technical indicators can spell a chance for profit. Now, just a rare of the ones most commonly used by swing traders, in ascending order of complexity.

Swing traders tend to have not the same goals as day traders, which goal to pick up on rapid intraday changes due to a catalyst.

Swing trades, on the other hand, tend to goal for "swings" moving from a short-term low back to a new high.

Swing trading signals tend to look not the same as day trading signals. Day traders frequently look for high volatility and volume and look to ride a trend, possibly buying at a pullback to VWAP.

Before we talk about the trading indicators, it is essential to understand what they represent and why and how they represent it are also important questions to think. Swing trading indicators are not better than any other method of technical analysis, and it should certainly not have seen as the divine grail. It is not assured that any trade that a trader makes will yield profit just for the reason that a trading indicator signaled it.

Here are few other factors that can have an influence on whether you end up creating a profit or bearing a loss in swing trading:

Market Conditions can frequently reduce the effectiveness of indicators. Even if it appears like security is nearby to go up, a broad bearish emotion could cause it to additional fall in value.

The timing of your trade needs to be rigorous. Receiving the right time can be authoritative to create a huge profit.

What many people call perception is simply know-how. Like all other things, you will turn out to be a better trader as you spend extra time trading and pick up on subtle market signals.

Swing Trading Indicators:

Swing trade indicators are important to focus on when selecting when to buy when to trade, and what to buy. Some of the top combinations of indicators for swing trading are given below.

1. Moving Averages:

The moving average is one of the foremost basic trading indicators in swing trading. A moving average smoothens erratic short-term price movements and comforts us to better understand the trend and in what way the safety is moving. Moving Averages are good indicators on their own, but they are also used as a base for other, more descriptive indicators. Swing trader should not forget this that moving averages approximately always lag behind the present price thanks to factoring in past data. The more data you think about, the larger the lag. Therefore, as a swing trader. It is smart to mix short term moving averages with longer-term moving averages. Doing so, you think about both the long and short term trend and have more ground on which to base your decisions.

When a trader is observing at moving averages, he will be observing at the calculated lines built on past prices. This indicator is not difficult to understand, and it is also difficult to look at whether you are doing day trading, swing trading, or else even trading longer term. They are used to either confirm a trend or identify a trend. To decide the average, a trader will need to sum up all of the concluding prices as well as the number for days the period covers and then divide the concluding prices via the number of days. To successfully use moving averages, a trader will need to compute different time periods and link them on a chart. This will give the trader a broader lookout of the market, as well as their average changes over time. When you have planned your moving averages, you then must use them to consider in on your trade decisions. You can practice them to:

Recognize the Strength of a Trend:

If the present price of the stock and trend is beyond from its moving average, then it is considered to be a weaker trend. Trend strength, shared by an indicator like volume, can help you create better choices on your trades.

Determining Trend Reversals:

You can use moving averages to recognize trend reversals with limits. You need to watch for instances where the current moving averages cross the longer moving averages after an uptrend. Though this is not the only instrument, you should use to regulate reversal, but it can comfort you to determine whether you should explore it further.

2. Relative Strength Index:

Welles Wilder developed the RSI indicator within the 1970s and distributed his findings in New Concepts in Technical Trading Systems. The book may be a classic text which presented multiple conventional technical indicators like RSI, Average True Range, and, therefore, the Average Directional Index. A simple explanation of RSI's calculation is linking this price strength relative to past price strength. For instance, a 14-period RSI on a daily chart will compare today's price to the last 13 closes. A high reading points out that today's price is powerful, relative to the previous 13 closes, and contrariwise. Wilder planned that RSI could be used as a momentum oscillator: measuring exactly how tough the momentum is during a market, but then RSI came to be used in a different way. RSI is mostly used by the traders as an overbought-oversold indicator, where a great reading means that the stock is "overbought" and is unavoidable for a pullback. In the comparison, an "oversold" reading indicates that the market is due for a rally because it's been sold-off an excessive amount of. This consumption of the indicator compares to the aim of a momentum oscillator, contained by which a great analysis indicates that this trend is further likely to last. In the conventional time series of 14-period RSI is used. The situation is the one suggested in also Wilders' work and is defaulting in maximum charting platforms. On the other hand, the study of Larry Connors's point towards the 14-period RSI comprises a miniature edge, in which shorter-term RSI analyses produce additional commercial signals.

Connors' research indicates that the 2, four, and blended RSI periods show the most effective long-term trade expectation. As a result of his research, Connors developed the Connors RSI indicator (which measures the speed of change of RSI), which is included with most charting packages nowadays.

Relative strength index (RSI) is one of the finest technical indicators for swing trading. This indicator is responsible for giving the information you need to determine once the ideal enters into the market. It allows traders to investigate small signals better. This will help the trader to regulate if the market has been oversold or overbought, is range-bound, or is flat. The RSI will give the trader a relative evaluation of how to secure the existing price by examining both past instability and performance. This indicator will be easily recognized by using a range of 1-100. The RSI indicator is most convenient for:

Determining the circumstances that led the market to oversold or overbought:

A trader will need to be able to classify these conditions so that a trader can find equally trend reversal and corrections. Overbuying can indicate a bearish trend even though overselling can be seen as more bullish. If the indicator is around 30, it could be indicated as an undervalue or oversold. Indicators about 70 may mean that the security was overrated or overbought.

Identifying Divergences:

Divergences are used to classify reversals in trends. When the value hits a new low, but then the RSI does not, then at that time, it would be considered as a bullish divergent signal. If the value hits a new high and the RSI doesn't, then that would be termed a bearish signal.

3. Volume:

A generally overlooked indicator that is easiest for beginners to use, even for new traders, is volume. Looking at volume is very critical when you are considering trends. Trends need to be maintained and supported by volume. A trader always wants to make sure that there is more significant volume going on when the trend is going in that way. Increasing volume means money supporting the safety, and if you do not see the volume, it may possibly be an indication that there are undervalued conditions at play.

4. Visual Analysis Indicator:

Despite the fact that technical indicators for swing trading are critical for making the right choices, it is helpful from many shareholders, both new and experienced, to be able to look at visual patterns. By generating visuals patterns, a trader can see the activities in the market with a quick glance to help support your decision.

5. The Flow of Net Imbalances:

Each day, there are a lot of orders to be found to urge the closing print (market-on-close orders). These are typically institutions like mutual funds and ETFs that need the large liquidity provided at the market close. Some minutes before they close every day, the interactions will distribute information on the order inequalities at the market close. That is, what number more shares are being accepted than sold at the close? For instance, if market-on-close buy orders are equaling 100,000 shares, and sell orders equaling 90,000 shares, that's a +10,000 share imbalance. Market makers arbitrage this within the short-term and make pennies, that's not a timeframe we are able to compete in. However, we are able to track the cash flow of a stock or sector by tracking the trend of the online imbalances over time.

If there are determined in closing the imbalances in one sector, it's indicating that institutions are collecting an edge therein stock. This provides us vital information that a major price move could be on the precipice. The tool I exploit to measure imbalance money flow is Market Chameleon. MC allows you to easily view 20-days or 50-days moving averages of capital inflows and outflows of sectors, industries, indexes, or watch lists.

Day Trading Indicators:

To find the simplest technical indicators for your particular day-trading approach, test out a bunch of them singularly and so together. You will find yourself sticking with, say, four that are evergreen otherwise, you may flip counting on the asset you're trading or the market situations of the day. Regardless of whether you are day-trading stocks, forex, or futures, it's often best to stay it simple when it involves technical indicators. You will find you like viewing only a pair of indicators to endorse entry points and exit points. At most, use simply one from each type of indicator to dodge avoidable and distracting repetition.

Combining Day-Trading Indicators

Consider a combination of sets of two indicators on your expense chart to classify points to initiate and get hold of out of a trade.

For example, Relative strength index RSI and moving average convergence/divergence will be combined on the screen to recommend and strengthen a trading signal. The relative strength index (RSI) can recommend overbought or oversold conditions by measuring the value momentum of an asset. The indicator was produced by J. Welles Wilder Jr, who proposed the momentum reaching 30 (on a scale of zero to 100) was an indication of an asset being oversold, and so a buying chance and a 70 percent level was an indication of an asset is overbought and so a selling or short-selling chance.

Constance Brown, CMT, refined the service of the index and assumed the oversold level in an exceedingly upward-trending market was fundamentally much above 30, and therefore, the overbought level in a downward-trending market was much below 70.3.Using Wilder's levels, the asset price can still trend higher for a few times, whereas the RSI is signifying overbought and the other way around. For that reason, RSI is best monitored only if its signal imitates to the value trend: as an example, hunt for bearish momentum indications when the value trend is bearish and pay no attention to those indications when the value trend is bullish.

To more easily identify those price trends, you'll be able to use the moving average convergence/divergence (MACD) indicator. MACD consists of two chart lines. The MACD line is made by eliminating a 26-period exponential moving average (EMA) from a 12-period EMA. An EMA is that the average value of an asset over a period of your time only with the key change that the foremost recent prices are given greater allowance than prices farther out.

The second line is the signal line and could be a 9-period EMA. A bearish trend is signaled once the MACD line crosses under the signal line; a bullish trend is signaled after the MACD line crosses directly above the signal line.

Choosing Pairs:

While selecting pairs, it is a good knowledge to decide on one indicator that's measured a number one indicator, i.e., RSI and one that's a lagging indicator, i.e., like MACD. Most important indicators make signals before the conditions for entering the trade have arisen. Lagging indicators make warning signs after those circumstances have looked as if, in order that they can act as verification of leading indicators and might prevent you from trading on made-up signals.

A trader must also first-rate a pairing that features indicators as of two of the four different types, never two of the same type. The four types are development like MACD, moments like RSI, volatility, and volume. As their names suggest, volatility indicators are supported volatility within the asset's price, and volume indicators are supported trading volumes of the asset. It's typically not useful to look at two indicators of the identical type since they'll be on condition that the identical information.

Using Multiple Indicators:

A trader might also opt to have live one indicator of every type; it might possibly be two of which are maximum substantial and two of which are lagging. Numerous indicators can provide even more strengthening of trading signals and might increase your probabilities of hunting down made-up signals.

Refining Indicators:

Whatsoever indicators you choose, make sure to research them, and take summaries on their effectiveness over time. Ask yourself: What are an indicator's disadvantages? Does it produce several made-up signals? Does it fail to signal, leading to missed chances? Does it signal too early (more probable of a number one indicator) or too late (more likely of a lagging one)?

You may find one indicator is actual when trading stocks but not, say, forex. You may want to switch out an indicator for an additional one amongst its type or make changes in how it's planned. Making such modifications could be a key part of success when day-trading with technical indicators.

Should You Trade on Technical Indicators?

Technical indicators practice past price-data in their calculation and, as a result, lagging this price. On the other hand, since historical data is that the only piece of knowledge that traders must do in advance for future price movements, technical indicators do have a very important role during a well-defined trading strategy.

Avoiding the addition of too adding too many indicators to your chart as indicators of the identical type generally return similar trading signals. As a replacement for, choose only one indicator out of every group (momentum, trend-following, and volatility) and mix their indications to verify a situation and trade supported it. An efficient mixture of indicators might be the moving be around, the RSI indicator, and, therefore, the ATR indicator, for instance.

Don't base your trading decisions totally on indicators and their signals. Trend-following indicators return a buy signal when prices start to maneuver higher, whether or not the market is trading sideways. In the same way, oscillators and momentum indicators will offer you a marketing signal when prices start to increase during an uptrend. There's no single greatest indicator, which is why you ought to combine different types of indicators and include them into a broader trading strategy.

5. PROS AND CONS OF SWING AND DAY TRADING

Swing trading is far and away one among the foremost popular ways to trade commercial markets. But like any style of strategy, there are both pros and cons when using it, and knowing those prior times may be crucial so as to choose if it's for you within the long term.

Advantages of Swing Trading

It allows you to require the benefit of the natural ebb and flow of markets. Financial markets never go into one way continually, and by having the ability to require the benefit of that, you'll rise your returns as you, in theory, are visiting be making money once the market rises over the subsequent few days, then make some while the market pulls back, because it will definitely do sooner or later.

By actuality in and out of the markets, you'll identify more chances. If you study any economic chart, you'll see that there's nearly always a precise long-term trend, but the market may not continuously be at a sustenance or resistance area. By being in an exceedingly and out of the market in a matter of some days (typically), you'll collect profits and identify other markets that are putting in for other trades. This enables you to spread the danger around and ties up lots less capital rather than continually having to come back up with margin for brand spanking new positions as you discover new trades. By closing your first position, you'll not deposit extra money in your account to hide the second.

Stop losses are typically smaller than long-run trades. The stop losses on a swing trade may well be 100 pips based upon a four-hour chart, while a stop loss on a weekly chart that's based upon the trend might need to be 400 pips. This enables you to put larger sized positions rather than extremely low leveraged ones via the longer-term trends.

You've got clear boundaries. The swing trader could be an extra technical based trader, and per se will normally have a particular area that they deem as being an indication the trade is functioning against them. Due to this, you recognize exactly when the trade isn't working and may limit the damage a nasty trade can do. Longer-term traders normally must provide a wide berth for the markets as they look forward to them to "go with the fundamentals."

Disadvantages of Swing Trading

You will get whipsawed often, simply because the market shows support or resistance at a particular area, doesn't mean they'll be respecting it today. Also, anytime you can place a trade, you're risking money. Due to this, as a swing trader, you're risking it more often. Odds are you'll have losses from time to time, irrespective of how good you're.

You will get to be knowledgeable in technical analysis. Whereas not necessarily a "disadvantage," it means extra work. Nearly any person can tell the trend on a chart that's going from the lower left to the upper right over time, but someone was trying to swing trade that a chart must identify entry and exit points. This is often something a technical analysis can do, but you would have to tell about it first. This takes time.

It takes a unique mindset than long-run trading and more nerves. While it isn't necessarily scalping, the swing trader does run the danger of being "alarmed out of the markets" as pullbacks in these lesser ranges appear to be more violent than to someone observing a weekly chart. This is often a psychological issue and one that the majority of traders will eventually accommodate during their careers.

As you'll see, there are pros and cons to swing trading, a bit like the rest. To be honest, most traders do a touch of varied different styles because the markets aren't necessarily always conducive to at least one particular style of trading and sometimes can involve others. An honest trader is able to use various styles of trading so as to extend their funds. The trader must befit the markets, not the opposite way around.

Swing Trading Example:

Find a stock in the market that has been trading in the direction of the upside for the past week, and has prepared short & sharp bottoms on its daily chart. Also, determine the stock's performance since the uptrend started and note if its price refunded to the moving average thrice. If it did, and also penetrated the moving average at a median of 1.5% of its price, a good buy order may be placed. This order may be approximately 1% of the stock's price below the moving average.

When the trade has been moving, it's advisable to put a stop loss near the entry point to curb losses. And profits may be taken near the upper channel line for weak markets, and at the upper station line, for strong markets. The purpose is to take profits in line with your trading plan, but an expert trader may favor holding for ages longer till when the market doesn't visit new highs.

Advantages of Day Trading:

Trading strategy:

Day trading lets you use a range of trading strategies across all major markets. Common day trading strategies contain breakout trading, counter-trend trading, and trend-following (or mean-reversion). In breakout trading, traders try and catch the early volatility that happens instantaneously after the worth breaks a very important technical level, like chart patterns. Incomplete orders tend to bunch above and below important levels, which ends up in a flow in momentum and volatility after the worth hits those levels and triggers the undecided orders. Breakout trading also lets day traders line an incomplete order to catch a breakout once it happens, as pending orders become market orders once the worth reaches the pre-specified level. Popular technical tools employed by breakout traders contain chart patterns, like head and shoulders patterns, triangles, double tops and bottoms, triple tops and bottoms, rectangles, wedges, and flags. Additionally, breakout traders also can make the most of the volatility that happens after the worth breaks above or below a channel, trend line, or horizontal funding or resistance levels. Trend-following strategies, as their name proposes, include opening day trades within the direction of the underlying intra-day trend. Trend-following is probably the foremost popular trading strategy among day traders because it returns a lovely risk-to-reward ratio with a comparatively high success rate. To open exchange the way of the underlying trend, await the worth to finish a pullback (e.g., to a very important intraday Fibonacci level) and use candlestick patterns to form sure the underlying trend is on the point of continue.

Counter-trend trading strategies include opening trades within the other way of the underlying trend. Counter-trend trader's goal to catch market corrections that occur after a chronic and powerful uptrend or downtrend. This trading strategy is slightly riskier than breakout trading and trend-following and may be used only by knowledgeable day traders.

More Trading Opportunities:

Since day trading could be a relatively fast-paced trading style, it offers an outsized number of trading opportunities – on a daily basis. Day traders base their choices totally on intraday timeframes, like the 15-min, 30-min, 1-hour, and 4-hour ones. Those timeframes offer way more tradeable setups than the daily or weekly charts employed by swing traders and position traders, which could be a major advantage of day trading.

However, keep in mind that shorter-term timeframes usually contain more market noise, which might quickly accumulate losses if you set your stop-loss levels too tight. To avoid this, try and measure the typical volatility of the security that you are trading (by means of the ATR indicator, for instance), and place your stop losses for that reason.

An advanced amount of trading chances doesn't essentially mean more income. A trader should follow your trading plan and only place those trades that are completely in-line with your strategy. Risk management also plays a very important role in day trading success, so confirm to risk a little percentage of your trading account on any single trade.

Higher Trading Costs:

Even though day trading the market, you'll have greater trading costs than once swing or position trading the market. Since day trading contains opening more trades throughout the day, choose a broker that has tight spreads and low trading fees. Some brokers offer stable spreads, which might be exciting for traders who want to trade around significant news releases and retain trading costs low. News releases tend to steer to high market slippage, volatility, higher trading costs, which are a few things you wish to grasp if you're about to trade important market reports. Within the long term, those trading costs can quickly add up and reduce your profits.

Limited Profit Potential:

Assumed the shorter holding periods of trades and shorter timeframes on which day traders base their choices, day trading includes a more restricted profit potential linked to swing trading. Additionally, traders close their trades by the tip of the trading day irrespective of their profit. While this practice removes overnight risk, it also limits the probable profits of promising trade setups.

Risk of Overleveraging Your Trades:

Most markets don't change much over the day. As a result, day traders utilize more leverage to squeeze out the foremost profits and make the most of these small price actions. While leverage is often very efficient, traders who over-leverage their trades also risk larger losses.

Leverage may be a double-edged sword and will be used only per your trading plan to ensure to make a strict risk management attempt to cap your influence or risk-per-trade in such how that removes the danger of ruin (i.e., blowing your account.)

Market Noise

The shorter the timeframe, you're trading on the more market noise you've got to handle. Market noise represents unpredictable and unpredictable price behavior with none technical reasoning or news that would have led to those movements. Market noise presents a true problem for short-term traders, and therefore the only thanks to avoiding getting stopped out too early are to widen your stop-loss level. Take a glance at the previous volatility within the pair, and take a look at to line your stop-loss above or below recent support and resistance levels, giving the market sufficient space to perform.

CONCLUSION

Swing trading is extremely popular because it is administrated on higher time-frame charts allowing a trader to trade the markets, hold down employment, study, or do other things with their time. It may also be accustomed to capture the big intraday moves for the traders who are looking to trade within the sessions and don't want to carry trades overnight or for extended periods of time. This is only one trading strategy of the many traders who can have their own toolbox. Before deciding if it's for you, confirm your test and excellent it on a demo trading account.

A trader should be disciplined and rigorous to start out day trading. A typical day trader problem is that they act and deviate from their strategy. Sometimes you can pass before you realize you're not strictly following your initial strategy. This will trouble the victory rate of the strategy and breaks the odds. An honest thanks to tackling discipline issues is to jot down the precise rules of your strategy and stick the note to your monitor so it'll always be ahead of you during trading sessions. This way, you'll continually be reminded to follow your strategy rules. In each of the above trades, we've carefully calculated the end result. You ought to do so, too, to be conversant in what exactly can happen to you in every trade. When you get extra established, it gets easier, and a few progressive day trading apps also will calculate everything for you spontaneously. Although being different to day trading, reviews and results propose swing trading could also be a nifty system for beginners to start out with. This can be due to the intraday that changes dozens of securities can be proven too hectic. Whereas swing traders will see their earnings within a pair of days, keeping motivation levels high. At the identical time vs. long-term trading, swing trading is brief enough to stop interruption.

Online trading is one of the most searched words on Google by those who plan to start making money from the financial markets. The doubts are various. There is the hope of earning easy money and solving all economic problems in a short time and there is also the fear of losing everything due to some scam.

These doubts and misconceptions arise from the fact that most people who dream of trading do not really know what it is.

For many it is only a vague hope of earning, something that generates easy money that they have heard about from some relative or friend. Online trading, of course, can be an extremely profitable activity as long as you have a basic preparation and, above all, to use serious platforms,

Those who start trading binary options for the first time may find themselves displaced by the need to use strategies to earn. The basic idea is that a trading strategy is something extremely complex and elaborate. Nothing could be more false. Strategies can be complex but they can also be simple. Never use complex strategies if you are at the beginning of a trader's career. We strongly recommend that you do only the things you can understand.

An alternative solution, perfect for those who really don't know anything about finance, is constituted by trading signals. Thanks to these signals it is possible to copy, in an absolutely automatic way, the operations made by expert traders. In this way it is possible to immediately get some profits even if it is evident that everything depends on the initial choice that is made

CPSIA information can be obtained
at www.ICGtesting.com
Printed in the USA
LVHW051603121220
674005LV00001B/42